TEACHING DIGITALLY:

A Guide for Integrating Technology
Into the Classroom Curriculum

TEACHING DIGITALLY:
A Guide for Integrating Technology Into the Classroom Curriculum

Lawrence Tomei
Duquesne University, School of Education

Christopher-Gordon Publishers, Inc.
Norwood, Massachusetts

COPYRIGHT ACKNOWLEDGMENTS

Every effort has been made to contact copyright holders for permission to reproduce borrowed material where necessary. We apologize for any oversights and would be happy to rectify them in future printings.

Excerpt from page 162, Table 9-2 from Applying Educational Psychology, 5th ed. Myron H. Dembo. Copyright © 1994, 1991, 1988 by Longman Publishing Group. Reprinted by permission of Addison-Wesley Educational Publishers, Inc.

Apple and Apple Logo are trademarks of Apple Computer, Inc., registered in the United States and other countries and are used with permission.

Netscape logos are registered trademarks of Netscape in the United States, used with permission.

Lycos Hotbot logo used with permission.

Excerpt from pp. 379–380, table 9-2 from APPLYING EDUCATIONAL PSYCHOLOGY, 5th ed. Myron H. Dembo. Copyright © 1994, 1991, 1988 by Longman Publishing Group. Reprinted by permission of Addison-Wesley Educational Publishers, Inc.

Christopher-Gordon Publishers, Inc.
1502 Providence Highway, Suite 12
Norwood, MA 02062
800-934-8322
781-762-5577

Printed in the United States of America

10 9 8 7 6 5 4 3 2 1   05 04 03 02 01

ISBN: 1-929024-27-4

DEDICATION

This book is dedicated to

my Mother—my first teacher—who

passed away during the writing of this book.

TABLE OF CONTENTS

FOREWORD

Introduction

Recent research sponsored by the federal government cites instructional technology as one of the two most critical challenges for administrators, teachers, and students as we approach the next millennium (Rowand, 2000). *Teaching Digitally in the 21st Century* addresses the skills and competencies needed to infuse technology-based resources into classroom instruction and serves as the definitive technical manual for today's practicing educator. This text is designed as an indispensable desktop resource and personal reference tool for integrating technology into the curriculum.

Intended Audience for the Book

Teaching Digitally in the 21st Century is specifically for:

- **Elementary teachers** who wish to infuse technology-based, integrated thematic units into their contained classroom;
- **Secondary teachers** who seek to concentrate on technology resources to strengthen their specific academic discipline;
- **Distance educators** who rely on technology as the primary vehicle for instruction; and,
- **Corporate trainers** who depend on technology to improve their bottom line.

How the Book is Organized

Specific learning objectives are provided at the outset of each chapter to establish the content and structure of the book and to introduce the key topics within each section. *Teaching Digitally in the 21st Century* is divided into four parts and eleven chapters.

Part 1: Understanding the Basics of Instructional Technology sets the stage with an introductory examination of the discipline of instructional technology. National and international standards and the use of personal computers for classroom instruction lay a foundation for this newest teaching strategy.

- **Chapter 1. "Technology for Teaching"** defines "instructional technology" and examines current occupations and job opportunities available in education and the corporate environment. It also presents instructional technology as a tool for classroom application and discusses technology standards proposed by national and international agencies. Lastly, readers are introduced to the accompanying CDROM containing megabytes of lesson examples and instructional resources. A web site has been created specifically for readers with an electronic bulletin board system, private email, and online chat rooms where they may request assistance, share ideas, or research successful implementations of teaching with technology.
- **Chapter 2. "A Primer on Personal Computers"** introduces the two most popular platforms on the educational scene: the Apple Macintosh desk top com-

puter and the Windows-based personal computer. Aspiring instructional technologists should gather the necessary skills to navigate the desktops, windows, and housekeeping functions of their favorite operating system before going further. *The more accomplished technologist is free to bypass this section.*

Part 2: Preparing Instructional Materials offers the tools to produce individualized student materials, classroom presentations, and interactive web-based resources. By the conclusion of Part II, readers will be able to prepare technology-based instructional materials designed specifically for their students.

- **Chapter 3. "Resources of the Internet"** explores the World Wide Web and familiarizes the reader with the concepts of search engines, copyright issues, and harvesting images, text, and files.

- **Chapter 4. "Text Materials for the Classroom"** utilizes the basic features of word processing to develop text-based handouts and study guides for students. A few simple techniques result in professional classroom products.

- **Chapter 5. "Visual Presentations for the Classroom"** introduces graphics packages as essential tools for designing student-centered, content-specific instruction. Using the capabilities of full-featured presentation software, educators tailor course content, classroom delivery, and learning applications to meet the needs of even their most challenged student.

- **Chapter 6. "Web Home Pages for the Classroom"** introduces readers to the World Wide Web and its power for classroom teaching. Imagine having the volumes of the Library of Congress at your fingertips, conversations with the most important people of the 20th century on your desktop, and the instructional materials of the world's most prominent educators in the memory of your personal computer.

Part 3: Preparing Instructional Lessons moves the reader to the advanced applications of technology necessary to prepare exciting, multimedia-rich, student-centered lessons. Readers are introduced to a new model for preparing technology-based lessons which takes the reader from goal-setting to lesson delivery.

- **Chapter 7. "A Model for Preparing Technology-Based Lessons"** introduces the 10-step model for designing, developing, and delivering technology-based instruction. Successful classroom lessons always begin with sound learning objectives; technology-based instruction is no different. Assessment of student learning is discussed, follow-up activities are considered, and academic standards involving technology are established. Behavioral, cognitive, and humanistic applications are presented. And, a new taxonomy for instructional technology is introduced.

- **Chapter 8. "The HyperBook Lesson"** applies advanced word processing skills to create a complex student workbook complete with images and hyperlinks harvested from the Internet. The HyperBook simultaneously addresses the needs of the tactile learner and classroom environments perhaps not equipped with the latest technology, appropriately trained teachers, or available time in the academic schedule.

- **Chapter 9. "The Interactive Lesson"** introduces a forum for delivering individualized instruction using the advanced features of graphics presentation software. The Interactive Lesson combines real-time formative assessment with a broad range of multimedia resources such as sounds, images, and video. The resulting lesson is especially appropriate for remedial instruction and classroom enrichment activities.
- **Chapter 10. "The Virtual Tour Lesson"** offers the advanced features of web design. The Virtual Tour format allows educators to expand instruction beyond existing Internet sites especially designed for particular academic content using validated information, dependable links, and immediate access.

Part 4: Assessing Instructional Technology recognizes that although successful technology must be grounded in the pedagogies of teaching and learning, evaluating the effectiveness of technology-based lessons demands its own perspective. Measuring student understanding of technology-based materials requires special considerations.

- **Chapter 11. "Evaluating Technology-Based Resources"** completes the examination of instructional technology by considering the ultimate indicators of success in the classroom. Checklists, rubrics, and portfolios assess each manner of technical resource offered throughout the book from handouts and study guides to classroom presentations and home pages, to the HyperBook, Interactive Lesson, and Virtual Tour.

Apparatus

Teaching Digitally in the 21st Century serves as both an instructional text and a ready reference source. The first-time reader finds practical examples, realistic applications of technology, and easy to follow instructions for implementing technology immediately. **Technology Bursts** and **Best Practices** target the more technically-demanding aspects of instructional design providing a "how-to" guide to advanced features and capabilities that find their way into the preparation of the more sophisticated technology-based instructional materials.

Technology Burst #1

A Technology Burst will show you how to employ an important skill or competency to prepare instructional materials. Look for these as reference guides throughout the book.

Technology Bursts pinpoint the most important skills and competencies required to prepare the technical elements discussed throughout the book. They provide detailed instruction of selected features followed by actual examples of how resources look, making the text an excellent tool for developing instructional materials.

> ### Best Practices #1
>
> Best Practices offer additional resources for better reader understanding of instructional technology as a teaching strategy. Look for these icons throughout the book as they point you to more current information.

Best Practices suggest how the various technologies are implemented in an actual classroom environment. They increase the reader's personal understanding of instructional technology applications and encourage professional development in the discipline. **Best Practices** are always found on the CDROM that accompanies this text or via a special web site offered to readers.

Featured Media

The book is only one component of *Teaching Digitally in the 21st Century*. The compact disk (CDROM) which accompanies this text offers examples of teacher-prepared materials. Readers are directed to this media throughout the book to explore in more detail various elements of teaching-learning theory, specific technology tools used in the preparation of instructional materials, and creative multimedia examples of lesson material with immediate applications in the classroom. All materials provided on this CDROM are without copyright restrictions; however, proper citations and credits are requested.

One of the most challenging problems with any text on technology is maintaining its currency. Readers may access a free web site provided by Duquesne University, Pittsburgh, Pennsylvania, offering additional resources updated on a regular basis. Resources include

- **Best Web Sites for Educators**—a list of prime sites for teaching and learning, updated by the vote of participating educators;
- **Private Chat Rooms**—for interactive discussions. Participating educators are alerted, via email, to periodic online chat sessions hosted by the author to discuss real-time, technology-related issues; and,
- **Bulletin Board System**—Educators may post to this 24-hour, 7-days a week forum for questions, answers, and tips for using technology in the classroom. A Calendar of Events includes upcoming instructional technology activities and is accessed directly from the Internet browser.

Accessing the Web Site

The web site requires a unique username and password to establish a user account. Complete the following information and cut and paste or attach the file to an email and send the request to the author at **tomei@duq.edu**. Accounts are established within 3 to 5 business days and a reply email is provided to verify activation of the account. Accounts not accessed for 120 days will be removed.

Your Name	User Name Requested	Password Requested (1)	Date of Request	Email Address

Note: Passwords may be changed online at any time. If a password is forgotten or misplaced, notify the author via email and the original password requested will be re-established.

Teaching Digitally in the 21st Century has been prepared for the novice and journeyman educator. As the journey into instructional technology begins, keep in mind that **technology is a tool,** no more or less important than other strategies in an educator's bag of teaching strategies. If the tools, models, examples, and resources presented in these pages help to increase student understanding and learning, then by all means use them. If a lesson is still better taught with textbooks, manipulatives, the blackboard, or field trips, use these media instead. **Teaching is paramount; learning is preeminent; technology remains subordinate.**

Bibliography

Rowand, C. (2000, April). Teacher use of computers and the internet in public schools. Washington, DC: National Center for Education Statistics. URL: nces.edu.gov/pubs2000/2000044.pdf.

PART 1

UNDERSTANDING THE BASICS OF INSTRUCTIONAL TECHNOLOGY

Chapter 1

TECHNOLOGY FOR TEACHING

Chapter 1 begins an in-depth examination of technology terms, educational foundations, careers, and standards. The strategic learning objectives for this first section of the book include:

- **Instructional Technology Defined**. Objective 1.1: Distinguish among the terms technology, educational technology, and instructional technology.

- **Educational Foundations of Instructional Technology**. Objective 1.2: Base applications of instructional technology on sound educational principles of teaching and learning and a proper understanding of its use in the classroom.

- **Instructional Technology as a Discipline**. Objective 1.3: Appreciate the possibilities and opportunities of instructional technology as a personal career choice.

- **Standards for Instructional Technology**. Objective 1.4: Consider the impact that emerging technology standards will have on the educator of the 21st century.

Instructional Technology Defined

Objective 1.1: Distinguish among the terms technology, educational technology, and instructional technology.

A common misconception held by many educators is that the terms **"technology," "educational technology,"** and **"instructional technology"** are synonymous—they are not. The professional educator recognizes the subtle differences and understands the distinctions when using technology to teach. Since these differences are at the very foundation of this book, it is best that any misconceptions regarding their meaning be cleared up now.

Technology

"Technology is the systemic and systematic application of behavior and physical sciences concepts and other knowledge to the solution of problems" (Seels & Richey, 1994). Technology per se is value free; that is, the presence of technology is neither good nor bad, effective or ineffective.

When applied to the classroom, technology encompasses all aspects of scientific endeavor that impact student learning. For example, while everyone would most likely agree that the personal computer is a 'piece of technology,' not everyone would so quickly place the electric fan, the light switch, or the perennial blackboard in the same category. Yet, climatic conditions, environmental surroundings, and visual aids most definitely contribute to successful learning outcomes. For our purposes, "technology" is far too broad a term to serve as the focus of this book.

Educational Technology

Educational technology is "the combination of instructional, developmental, managerial, and other technologies as generally applied to the solution of educational problems" (Seels & Richey, 1994). This definition strikes at the heart of teaching and learning and characterizes the appropriate uses of technology in the classroom. The term seems to transcend the idea of science applied merely to the solution of generic problems and concentrates instead on the more consequential task of solving academic investigation. However, the term educational technology still lacks a critical element of teaching and learning.

Instructional Technology

Teaching Digitally in the 21st Century deals with instructional technology; specifically, "the *application* of technology to the solution of explicit instructional problems" (Seels & Richey, 1994). Instructional technology deals with the practice of *using* technology to teach—plain and simple. And only this term adequately defines a process which includes the analysis, design, development, implementation, and evaluation of technology specifically for classroom teaching. This text, then, considers the most common technology-based tools; tools that educators have available to improve student understanding, enhance scholarly achievement, and satisfy expressed curriculum objectives.

Educational Foundations of Instructional Technology

Objective 1.2: Base applications of instructional technology on sound educational principles of teaching and learning and a proper understanding of its use in the classroom.

Teachers, technology coordinators, computer consultants, curriculum designers, and trainers are tasked to create technology-based materials grounded in sound pedagogical practice. A wealth of preparatory material is provided on the accompanying CDROM to support the instructional technologist in the following areas:

- Learning Theories
- Technology in the Classroom
- Instructional Technology as Pedagogy
- Technology Support for Professional Development

Learning Theories

Before using technology as a teaching strategy, the educator must demonstrate an understanding of the three most popular psychologies of learning: behaviorism, cognitivism, and humanism. The Interactive Lesson presented in chapter 9 uses behavioral principles of sequenced instruction, stimulus-response, and reinforcement to guide its construction. Likewise, the HyperBook found in chapter 8 supports the cognitive building block approach for constructing new knowledge for the learner. Finally, the Virtual Tour is most closely aligned to the humanistic approach to personalizing knowledge for the prospective learner.

Without an understanding of the strengths and weaknesses of each psychology, technology-based lessons are prone to failure. At the very least, ignoring these foundations guarantees that even a successful lesson cannot be attributed to the skillful application of sound teaching and learning principles.

If a review of educational psychology is in order before going further, **"Learning Theories—A Primer Exercise"** is highly recommended. **Best Practices #2** examines these theories and triggers your prior knowledge of how students learn best in the diverse environment of today's classroom.

Best Practices #2

On the CDROM, locate the folder entitled Learning_Theories. In this folder, locate the "Learning Theories -- A Primer Exercise." The file name for this exercise is: theories.htm and it will introduce the three most widely recognized schools of educational psychology.

Technology in the Classroom

Educational technology spans the gamut of technology from the hand-held calculator, film projector, videotape player, and overhead projector to the laser disk player, whiteboard display, and desktop computer.

The **"Impact of Educational Technology in the Classroom"** found in the IT Reports recommended in **Best Practices #3** offers an online review of the very best applications of technology found in today's instructional technology market. Choose from among dozens of reports prepared by post-graduate doctoral students who rate the candidate technologies against the popular prevailing ideologies of teaching and learning.

Best Practices #3

On the CDROM, locate the folder entitled IT_Reports. In this folder, locate the "List of Instructional Technology Reports." The file name for the reports is reports.htm and contains links to excellent reviews of technologies that support classroom teaching and learning.

Instructional Technology as Pedagogy

Instructional technology has moved to the forefront of education in a big hurry. Leading educational journals tout endless sources of grants and funding opportunities earmarked for new programs. Multimedia computer classrooms, video distribution centers, satellite downlink conference rooms, and network connections to the information super highway are common themes in many professional periodicals. Technology may be advancing, but are changes in the pedagogy that will make the best use of these new teaching tools keeping pace?

Best Practices #4 examines three new learning paradigms and proposes matching the most popular instructional technologies to the best classroom practices. The three paradigms include

- Enactive Classroom Learning;
- Learning and Classroom Focus; and
- Presenting Student Learning.

Best Practices #4

On the CDROM, locate the folder entitled Pedagogy. In this folder, locate the "Pedagogy for the Future." The file name is pedagogy.htm and contains three new learning paradigms especially suited for instructional technology.

Technology Support for Professional Development

A Smart or Intelligent portfolio is recommended for collecting and showcasing personal efforts with respect to instructional technology. Portfolios also provide continuous self-assessment and professional development as a learner, expert, or scholar.

The CDROM exercise, **"Teacher Educator Portfolios"** advocated by **Best Practices #5** acquaints the educator with the concepts and advantages of portfolios and provides the electronic formats for using folders and files to complete a personal portfolio.

Best Practices #5

The CDROM contains an extensive exercise entitled "Teacher Educator Portfolios." Locate the folder entitled Portfolios and find the file name portfolios.htm containing a 'how to' guide in selecting, designing, and building an appropriate portfolio. If you do not already have a professional portfolio, now is the time to start one.

Instructional Technology as a Discipline

Objective 1.3: Appreciate the possibilities and opportunities of instructional technology as a personnal career choice.

Increasingly over the last 20 years, society has grown to recognize technology as an academic discipline worthy of attention. Its many contributions to modern society include the study of computer science which advances technology as a body of knowledge, laws, and principles. Business schools offer programs in management information systems with their technologies for planning and decision-making. Computer technology prepares programmers, analysts, and information scientists for jobs throughout industry, kept particularly busy with the challenges of Y2K (Year 2000) and the new millennium.

Technicians train for the responsibilities of installing, troubleshooting, and repairing these evolving technical marvels. And engineering programs offer computer-aided design and manufacturing skills to a society seeking improvements of its environment, cities, and future.

However, it is the educational focus of technology—one that includes multimedia-rich tools for learning—that has gained the attention of the academic community and prompted their eventual acceptance of television, computers, laser disks, video conferencing, chat rooms, and CDROMs in the classroom.

Career Choices in Instructional Technology

In truth, as educators, we are only now beginning to flex our collective muscle, advocating for instructional technology alongside other subject areas as a viable discipline in its own right. This particular species of academic content is growing at a phenomenal rate to encompass many related categories. Simply take a close-up look at several job ads extracted from the classifieds of a few selected metropolitan newspapers.

> **Middle school computer teacher position** available for the Fall. Candidates must be certified in Technology Education. Proficiency in the use of various educational technologies required. Experience in the classroom, specifically in the application of personal computers, is a prerequisite. Salary and benefits very competitive. Closing date May 31. Send resume, clearances, transcripts, and *Instructional Technology Certificate* to Valley School District, St. Clair, PA 15111.

Computer Teacher. Schools are no longer content to place individuals in computer classrooms who have not been adequately prepared and professionally certified in instructional technology. Computer technicians do not understand the educational foundations necessary to ensure successful learning outcomes for the student—they have not been schooled in the psychology of education. Conversely, science or mathematics teachers, regardless of how well versed they are in their content areas, cannot count instructional technology among their strengths simply because of an in-service training workshop or a self-study program of classroom technology. Instructional technology is fast becoming its own area of teacher certification with 17 of 50 states currently offering its teachers an instructional technology specialists certification (Rogers, Honig, & Ambach, 1999).

> **Technology Coordinator.** Twelve-month position, experience in technology planning and implementation; experience with Windows and Macintosh required; networking knowledge a plus. Certification as an *instructional technologist* mandatory. Send resume, all college transcripts, and three letters of reference to Dr. David Michaels, Assistant Superintendent, Allied Unified School District, All Saints, NM 53891.

Technology Coordinator. School administrators are clamoring to secure the services of qualified technicians with computer software, networking, and hardware maintenance experience. For the most part, these positions go unfilled because schools are unable to compete with the seemingly extravagant salaries in the corresponding corporate sector. When schools do find competent individuals to fill their positions, odds are this person has little, if any, familiarity with needs of educators. Many are unprepared for the uncommon demands of an elementary, middle, or high school classroom environment. They probably do not understand their "client-teacher" and the nuances of using technology as an instructional tool. They may not even possess the credentials to make them credible collaborators with the teachers they serve. Instructional technology removes these barriers.

> **Curriculum Designer.** Twelve-month position available July 1. Seeking creative and articulate leader for effective development and implementation of innovative, technology-based K–12 curriculum instruction and staff development programs. Qualifications: *certification in instructional technology*, knowledge of state academic requirements, *experience in technology/curriculum integration*.

Curriculum Designer. A longstanding weakness of teaching with technology has been the educator's dependence on the computer professional to prepare technology-based materials. The first generations of computers were simply too difficult, their programming languages too exotic, interfaces too mysterious, and cost too exorbitant for any but the computer professional. Educators had neither the time, money, or inclination to tackle the intricacies of technology-based materials—until recently, that is. Today's desktop computer offers the first real opportunity to recapture the tasks of curriculum designer. Using tools common in state-of-the-art integrated software packages, educators no longer need the skills of a computer technician to implement curriculum. The teacher is once again in charge of all aspects necessary to guarantee successful student learning.

> **Educational Computing Consultant**, State University. The successful candidate will be able to manage multiple projects, coordinate student employees, adapt to emerging technologies and be comfortable with both Macintosh and Windows environments. This position requires a *Certificate in Instructional Technology* and 4 years professional experience.

Educational Consultant. With increasing emphasis on preparing its graduates, higher education has tenaciously embraced Instructional Technology. The problem that persists, however, involves faculty members who find it difficult mastering the skills required to integrate technology into their courses. Often, higher education turns to consultants to assist their faculty. Educational consultants are typically trained to appreciate the impact of instructional technology on the teaching-learning experience; those who come to understand this practice find their services increasingly in demand.

> **Corporate Trainer**. Check into New Vistas. We are the world's largest computer training organization with over 300 independent training locations. Our explosive growth has created the need for additional full-time instructors. Candidates must possess a documented history of successfully applied classroom presentation skills, an eagerness to learn, and a willingness to work. Do not apply for this position without the necessary credentials including three letters of reference, a vita depicting increasingly more complex responsibilities, and a *certification in the use of classroom-appropriate technologies*. Take an hour to see what New Vistas has to offer by visiting our Web site at newvistastraining.com.

Corporate Trainer. Instructional technology as a discipline has made its mark throughout the corporate world. The effect of computers on the administrative, managerial, and decision-making aspects of business is well established. Companies reap the benefits of distance learning with reduced travel budgets and employee time away from the office. They do not hesitate to prepare trainers in the more subtle points of company products hoping they, in turn, will share this expertise with colleagues and customers. However, few corporate trainers are accomplished in the foundations of education that allow them to correctly diagnose adult learning strengths and weaknesses. Instructional technology offers the best applications of technology in the teaching of adults.

It is apparent from the professional classified section of a major city newspaper that employers across the board are seeking credentialed, certified candidates with practical hands-on experience with technology. New advertisements similar to those above appear daily in newspapers, professional journals, and newsletters of national educational organizations. Expect to see even more in the years to come as technology takes its rightful place among the important teaching and learning strategies of the new millennium.

Standards for Instructional Technology

Objective 1.4: Consider the impact that emerging technology standards will have on the educator of the 21st century.

Organizations such as the International Society for Technology in Education (ISTE) and the National Council for the Accreditation of Teacher Educators (NCATE) have adopted a set of expertise which all teachers should master before taking leadership roles in the classroom. From the efforts of these two organizations, a composite list of the *competencies, skills, and instructional strategies* for the classroom teacher of the 21st century was developed (ISTE Accreditation and Standards Committee, 2000).

Computer Competencies

Educators in the new millennium will *demonstrate* and *model* technology in the classroom; so says the introduction to the new set of technology-based standards from ISTE and NCATE. Demonstrating involves the presentation of instructional technologies such that students are both familiar and proficient in their use. Modeling implies that the instructor "practices what is preached"; that is, technology must become an active teaching strategy as visible poof of its importance and the teacher's commitment to making it an effective learning tool. To satisfactorily champion this position, educators are expected to

- Become a competent user of both Apple Macintosh and Windows-based computers, equipped with CDROM, hard disk, and telecommunications hardware.
- Master multimedia computers connected to the Internet to teach targeted lesson objectives in the classroom, school library, or computer lab.
- Serve as a technical authority to resolve questions related to technology from both students and colleagues.
- Troubleshoot technical obstacles to the routine operational demands of the classroom.
- Advocate for the growth of technology use in schools based on the sound pedagogical underpinnings of recently published educational research.

Computer Skills

In the future, educators will require various technology-based skills to enhance their professional growth and personal productivity. They will use these tools for both formal and informal communication; peer and colleague collaboration; content area research, and on-going curriculum development. They will share this knowledge with fellow educators via in-service training sessions, professional seminars/conferences, and cooperative learning situations. The most widely accepted skills will include mastery of

- Office productivity software, as a minimum: word processing (text-based materials), graphics presentation (visual-based lessons), spreadsheet (mathematics-based lesson), and database applications (management-oriented applications).
- Multimedia applications with CDROM and Internet resources supporting essential academic content.
- Telecommunications (both modem and network) packages accessing the Internet and online library resources.
- Adaptive technologies to assist students with special needs.
- Computer-managed instruction (CMI) supporting routine classroom decisions and computer-assisted instruction (CAI) for tutorial, drill and practice, and simulation-based learning.
- Technology to acquaint students with the key social issues of the day related to ethics, values, legal and moral development, and compelling social questions.

Instructional Strategies

Classrooms will integrate technology into every fiber of the academic curriculum; subject areas such as mathematics, science, language arts, social studies, and so forth will use technology in a fitting manner to enhance student learning. To remain current with these imaginative applications, educators will embrace

- Text-based materials including student handouts, study guides, and the HyperBook. Hard copy commodities have long been part of the instructional scheme. Historically, they have depended on curriculum designers and costly publishing agencies to create, publish, and distribute classroom-ready materials. Technology is once again placing this responsibility in the hands of teachers who are ultimately accountable for the learning of their charges. Educators can develop their own text-based materials, taking full advantage of the particular strengths of each student.

- Visual-based materials have taken many forms since the introduction of the blackboard and classroom bulletin board. Graphics resources surfaced with the introduction of the computer yet remained the domain of the technology specialist for most of the last 50 years. Venerable first- and second-generation computers depended on the bytes and bits of arcane programming languages before they could be brought to serve the classroom. State-of-the-art technology has changed all that—graphics packages now design and present complex instructional lessons using auto-formatting utilities and template-based aspects.

- Web-based assets are an invention of the 1990s and the introduction of powerful multimedia-capable desktop computers. Course web pages now count among the most prolific applications of technology found online. The Virtual Tour integrates the many advantages of the World Wide Web to produce a new phylum of technology-based instructional materials. Once the educator understands the rudimentary elements of web page design, the opportunities for individualized lesson development and implementation are limited only by the imagination.

Teaching Digitally in the 21st Century engages theories as well as practices of successful student-centered, technology-based applications for the classroom. Table 1-1 summarizes the skills, competencies, and instructional strategies that serve to prepare winning text-based materials, design the best in visually strong classroom presentations, and produce imaginative online learning opportunities.

Conclusion

Teaching Digitally in the 21st Century is a "how to" manual for educators in the new millennium. "Technology" is no longer adequate to define the classroom environment. Even "educational technology" is not sufficient to explain how student learning occurs in computer labs and multimedia classrooms. "Instructional technology" supplants the vocabulary with an explanation of how the integration of technology is used to foster student achievement.

This book is not for the faint of heart. Before continuing, reaffirm the commitment to the basic precepts of education that first inspired you to become a teacher. Rededicate whatever energies are required to give rise to successful student learning. Advocate the profession and vow to become a student again. And, perhaps most importantly, apply the principles of teaching and learning that initially prompted you to embark on education as a career.

Chapter 2, "Primer on Personal Computers" introduces the two most popular platforms found in education today, the Apple Macintosh and Windows-based personal computer. It is intended for the novice technologist who needs a guide to computer hardware, software, and operating systems. Chapter 2 also serves as a refresher for using either the Apple or Windows machine as your primary system.

(Author's Note: If you already have sufficient skills to navigate the desktop, launch applications, and create, copy, and move files, simply bypass this chapter.)

Abilities	Goals	Applications
Competencies	Competent user	Macintosh and Windows systems
	Multimedia	Images, sounds, video, the Internet
	Technical authority	Resolve questions from students, faculty, and staff
	Troubleshooter	Hardware and software solutions
	Advocate	Of the IT discipline
Skills	Office productivity software	Word processing, graphics, spreadsheets, and databases
	Multimedia applications	CDROM, images, sounds, video, the Internet
	Telecommunications	Modems and networks
	Adaptive technologies	Special needs students
	CMI and CAI	Classroom management and instruction
	Social issues	Ethics, values, legal, and moral
Strategies	Text-based resources	Student handouts, study guides, and the TechBook with its imbedded technologies
	Visual-based resources	Classroom presentations and the high-tech Interactive lesson
	Web-based resources	Internet-based course pages and the innovative Virtual Tour

Table I-I. Skills, Competencies, and Strategies of Instructional Technology

Bibliography

ISTE Accreditation and Standards Committee, 2000. Contact Person: Lajeane Thomas, Louisiana Tech University. URL: www.iste.org/Standards/index.html.

Rogers, W., Honig, W., & Ambach, G. (1991, 1999). *Improving student performance through learning technologies.* Washington, DC: Council of Chief State School Officers.

Seels, B., & Richey, R. (1994). *Instructional technology: The definition and domains of the field.* Washington, DC: Association for Educational Communications and Technology.

Chapter 2

A PRIMER ON COMPUTERS

Instructional technology rightfully traces its roots to the first electronic computer. In February1946, the public saw its first glimpse of the future with the introduction of ENIAC, a machine built by John Mauchly and J. Presper Eckert that improved by some 1,000 times the processing speed of any of its contemporaries. The "Electronic Numerical Integrator and Computer" was the first large-scale general-purpose electronic computer and laid the foundation for the modern electronic computing industry. It has been written in contemporary journals of the time that the first viable application of the ENIAC was a diagnostic routine that would train its designers in the identification and correction of malfunctioning components in the machine itself (Shelly, Cashman, Ganter, & Ganter, 1999). Think of it—one of the very first uses of the computer was to teach!

As a result of this historical link to computers of the past, an understanding of how computers have evolved into the tools of instructional technology that we see in today's classrooms seems appropriate. Chapter 2 supports the construction of this knowledge base with the following objectives:

- **The History of Personal Computers.** Objective 2.1: Appreciate the history and traditions of technology as it evolved during the last half of the 20th century.

- **Personal Computers for Classroom Application.** Objective 2.2: Become familiar with the contributions of personal computers to student learning and classroom instruction.

- **The Apple Macintosh Operating System.** Objective 2.3: Identify the basic operations of the Macintosh operating system. Navigate the Apple desktop and format its disk storage media for classroom applications.

- **The Windows Operating System.** Objective 2.4: Identify the basic operations of the Microsoft Windows operating system. Navigate the Windows desktop and format its disk storage media for classroom applications.

The History of Personal Computers

Objective 2.1: Appreciate the history and traditions of technology as it evolved during the last half of the 20th century

Three autonomous events factored into the evolution of technology during the last 50 years to produce the set of integrated tools discussed in the subsequent chapters of this book. While instructional technology has resulted in its own particular strategy for teaching, its components are fairly simple and straightforward. To fully implement this strategy in the classroom, the educator must come to understand the rich heritage of the personal computer, its common software applications, and the Internet.

Steve Wozniak must be considered one of the first visionaries of classroom technology—whether intentional or otherwise. In 1976, he designed the Apple I, the first commercially available, single-board computer designed for mass consumption. A year later, the Commodore PET (Personal Electronic Transactor) became the first personal computer to be sold fully assembled. Apple returned to market prominence with the Apple II in 1977 and became a legend in its own time when the company released its printed circuit motherboard, switching power supply, keyboard, case assembly, manual, game paddles, and cassette tape storage device with several graphics-enhanced games. Just one month later, Tandy Radio Shack's first desktop computer, the TRS-80, sold 10,000 units in a 30-day period exploding previous industry predictions of 3,000 units for the entire year. And, in 1981, IBM introduced its personal computer, igniting a phenomenon in the personal computer market. The computer wars had begun.

In 1984, Apple Computer launched its first line of Macintosh computers, a mouse-driven computer with a graphic user interface. Later releases from a variety of manufacturers would hail ever-faster processors, smaller disk drives with larger storage capacity, enhanced audio and video hardware, CDROM players, plus a seemingly endless host of printers, scanners, and modems.

At the threshold of computer history, software was as proprietary as the hardware on which it was installed. Purchasing so-called improved versions of software almost always resulted in the purchase of a brand new suite of computers. Until, that is, a company named Micro-Soft was formed in 1971 by Bill Gates and Paul Allen. The hyphen in the company name was later dropped but not before they succeeded in embracing the vision of a common operating system with non-propriety applications from any number of software developers.

For the classroom teacher, common software applications once encompassed only five components: word processing, electronic spreadsheets, data base management systems, graphics presentation, and communications. With unlimited potential for sales and profits, the "big five" were eventually bundled into a single package and termed "groupware." Today, one of the most distinctive features of instructional technology is its reliance on commercially available and teacher-friendly software tools for developing individualized instructional materials and technology-based curriculum.

There have been three truly noteworthy advancements in the personal computer since its inception. First was the geometric increases in capacity. Memory, processor speed, and disk storage are multiple times faster and larger than any systems from only five years ago. Second was the incredible rise of digitized information. Multimedia has opened new horizons to any user hovering over a desktop computer. Scanners transform text and images into a string of zeroes and ones while video cameras create permanent digital photo albums. Sound cards digitize music and speeches as timeless commodities while CDROMs revolutionize the way music is performed. Third, few innovations match the impact of computer networks. As far reaching as the first two improvements were in the advancement of technology, neither exceeds the impact of the Internet. Designed at the outset by think tanks and the military to provide reliable communications in the event of nuclear war, the early Internet was used almost exclusively by computer experts, engineers, and scientists. Users were forced to learn a very complex and technically challenging system of imperceptive hardware and an even more obtuse language of instructions and commands. Since the Internet was originally funded by the federal government, it was initially restricted to research and government use. Commercial applications were prohibited unless they directly served the goals of research; a policy that continued until the power of the desktop computer and multimedia capabilities seeded the growth of independent commercial networks. The Internet is only beginning to realize its potential as a tool for teaching and learning.

Personal Computers for Classroom Application

Objective 2.2: Become familiar with the contributions of personal computers to student learning and classroom instruction.

Educators often find themselves in situations in which they are responsible for purchasing computer systems for their school, school district, or even personal home use. The following discussion offers some guidelines and suggestions for computer purchases in the hopes that this experience might increase your personal access and use of technology and software to support instruction and foster collaboration with colleagues, students, and fellow professionals.

Earlier, the personal computer, common software applications, and the Internet were introduced in an historical context. Purchasing computers for classroom application entails a thorough consideration of each of these critical components. Keep in mind as you read the following recommended configurations that the research for this book was begun in 1999 and completed in 2000. As the years have already proven, technology waits for no one and the suggestions for hardware and software provided below will undoubtedly be superceded by bigger, better, and faster components probably before this book is printed. Still, an understanding of the components that should be evaluated in the purchase of hardware and software will serve you well in any similar experience.

The Personal Computer

An examination of current manufacturers produced a recommended suite of hardware components for a desktop machine suitable for classroom instruction. Portable laptop computers will vary only slightly in capability in the areas of display size and imbedded peripherals. When purchasing new computers for a school or classroom consider the following elements:

- **Processor Speed**. Expect processor speeds to approach or exceed 700-900 MHz by 2001; however, a 500 MHz processor should suffice as an educational computer system for many years to come.
- **Memory**. One of Murphy's Laws of Computers states that "programs will expand to fill all available memory — regardless of how much is available." Truer words were never spoken. A minimally configured system should contain at least 128 megabytes of memory at a cost of about $1 per megabyte.
- **Hard Disk Drive.** These are available in the range of 13–15 gigabytes but any-

thing over 10 gb may be relatively too expensive when compared with the additional storage provided.

- **Display**. Anything less than a 17-inch screen strains the eyes; anything bigger intrudes on an already busy desktop.
- **CDROM Drive**. Current speeds are approaching 20X, or some twenty times faster than the original drives offered back in the mid-1980s. Also consider the DVD format that is fast becoming the industry standard.
- **Sound Card with Speakers**. Clarity is an issue here; the trade-off between quality and cost must be considered.
- **Modem**. To access Internet service from home, a 56 kilobyte modem is essential until cable-ready network connections become the norm.
- **Maintenance**. Consider the maintenance policy that accompanies any purchase. Most reputable manufacturers are offering multi-year warranties at no additional cost; some even provide on-site service without charge.
- **Mouse** and **Keyboard** are essential. Check out the performance of the keyboard before purchasing a machine and consider an upgrade if the keys are not smooth or the mouse does not track easily.
- **Peripherals**. In addition to the basic desktop system, consider the following peripheral items:
    - **Color Printer**. Color Ink-Jet printers are becoming the output device of choice for the classroom, but the cost versus capability question remains.
    - Master **Power Consoles** protect the investment of hardware components from unpredictable power strikes.
    - Digital **Scanners** transform text and images into digital files and facilitate the development of technology-based student materials.
    - **Zip Drives** offer megabytes of additional storage at near hard-drive speeds making backups less arduous.

Computer Software

Most educators select their word processor, spreadsheet, and graphics packages early in their professional careers and convincing them to change is always difficult. Fortunately, there are only minor user-interface differences among most commercially available packages. An example of a reputable groupware package is Microsoft Office, which includes:

- **Microsoft Word** word processor
- **Power Point** graphics presentation system
- **Excel** spreadsheet
- **Access** database system
- **Outlook** for electronic mail and personal information manager
- **Publisher** desktop publishing

In addition, an Internet browser is an essential component of a viable instructional computer system. **Netscape Communicator** is an example of a popular browser with a range of features, which include:

- **Navigator** for exploring the Internet
- **Composer** for creating, editing, and publishing online web documents

Access to the World Wide Web

Most city yellow pages contain a comprehensive list of Internet service providers, or ISPs, offering a basic suite of web-based services and an unlimited menu of additional options. When contracting for an ISP, consider the following list of services:

- **Telephone vs. Cable Access**. Telephone dial-up service remains the most common method of accessing the Internet; however, many schools and homes are opting for the faster and more reliable cable service. Regardless, a monthly service fee for telephone or high-speed cable connectivity should provide:
  - **unlimited, toll-free access** to the Internet;
  - free updates to **communications software** such as Netscape, Telnet, and File Transfer Protocol (FTP) ; and
  - at least one World Wide Web **personal home page**. However, do not expect to use this free page to conduct school business; there are separate accounts and associated fees for this service
- **Electronic Mail**. Opt for a provider who offers email accounts with at least 5 to 10 megabytes of disk space for incoming mail. Also, ensure that additional disk space is available should it be necessary for some teachers and students to download large attachments such as images and multimedia files.
- **Technical Support**, both online and by phone. Conduct a "test call" before subscribing to gauge the caliber of service. For example, a service call should be handled by a human not a voice mail system and service should be readily available during the school day when it will be needed most.
- **Documentation**, both online and hard copy.
- Online **Account Information** to track monthly usage, payment balances, and contact information.

The Better Question to Ask

Whenever educators contemplate purchasing computers for the school or classroom, two questions inevitably surface. First, if we purchase a particular computer today, will there be a bigger, better, faster model on the market in six months? To resolve this issue immediately, the answer will always be "Yes!" Within six months, if not the same month a new system is installed in the computer lab, the manufacturer will announce a newer model with faster processor speeds, larger memory, and a heftier hard disk drive capacity.

And, here is the second question. If we purchase a particular computer today, will this particular computer model be less expensive six months from now? Again, and this is something no one wants to hear, the answer is always "Yes!" Nothing loses its resale value faster than a computer.

Now for the good news. Schools should know that they may be asking the wrong questions. Rather than concentrating on speed and cost, ask: "If we purchase these computers today, will they provide the capabilities our students need now at a price we can afford now?" Computers may continue to provide the tools their students need for the technology-based curriculum created by the teacher well after the next generation and the generation of machines after that have come and gone. To make the experience of shopping for a personal computer more rewarding, the following table is provided. Remember, these minimum requirements continue to change as quickly as new machines are introduced to the market.

Hardware/Software Feature	Minimum Requirements
Operating Systems	Windows: Windows 98
	Apple: Macintosh System 9.0
Processor Speed	Windows: Pentium III
	Apple: 68040 or Power PC
Memory (RAM)	Windows/Apple: 128 RAM
Hard Drive	Windows/Apple: 8 gigabytes of free disk
WWW Browser	Netscape 4.0 or higher
	Internet Explorer 4.0 or higher
Plug-ins	Real Audio Plug-in
	Adobe Reader
	Quicktime Movie/CD/DVD Player
Modem	56 kilobyte per second
	Cable Modem preferred
CDROM	Required
Sound Card	Required
Printer	Inkjet or Laser

Table 2-1. Shopping List for the Purchase of a Personal Computer for Education

With this cursory look at the history of personal computers in education, chapter 2 continues with a look at the two most popular platforms in education today. The Apple Macintosh instructions are displayed first followed by Windows-based examples. Become familiar with both platforms or concentrate on the format found in your school or classroom.

The Apple Macintosh Operating System

Objective 2.3: Identify the basic operations of the Macintosh operating system. Navigate the Apple desktop and format its disk storage media for classroom applications.

> A local university sponsors a broad student base including students from many foreign countries. The technology faculty member forgot about a young man from Uganda who had been in the United States a mere 3 weeks before classes began. The student was apparently quite familiar with cable television, so when asked to use the mouse to point and click an icon, he raised the mouse at eye level and proceeded with unbridled enthusiasm to click the mouse button with little success. He had used a TV remote, but a computer mouse—that was a different animal.

Consider the scenario above; it actually occurred in a university classroom. There will be no assumptions about prior technology knowledge during this primer. Much of what is covered during the remainder of this chapter is best learned through practical, hands-on trial and error. So, power up your computer and follow along. *Whenever a sentence is shown in bold and italicized, avail yourself of the opportunity to try the commands or operations discussed.*

Mouse

The primary purpose of the mouse is to position the cursor on the screen and initiate a command. The Macintosh mouse has only one button so a single click typically selects a command, option, or a specific icon from within a folder's contents while a double click launches the application. A click and hold triggers pop-down menus.

Drag the Mouse (do not click any buttons yet) to get the feel for its movements across the screen. Go ahead—up, down, left, right. Be sure to work on re-positioning the mouse by picking it up and setting it down in a different place on the mouse pad. Some novices become very frustrated when they "run out of desk."

The Macintosh Desktop

With the computer powered on, the Desktop (see Figure 2-1) appears containing the key elements of the operating system.

- **Apple Menu**. At the top left corner of the screen is the Apple menu for system controls which includes important options such as Recent Applications and Recent Documents, Control Panels, and Find Files. Often overlooked as a time-saving shortcut, the Apple menu also includes several accessory applications such as a calculator, notepad (a simple word processor), and stickies (notes that can be placed on the screen as reminders).
- **Finder**. The Finder, located on the right side of the desktop, tracks open applications. Switching from one application to another is facilitated by clicking the icons found in the Finder.

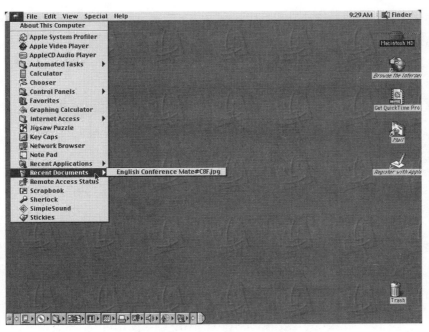

Figure 2-I. The Macintosh Desktop

- **Desktop Icons**. The Hard Drive icon is labeled "Macintosh HD" and located on the right side of the Desktop just below the Finder. Double-click the icon to display the contents of the hard drive. Other icons typically available on the Desktop include printers, the trash can, and, when inserted into the proper drives, floppy and zip diskettes.
- **Aliases** provide immediate point and click access to the most popular applications.

Navigating Macintosh Windows

Understanding the Desktop is the first step in using Macintosh Windows.

Opening a Window. To open a Macintosh window, click a desktop icon. ***Try it now. Point the mouse to the Hard Drive icon and click.*** A detailed list of all the folders and files contained on the hard drive is displayed.

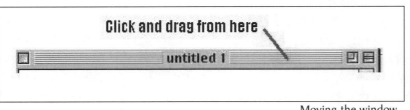

Moving the window

Moving the Window. When a window is opened, it most likely is not at the desired screen location. The window may be moved to any location on the screen. The top of any application window is called the **Title Bar** and contains the name of the application and the file that is currently open, as shown in the graphic above. *Drag the mouse to the Title Bar, click and hold the mouse button and drag the window to another location on the screen.*

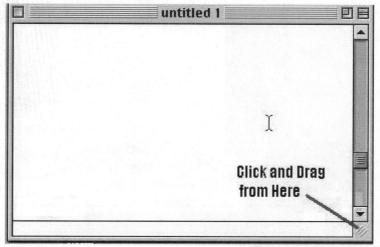

Resizing the Window

Resizing the Window. Is the window too small or too large? To resize the window, look for the small diagonal icon at the bottom right corner of the window. *Move your mouse to the Resize icon, click and drag the window to the desired size.* The window may need to be moved again to place it aesthetically on the screen.

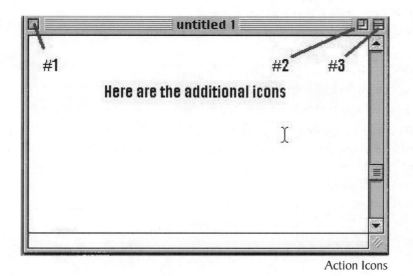

Action Icons

Action Icons. At the top of the window, three action icons are available. From the left, the **Close Box** (#1) quits the application and closes any files. The **Resize Box** (#2) changes the size of the window to pre-set dimensions. *Click the Resize Box once to return to the original dimensions of the window best suited for the screen size.* The **Collapse Button** (#3) minimizes a window so only the Title Bar appears on the screen, allowing additional desktop space to launch multiple windows. A second click on the **Collapse Button** returns the window it to its original size.

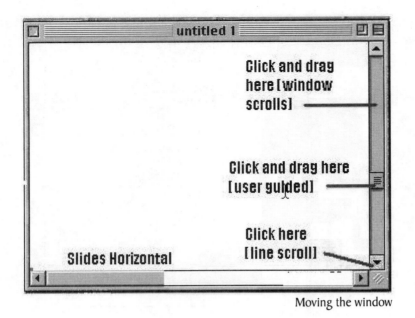

Moving the window

Slide Bars and Arrows. A Macintosh hard disk contains many folders and files; too many to be viewed on the screen at one time. To navigate some of the larger windows, a horizontal and vertical **Slide Bar** provides scrolling. *Move the mouse to the vertical Slide Bar. Click and hold the* **user-guide** *button (see figure above) and drag the bar up and down the entire page.* Clicking **window scroll** moves the viewing area up or down one screen at a time. The **line scroll** moves through the screen one line at a time.

Closing the window

Closing the Window. To close a Macintosh Window, click the **Close Box** icon or choose from the **File** pop-down menu at the top left of the window. *Click on File, drag down to Quit, and close the window.*

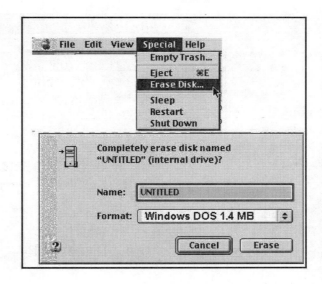

Formatting Diskettes

Before saving files to any floppy diskette or zip disk, the surface of the media must be prepared. In computer terminology, the disk must be formatted. Insert a diskette into the floppy drive and click on the diskette icon when it appears on the Desktop. It may take a few seconds for the diskette icon to appear if the computer checks for viruses before it accepts the media for use. From the Menu Bar, click on **Special** and drag down to **Erase Disk**.

Macintosh computers are able to read DOS-formatted diskettes but Windows systems cannot read the Macintosh format. This is especially important to remember when moving between the two platforms. Since Macintosh computers read either configuration, storage media should be formatted as DOS disks to avoid problems. *For practice, begin formatting a floppy diskette following these instructions. Select the Windows DOS format from the dialog box. When prompted, enter a Name for the diskette that is meaningful*. Formatting takes approximately 60–90 seconds to complete.

Creating Folders

Creating Folders

A typical hard drive holds upwards of 13 gigabytes of information. Without organization, finding files and locating documents is difficult at best. Folders are created for just this purpose.

To create a Folder, ***double-click the hard drive icon, click the File Menu*** at the top of the application and ***drag the mouse to New Folder***. An "Untitled Folder" icon appears in the window with a flashing cursor to rename the folder. For this example, ***enter the name "Teacher Folder." Store all documents, presentations, and Web pages in this location***.

Copying Files

To copy any file, locate the file on the appropriate drive. ***Click the file name, then hold the mouse button and scroll down the menu to Duplicate***. Open a receiving folder to hold the new file. ***Click the copy*** created in the previous step ***and drag the icon to the new folder***.

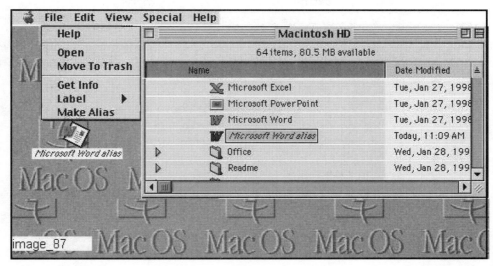

Creating an Alias

Creating an Alias

An "alias" offers an easy path to the most popular software applications. Follow these steps to create a Macintosh alias.

- Locate the target application icon and *click File* to open the pop-down menu. Scroll to the *Make Alias* option and click to accept the command.

-  Next, *click and drag the new alias to the Desktop*. Notice that the icon uses the word "alias" as part of the icon name. Click the new alias to launch the application.

Summary of the Macintosh Operating System

The Macintosh operating system provides basic capabilities critical to the use of the personal computer. It includes the following elements:

- The **Macintosh Mouse** only has one button. A single click selects an option or menu while a double click launches applications.

- **The Desktop** contains four common icons: the Apple Menu, Finder, Macintosh HD (hard disk), and the Trash Can.

- **Navigating the Macintosh** involves launching applications; moving and resizing the window; and, using the additional icons to collapse, maximize, and close the application. The Slide bar and arrows scroll the window up and down the page.

- **Formatting diskettes** prepares the storage media for saved files. Diskettes should be DOS formatted to ensure that they are compatible on both Macintosh and PC platforms.

- **Creating Folders** is part of sound disk management and benefits the user when it comes to locating files and applications.

- **Copying** files and **Creating an Alias** provides duplicate files and creates a shortcut to important applications.

The Windows Operating System

Objective 2.4: Identify the basic operations of the Microsoft Windows operating system. Navigate the Windows desktop and format its disk storage media for classroom applications.

(Author's Note: Introductory paragraphs are repeated here for readers who skipped over the Macintosh portion of this chapter.)

A local university sponsors a broad student base including students from many foreign countries. The technology faculty member forgot about a young man from Uganda who had been in the United States a mere 3 weeks before classes began. The student was apparently quite familiar with cable television, so when asked to use the mouse to point and click an icon, he raised the mouse at eye level and proceeded with unbridled enthusiasm to click the mouse button with little success. He had used a TV remote, but a computer mouse—that was a different animal.

Consider the scenario above; it actually occurred in a university classroom. There will be no assumptions about prior technology knowledge during this primer. Much of what is covered during the remainder of this chapter is best learned through practical, hands-on trial and error. So, power up your computer and follow along. *Whenever a sentence is shown in bold and italicized, avail yourself of the opportunity to try the commands or operations discussed.*

Mouse

The primary purpose of the mouse is to position the cursor on the screen and initiate a command. For Windows users, the left button activates many of the commands and options while the right button triggers elective pop-down menus. A single click typically selects a command, option, or a specific icon whereas a double click launches an application.

Drag the Mouse (do not click any buttons yet) to get the feel for its movements across the screen. Go ahead—up, down, left, right. Be sure to work on repositioning the mouse by picking it up and setting it down on a different place on the mouse pad. Some novices become very frustrated when they "run out of desk."

Figure 2-2. The Windows Desktop

The Windows Desktop

With the computer powered on, the Desktop appears on the screen (see Figure 2-2) containing the key elements of the operating system.

- **Task Bar,** located at the bottom of the screen, accesses the Start Menu and includes a button for each open application.
- **Recycle Bin** temporarily holds discarded files. Until they are discarded, files may be restored to their original directories.
- **My Computer** holds icons for each storage device such as the hard drive, floppy drive, and CDROM drive. In addition, My Computer houses two folders common to all Windows-based systems: Printer and Control Panel settings.
- **Shortcuts** provide immediate point and click access to the most popular applications.

Navigating Windows

The **Start Button** on the **Task Bar** provides ready access to a host of commands and files including the **Find** command for those hard to locate files, system settings, online help menus, and software applications.

Opening a Window. To open a window, click a desktop icon. *Try it. Point the mouse to the My Computer icon and click.* A detailed list of all the primary storage devices available is displayed. *Click on the "[C:] Local Drive" icon to list all the folders and files contained on the hard drive.*

Moving the Window

Moving the Window. When a window is opened, it most likely is not at the desired screen location. The window may be moved to any location on the screen. The top of the application window is called the **Title Bar** and contains the name of the application and the file currently open, as show in the graphic above. *Drag the mouse to the Title Bar, click and hold the mouse button and drag the window to another location on the screen.*

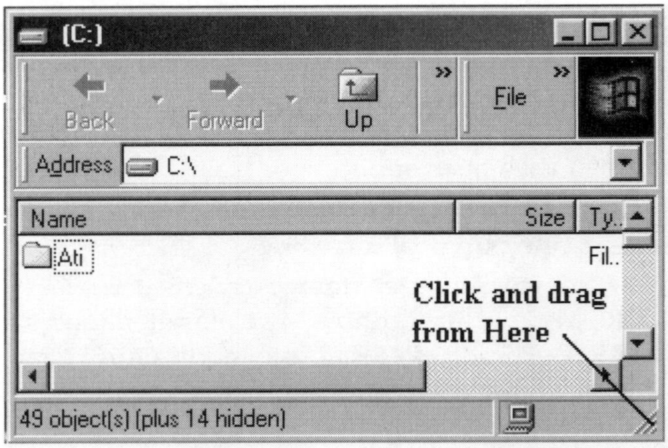

Resizing the window

Resizing the Window. Is the window too small or too large? To resize the window, look for the small icon at the bottom right corner of the application. *Move your mouse to the Resize icon, click and drag the window to the desired size*. The window may need to be moved again to place it aesthetically on the screen.

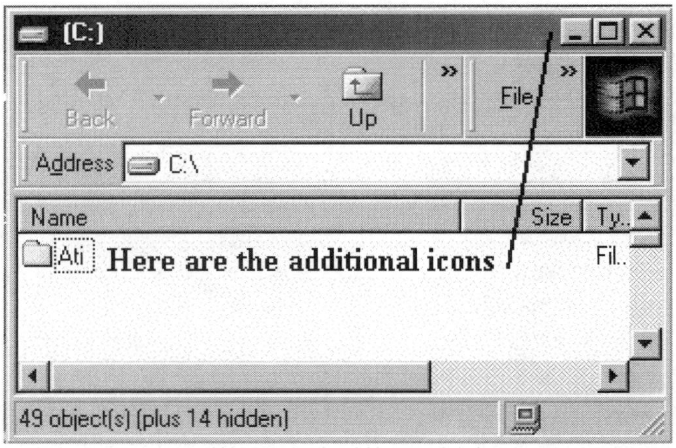

Action Icons

Action Icons. At the top right of the window, three additional icons are available. The _ (underline) icon **Minimizes** a window and collapses the application to a button on the Task Bar providing necessary desktop space to launch multiple windows. The box-like middle icon **Maximizes** the window to a full screen and returns it to its original size. The rightmost X icon **Closes** an application.

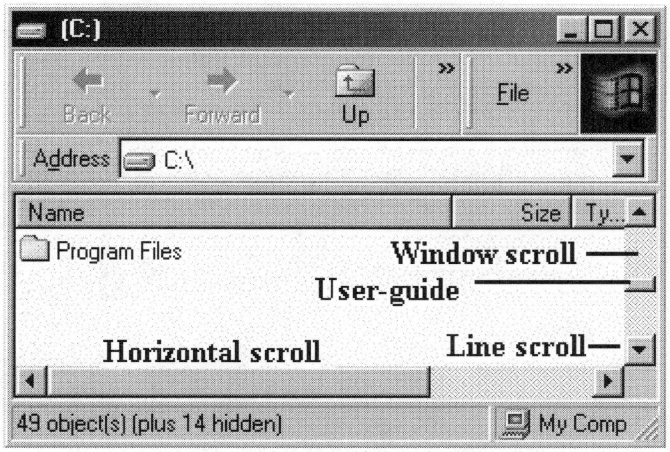

Slide Bars and Arrows

Slide Bars and Arrows. To navigate some of the larger windows, a horizontal and vertical Slide Bar provides scrolling. *Move the mouse to the vertical slide bar. Click and hold the* **user-guide** *button (see figure above) and drag the bar up and down the entire page.* Clicking **window scroll** moves the viewing area up or down one screen at a time. The **line scroll** moves through the screen one line at a time.

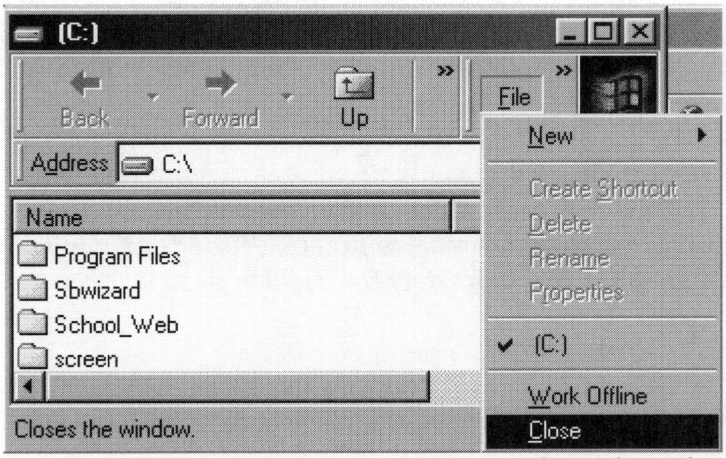

Closing the window

Closing the Window. To close a Window, click the X icon or choose from the **File** pop-down menu at the top of the window. *Click File, drag down to Close and exit the window.*

Formatting Diskettes

Formatting Diskettes

Before saving files to any floppy diskette or zip disk, the surface of the media must be pre-pared. In computer terminology, the disk must be formatted. Insert a diskette in the floppy drive and double click on **My Computer** to view its contents. Using the right mouse button, click on the **3 1/2 Floppy [A]** icon, then select **Format**. Respond to the prompt window; select **Quick (erase)** or **Full** if there were any problems with reading the diskette.

Macintosh computers are able to read DOS-formatted diskettes but Windows systems cannot read the Macintosh format. This is especially important to remember when moving between the two platforms. Since Macintosh computers read either configuration, storage media should be formatted as DOS disks to avoid problems. *For practice, format a floppy diskette following these instructions.* Formatting takes approximately 60–90 seconds to complete.

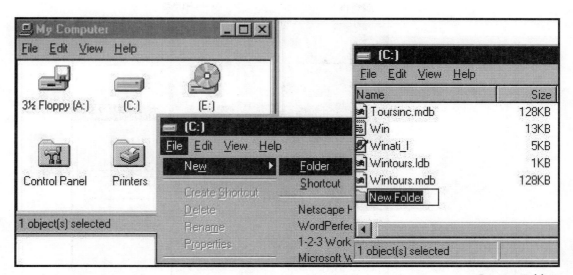

Creating Folders

Creating Folders

A typical hard drive holds upwards of 13 gigabytes of information. Without organization, finding files and locating documents is difficult at best. Folders are created for just this purpose.

To create a Folder, *double click the C: Drive icon from My Computer. Click the File Menu* and *drag the mouse to New, then Folder*. A "New Folder" icon appears in the window with a flashing cursor to rename the folder. For this example, *enter the name "Teacher Folder." Store all documents, presentations, and Web pages in this location*. The **F-5** function key refreshes the display and the newly titled folder is relocated alphabetically within the table of contents.

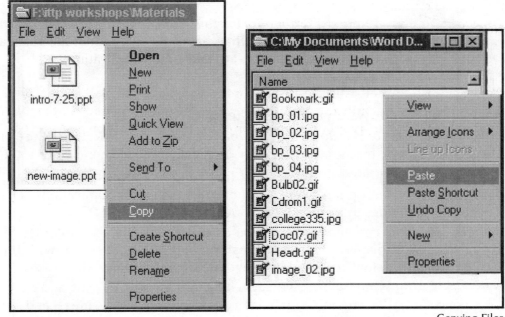

Copying Files

Copying Files

To copy a file, locate the file on the appropriate drive. Use the *right mouse button to open the pop-down menu and click the Copy command* to place the file onto the "clipboard." *Click the folder to hold the new file* and use the *right mouse button to Paste* the icon into the new location.

[context menu image showing Eudora file list with right-click menu: Open, Quick View, Scan with Norton AntiVirus, Add to Zip, Send To, Cut, Copy, Create Shortcut, Delete, Rename, Properties]

Creating a Shortcut

A "shortcut" offers an easy path to the most popular software applications. Follow these steps to create a shortcut:

- Locate the target application icon and *right click the mouse* to open the pop-down menu. Scroll to the *Create Shortcut* option and *left click* to create the shortcut.

-  Using the *left mouse button, click and drag the new shortcut to the Desktop*. Notice that the icon is marked with a small arrow. Click the new shortcut to launch the application.

Summary of the Windows Operating System

Each of the elements of Windows provides basic capabilities critical to the use of the personal computer as a tool for instructional technology. To revisit these elements briefly, they include:

- The left button of the **Mouse** most frequently activates a command; a single click selects an option while a double click launches applications. The right button provides the optional pop-down menus.

- The **Desktop** contains two common icons; namely, My Computer and the Recycle Bin. It displays the Task Bar at the bottom of the screen with the Start Menu and buttons representing each active application.

- **Navigating Windows** involves launching applications; moving and resizing the window; and, using the additional icons to minimize, maximize, and close the application. The Slide bar and arrows scroll the window up and down the page.

- **Formatting diskettes** prepare them for use as storage media for saved files. Diskettes should be formatted using Windows to ensure they are compatible on both Macintosh and PC platforms.

- **Creating Folders** is part of sound disk management and benefits the user when it comes to locating files and applications.
- **Copying** reproduces files and folders while **Creating a Shortcut** creates a link to important applications.

Conclusion

Part 1: Understanding the Basics of Instructional Technology introduced the concept of instructional technology and offered a primer on the personal computer geared to the practicing educator.

Part 2 focuses on **Preparing Instructional Materials**. Chapter 3 presents the Resources of the Internet and chapters 4, 5, and 6 follow with a practical guide in the preparation of text materials, visual presentations, and web home pages for the classroom. At the conclusion of Part 2, the reader will become an accomplished designer, composer, and user of the most popular technology-based tools provided in schools and corporate training environments.

Bibliography

The following is a list of books and articles on the subject of computers and education.

Agnew, P. W., Kellerman, A. S., & Meyer, J. M. (1996). *Multimedia in the classroom*. Boston: Allyn & Bacon.

Alavi, M. (1994). Computer-mediated collaborative learning: An empirical evaluation," *MIS Quarterly: Management Information Systems, 18* (2), p. 159–173.

Albright, M. J., & Graf, D. L. (Eds.). (Fall 1992). Teaching in the information age: The role of educational technology. *New Directions For Teaching and Learning, 51.* San Francisco: Jossey-Bass.

Anglin, G. J. (1999). *Critical issues in instructional technology* (Instructional Technology Series). Englewood, CO: Teacher Ideas Press.

Bantz, D. (1990). *Beyond courseware: A report and bibliography prepared for the Alfred P. Sloan Foundation on Computing Technology in Higher Education*. Hanover, NH: Dartmouth College, ERIC Document.

Barrett, E. (Ed.). (1992). *Sociomedia: Multimedia, hypermedia, and the social construction of knowledge*. Cambridge, MA: MIT Press.

Blackett, A., & Stanfield, B. (1994). A planner's guide to tomorrow's classrooms. Planning For Higher Education, 22 (3), 25–31.

Special classroom design needs implied by different teaching methods (lecture, discussion, lecture with audiovisuals, group instruction via computer, etc.) are examined.

Cashman, T. J.; Gunter, G. A., Gunter, R. E., & Shelly, G. B. (1999). *Teachers discovering computers: A link to the future.* Cambridge MA: Course Technology,

Castro, C. M. (Ed.). (1998). *Education in the information age: What works and what doesn't.* Washington, DC: Inter-American Development Bank.

Changing the process of teaching & learning: Essays by Notre Dame Faculty. (1994). Notre Dame: University of Notre Dame.

Educational Multimedia and Hypermedia Annual Report, 1998: Proceedings of ED-MEDIA 98. World Conference on Educational Multimedia and Hypermedia. Charlottesville, VA: Association for the Advancement of Computing in Education.

Egan, K. (1998). *The educated mind: How cognitive tools shape our understanding*. Chicago and London: University of Chicago Press.

Eidgahy, S. Y., (Mar. 1, 1992). Educational technology services in higher education: A synthesis report. *Techtrends, 37* (2), 37.

Erickson, F. L., & Vonk, J. A. (1994). Computers: Concepts and implications. *Business and Educational Technologies.*

Farrington, G. C., & Eleey, M. (Oct. 1994). Penn's plans for integrating emerging technologies, *The Journal: Technological Horizons in Education, 22* (3), 104–106.

Forcier, R. C. (1999). *The computer as an educational tool: Productivity and problem solving.* Englewood Cliffs, NJ: Prentice Hall.

Jonassen, D. H., Peck, K. L., & Wilson, B. G. (1999). *Learning with technology: A constructivist perspective.* New York: MacMillan.

Laurillard, D. (1993). *Rethinking University teaching: a framework for the effective use of educational technology.* London and New York: Routledge.

Lockard, J., Abrams, P. D., &, Many, W. A. (1997). *Microcomputers for twenty-first century educators.* 4th Edition. Longman, Publishers.

Maddux, C. D.; Johnson, D. L., & Willis, J. W. (1996). *Educational computing: Learning with tomorrow's technologies,* 2nd Edition. Boston: Allyn & Bacon.

Massy, W. F., & Zemsky, R. Using information technology to enhance academic productivity. Internet file.

Morrison, G. R., Lowther, D. L., & Demeulle, L. (1999). *Integrating computer technology into the classroom.* Englewood Cliffs, NJ: Prentice Hall.

Provenzo, E. F., Brett, A., & McCloskey, G. N. (1998). *Computers, curriculum, and cultural change: An introduction for teachers.* Hillsdale, NJ: Lawrence Erlbaum Associates.

Sammons, M. C. (1993). Motivating university faculty to integrate multimedia into classroom presentations. Educational Multimedia and Hypermedia Annual Report, Charlottesville, VA: Association for the Advancement of Computing in Education. pp. 457–462.

Sharp, V. (1996). *Computer education for teachers.* Brown & Benchmark Publishers.

Shelly, G. B., Cashman, T. J., Gunter, R. E., & Gunter, G. A. (1999). *Teachers discovering computers.* Cambridge, MA: Course Technology.

Technology across the curriculum. (Sept. 1995). *Syllabus, 9,* (1), p. 26–35.

Tucker, R. W. (Sept. 1995). The virtual classroom: Quality and assessment. *Syllabus, 9* (1), 48–51.

Tyner, K. (1998). *Literacy in a digital world: Teaching and learning in the age of information.* Hillsdale, NJ: Lawrence Erlbaum Associates.

Watabe, K. An internet based collaborative distance learning system: CODILESS. (Apr. 1995). *Computers & Education, 24* (3), 141–155.

Part 2

Preparing Instructional Materials

Chapter 3

RESOURCES OF THE INTERNET

The Internet celebrated its 30th anniversary in 1999. Another scarcely-known fact is that the Internet was designed to provide a survivable communications network to operate during a nuclear war. The concept stemmed from a news report that telephones would be unreliable and video transmissions impossible due to the electromagnetic pulse effects of atomic fallout. The Internet would provide intelligent alternate rerouting of critical command and control traffic via dedicated telecommunications. The military was quick to adopt the Internet as a national security project and the race was on (Shelly et al., 1999). The importance of the Internet is the subject of much contemporary research. Chapter 3 introduces some of this investigation including:

- **A History of the Internet and Its Impact in the Classroom.** Objective 3.1: Recognize the importance of the Internet from its earliest stages of development to present day applications in teaching and learning.

- **Components of an Internet-Ready Computer System.** Objective 3.2: Identify the essential components of an Internet-ready personal computer system.

- **Exploring the Internet Using Netscape Navigator.** Objective 3.3: Demonstrate the degree of mastery of Netscape Navigator required to successfully explore the World Wide Web.

- **World Wide Web Sites for Educators.** Objective 3.4: Become familiar with some of the best Internet sites related to educational applications.

- **Evaluating an Internet Site.** Objective 3.5: Apply the three steps for evaluating the content of an Internet site to determine the value of information found on the World Wide Web.

- **Copyright and the Use of Internet Resources.** Objective 3.6: Understand the concept of copyright protection and the limitations provided by the Fair Use laws applied to the field of education.

- **Harvesting the Internet.** Objective 3.7: Employ the tools of Web harvesting to capture text and images from the Internet.

A History of the Internet
and Its Impact in the Classroom

Objective 3.1: Recognize the importance of the Internet from its earliest stages of development to present day applications in teaching and learning.

The early Internet was the exclusive domain of the computer expert, engineer, and scientist; there was nothing user-friendly about it. Until an upstart company with an Apple logo introduced its microcomputer in the mid-1970s, there were virtually only a handful of personal computers in existence and those were typically built by hand. Those who used the Internet learned a very complex system of keyboard commands with an even more enigmatic vocabulary.

The Internet would mature as a direct result of the rapidly evolving architecture initially embraced by the Defense Department in 1980, universally adopted by industry in 1983, and supported by the increased attention on graphical interface tools. First on the technology scene in 1979, newsgroups provided a means of exchanging information around the world and almost overnight became the symbol for community building that was to characterize the future of the network. A few years later in 1981, list-server software was introduced and further nurtured the exchange of electronic mail, particularly for collaboration (Smith & Gibbs, 1994).

As more and more universities and organizations connected, the Internet became harder and harder to control. Users continued to seek tools that would aid them in indexing the vast resources already available. In 1991, the first amicable search interface to the Internet was developed at the University of Minnesota. Their simple menu system, christened "Gopher" after their school mascot, organized files and information located throughout their network. It was soon to become the adopted standard for the world until the advent of the World Wide Web.

In 1989, arguably the single most significant event occurred that would have far-reaching impact on the Internet. A new protocol for information distribution emerged based on "hypertext" —a system of embedded links, images, sounds, and video. The debate continues whether hypertext accelerated the advance of desktop technology or multimedia computers fueled the advancement of the World Wide Web.

By 1993, development of the graphics-based browser called Mosaic gave the Internet its biggest commercial promotion. The Netscape Corporation would follow with its browser software and serve as the industry standard until Microsoft introduced Internet Explorer. Today, only Netscape and Explorer remain as viable commercial desktop applications for the millions of Internet users.

Since the Internet was initially funded by the government, it was limited to research, education, and government use. Commercial applications were actually prohibited unless they directly served the objectives of the military, research, or education. By the early 1990s, this policy began to change as independent commercial applications found a ready market. Combined with an explosion of desktop capabilities—megabytes of memory, gigabytes of storage, and megahertz of processor speeds—the only aspect of the technology that appeared to be lacking was the area of high speed connectivity.

Current trends focus on the growth of high speed connections. Faster and faster modem technology provides access to telecommuters and home users. However, even 56kb speeds are not fast enough to carry high quality multimedia sound and video. New technologies such as cable modems, digital subscriber lines, and satellite broadcast are now available in homes and schools.

Educators are embracing this technological revolution and leading their students into the future of fingertip information, real-time collaboration, and distance learning. Teachers access the Internet on a daily basis from their classroom, computer lab, and home. The following discussion offers a guide for obtaining a suite of Internet-ready technology.

Components of an Internet-Ready Computer System

Objective 3.2: Identify the essential components of an Internet-ready personal computer system.

Criteria for an Internet-Ready Computer System

Chapter 2 guided the reader through the murky waters of computer acquisition by concentrating on three critical components of instructional technology: the personal computer, common software applications, and access to the Internet. The following discussion expands this initial look by focusing on the specific qualities of a complete Internet-ready computer system with multimedia computer, network connection, and software browser. Specific capabilities are highlighted in *bold italic text* for easy identification.

Multimedia Computer. The Internet revolves around enhanced text, images, sounds, and video making the selection of certain key elements of desktop technology critical.

- **Processor Speed**. The Internet depends on the speed of the computer's processor; the faster, the better. It is wise not to consider any machine with a processor operating at less than *300 megahertz*.

- **Memory**. Processor speed combines with memory capacity to host multimedia. Any machine connected to the World Wide Web should sport *at least 128 megabytes of memory; 256 mb is recommended*.

- **Hard Disk**. Downloading megabytes of graphics and audio saturates hard drives quickly. An Internet-ready system includes at least *8 gigabytes* of hard disk. The rule of "the bigger, the better" still applies.

- **Sound System and Video Display**. To enjoy the full effects of enhanced graphics and audio, an Internet-ready multimedia system includes *external speakers* and an *expanded video display* card. Once the most costly add-ons, these peripherals typically come with systems manufactured in the last few years.

High Speed Connectivity. Educators access the Internet most often in classrooms, computer labs, or home. For classrooms and labs, networks ensure ample speed for educational applications. Home, however, is another story. While most Internet Service Providers (ISP's) offer 56 kilobyte (kb) connectivity, users realize that even 56,000 characters per second is painfully slow when images, sounds, and video clips demand megabytes of storage. The typical on-campus connection transfers files at the rate of 10 million characters every second; the best modems on today's market operate closer to 200 times slower. A 1.5 megabyte video animation clip downloads via a network connection in about 4–6 seconds. That same file on today's fastest modem would take at least 10 minutes; older 28.8 kb modems take 20–30 minutes. So, the second component of the Internet is perhaps the most critical. The *fastest modem speeds* affordable and technically available remain an essential consideration when purchasing a new computer or signing up with a local ISP.

Internet Browser Software. The final key ingredient is the Internet browser. The battle is over and the dust has settled on two apparent winners. Netscape's Communicator and Microsoft's Internet Explorer each offer an excellent graphical interface for navigating the World Wide Web. Netscape has been most generous with pro bono versions for education while Explorer comes prepackaged with the newer versions of Windows. The instructions provided in *Teaching Digitally in the 21st Century* center around Netscape's Communicator software. However, with very few exceptions, either browser offers similar features.

Exploring the resources of the Internet requires three components. First, a multimedia-capable computer fast enough and with sufficient memory and hard disk capacity to access, download, and store image, sound, and video resources. Second, a dependable, high speed connection either from home or school—the faster, the better. Third, Internet browser software to explore web sites. It is now time to put theory behind us and embark on the more practical and certainly more enjoyable aspects of actually using the Internet.

Exploring the Internet
Using Netscape Navigator

Objective 3.3: Demonstrate the degree of mastery of Netscape Navigator required to successfully navigate the World Wide Web.

Netscape Navigator provides a graphical interface for exploring the World Wide Web. The fundamental commands, once mastered, become an indispensable tool for research, teaching, and learning. The **Dinosaurs of North America** is an excellent vehicle for demonstrating the technologies presented in the following chapters. Follow **Best Practices #6** to locate the **Dinosaur Home Page**. **A copy of this web site is available at the appendix to this chapter.**

Best Practices #6

On the CDROM, locate the folder entitled Dinosaur_Page. In this folder, locate the "Dinosaur Home Page." The file name for this site is: dinosaur.htm

Double-click the file name to launch Netscape.

Launching Netscape Navigator

There are two ways to launch a web site. First, locate the specific ".htm file" and double-click its icon. Or, open the file from within Navigator by clicking *File → Open Page*. Click *Choose File* to browse the CDROM and *click on dinosaur.htm*.

Navigation Window (Area 1). This area contains the text, images, and links to other web sites (see Figure 3-1). The scroll bar along the right side of the screen advances the page up or down and is necessary when viewing particularly lengthy pages.

Navigation Toolbar (Area 2). Across the top of the browser, a series of icons perform the functions of moving **Back** and **Forward** through selected web sites, reloading pages if transmission errors occur, returning to the **Home Page**, linking to Internet **Search** engines, and **Printing** the contents of the current web page.

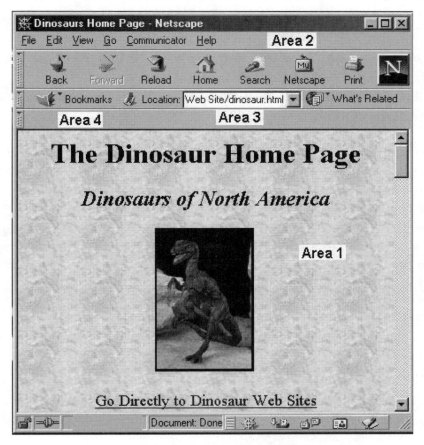

Figure 3-1. Communicator Navigation Window

Location Window(Area 3). The Location Window provides the address of the current Web site. Also called an **Uniform Resource Locator** (or URL), the Web address is very important since it is the only way of returning to a site. Scroll to the *Web Sites for Student Exploration* near the bottom of the page and *click on Jason's Dinosaur Site*. Identify the specific address of the site being displayed. The URL should show **http://members.aol.com/Ermine/index.html** and contains the following elements.

- **http://**—alerts the browser that the selected site contains hyper text transfer protocol (http) images, sounds, and video in addition to text.
- **members.aol.com**—This portion of the URL is a registered Internet site. A fee ensures that no one else uses this particular name. The ".com" segment is called the "domain" and provides important information about the type of site. Table 3-1 offers some of the more common Internet domain names and their typical content. Others are being added almost as frequently as new telephone area codes.

Extension	Domain	Typical Site Content	Example Sites
.edu	Education	Higher Education, including 4-Year Colleges and Universities	duq.edu (Duquesne University) pitt.edu (University of Pittsburgh)
.org	Organization	Non-profit organizations and other professional associations	family.org (Focus on the Family) nea.org (National Education Association)
.gov	Government	Federal Government	whitehouse.gov (White House Site)
.com	Commercial	Commercial sites with a wide variety of applications	disney.com (Disney World)
.net	Internet Providers	Sites for ISP services	telerama.net (Telerama Communications)

Table 3-1. Common Internet Domain Names

- **/Ermine**—An entry preceded by the forward slash indicates a subdirectory, usually an individual's personal folder. Jason's files are contained in the /Ermine subdirectory.
- **index.htm**—As Netscape navigates the Internet for text, images, sounds, and video, it actually searches for files. The **index.htm** is a file name downloaded from **members.aol.com**. The Internet connects thousands of individual host machines in this manner, each containing millions of unique files. Once a file is downloaded, it may be saved directly to a local computer—a process called "web harvesting."

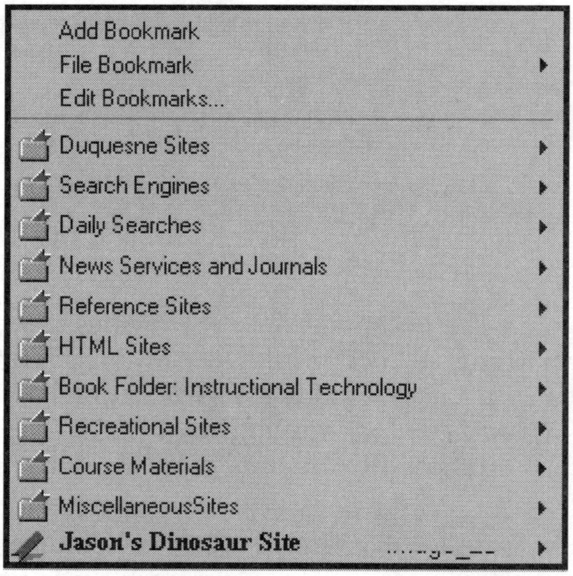

Figure 3-2. Bookmark Window

Bookmarks (Area 4) This area is for marking favorite sites on the Internet for access later (see Figure 3-2). Rather than manually tracking popular sites, bookmark them instead and organize them into folders. Creating bookmarks is easy:

- *A bookmark only saves the current site displayed.* If Jason's Dinosaur Site is still on screen, *click the Bookmark icon.*
- *Click Add Bookmark* to append the current site name and its URL to the end of the list of current bookmarks.
- To access a bookmarked site, *click the Bookmark icon again and drag the mouse down the list until it points to the desired site.*
- To delete an existing bookmark, *click Bookmark → Edit Bookmarks. Press the Delete key to remove the highlighted site.*
- To organize your bookmarks into folders:
    - Click **Edit Bookmarks**
    - Click **File → New Folder** to create a new folder anywhere in the Bookmark list
    - Scroll to find the location name appended to the end of the list.
    - Click the bookmark and drag the name to the desired location within Bookmarks or to one of the bookmark folders.

World Wide Web Sites
for Educators

Objective 3.4: Become familiar with some of the best Internet sites related to educational applications

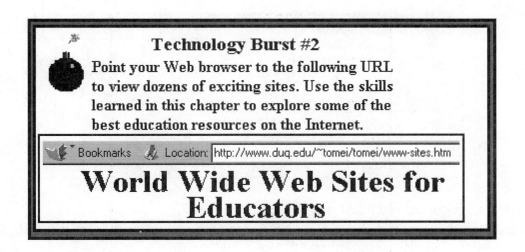

Follow the instructions for **Technology Burst #2** above and enter the URL provided in the Location window: **http://www.duq.edu/~tomei/tomei/www-sites.htm.** (Note: the tilde (~) is an *uppercase* character on the left side of the keyboard.)

Explore these sites before continuing with the chapter. The **Appendix** to this chapter contains a copy of this web site to serve as a personal directory. Add new addresses to this list when discovered and share them with fellow educators. While exploring the Internet, error messages may have warned of various problems, such as those shown in Table 3-2.

Error Message Received	Explanation	Resolution
Not Found. The requested URL was not found on this server.	1. Web site removed 2. Erroneous URL	1. Select another Web site to visit 2. Re-enter the URL
Unable to locate the server.	1. Key elements of the URL were incorrect	1. Ensure a correct URL 2. Re-enter the URL
Server does not respond.	1. Web site busy 2. Network delays 3. Too many users	1. Link to the site again later 2. Access the site during a less busy time of the day

Table 3-2. Common Internet Error Messages

Evaluating an Internet Site

Objective 3.5: Apply the three steps for evaluating the content of an Internet site to determine the value of information found on the World Wide Web.

With so much material to examine and so many sites to explore, the following graphic suggests an approach for assessing the value of information found on the web.

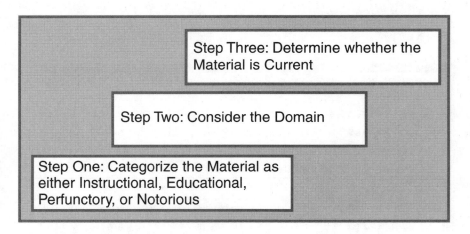

Step Three: Determine whether the Material is Current

Step Two: Consider the Domain

Step One: Categorize the Material as either Instructional, Educational, Perfunctory, or Notorious

Step One: Categorize the Material

Instructional information is prepared by the academic community for students, fellow educators, or research. These materials often take the form of online journals, magazines, and periodicals. The best are typically refereed (reviewed by committee) and offer online versions.

Scholarly information generally covers news and other similar events often reported in a way that is easily understood by the larger audience of educated people. It is more elementary than instructional material and often contains illustrations for the layperson. They are typically written by editors or reporters.

Perfunctory information contains illustrations written at a level that the casual reader understands. The main purpose of popular information is to entertain, sell products, or advocate a particular viewpoint.

Notorious information is intended to create disbelief or induce a reaction. Unfortunately, the Internet is replete with these sites, often causing schools and districts to install Internet filtering software to ward off student access to such material.

Step Two: Consider the Domain

An educator once described the Internet as the "largest, unorganized, uncataloged, unsupervised resource the world has yet seen." That observation is probably on the mark. For the first time in the history of technology, literally everyone can be a writer or publisher. Earlier in this chapter, the concept of Internet domains was introduced. To recap, a domain provides important information about the character of the site accessed. Let the domain offer some indication about the content of the information contained on the site.

Step Three: Determine Whether the Material is Current

When was the information created and, maybe more importantly, when was the last time it was updated? Most authors offer this information at the bottom of the Web page and it should be regarded when considering time-sensitive information such as news reports or stock quotations.

Copyright and the Use of Internet Resources

Objective 3.6: Understand the concept of copyright protection and the limitations provided by the Fair Use laws applied to the field of education.

Copyright Defined

Copyright is a form of protection provided by the laws of the United States (Title 17 USC) to the authors of "original works of authorship." This protection is available to both published and unpublished works and the copyright holder retains exclusive rights to reproduce or copy material and to benefit from the sale of this material directly; modify the copyrighted knowledge, including the right to produce derivative works based on the contents of the material; distribute, for cost or pro bono, copies of the work; and, perform or display the work publicly, again for cost or pro bono. (U.S. Copyright Office. URL: http://www.loc.gov/copyright).

Resources That *are* Copyrightable

Any of the following items can receive the protection of U.S. copyright laws as currently enforced:

- **Literary works** including novels, nonfiction prose, poetry, newspaper articles and newspapers, magazine articles and magazines, software manuals, training manuals, manuals, catalogs, brochures, ads (text), and compilations such as business directories.
- **Musical** works such as songs, advertising jingles, and instrumentals.
- **Dramatic works** including plays, operas, and skits.
- **Pictorial, graphic, and sculptural works** such as photographs, posters, maps, paintings, drawings, graphic art, display ads, cartoon strips and cartoon characters, stuffed animals, statues, paintings, and works of fine art.

- **Motion pictures, sound recordings, and other works** including movies, documentaries, travelogues, training films and videos, television shows, television ads, and interactive multimedia works. Recordings of music, sounds, or words.
- **Other intellectual works** such as computer software and personal electronic mail.

Resources That *Are Not* Copyrightable

There are materials that do not receive protection under the U.S. copyright laws. They include ideas or concepts; lists showing no originality, including alphabetically sorted lists; factual information; public records, court transcripts, and statistics; and titles or short phrases.

How to Avoid Violating Copyright Laws

To avoid problems associated with copyright materials: create your own content materials, stay within the Educational Fair Use Guidelines, use public domain materials, or obtain the permission of the copyright holder.

Educational Fair Use of Online Resources. Fair Use laws allow for educational application of a reasonable quantity of resources without the need for obtaining permission from the copyright holder. Permission is required if selections are larger than the Fair Use considerations provide, if the use will be recurring or permanent, if the resources are to be widely distributed, or if the uses of the copyrighted material has potential commercial applications. Fair Use considerations are provided in Table 3-3 below.

Text	Up to 10% or 1,000 words of a work.
	Poems of less than 250 words.
	No more than 3 poems by one poet.
	No more than 5 poems from an anthology.
Illustrations and Photographs	No more than 5 from any individual artist.
	No more than 10% or 15 items from a collective work.
	If the image is available at a reasonable cost, purchase it.
	If you can link to a site with the image, then do that.
Video Clips and Music	No more than 10 items or 3 minutes from any video or animation.
	No more than 10% or 30 seconds from a collective work.
Additional Information Regarding Copyrights	Copyright Basics—http://lcweb.loc.gov/copyright/circs/circ1.html
	US Copyright Office Home Page—http://lcweb.loc.gov/copyright/
	Copyright Clearance Center Online—http://www.copyright.com

Table 3-3. Fair Use Limitations

Harvesting From the Internet

Objective 3.7: Employ the tools of web harvesting to capture text and images from the Internet.

One of the most attractive features of the Internet is the ability to capture images, charts, graphics, and text from any web page. While the issues of copyright protection are never abandoned, the fact that the Internet connects directly with other computers makes harvesting possible. The process consists of two or three short steps, depending on whether you are using a Macintosh or Windows computer.

Step 1. Locating the Target Item for Harvesting

Select the graphic or text to be captured. The **Dinosaur Home Page** contains several images and paragraphs of text for teaching a unit of instruction. Return to the **Dinosaur Home Page** now (refer to Figure 3-1). The instruction begins by capturing the picture of the **velociraptor** at the top of the page.

Step 2. Capturing Images

Before capturing an image, view the image first to ensure it is exactly what you want. When composers design images, they sometimes add text or combine several images that might make them unusable or require an inordinate amount of work to crop the undesired portion of the image. To view an image

For **Windows-Based Systems**	For **Macintosh Systems**
1. Move the mouse to the selected image.	1. Move the mouse to the selected image.
2. With the pointer on the image, *right-click the mouse*.	2. With the pointer on the image, *click and hold the mouse button*.
Back Forward Reload Stop View Source View Info View Image (velociraptor.gif) Set As Wallpaper Add Bookmark Create Shortcut Send Page Save Image As... Copy Image Location	Back Forward Reload Stop View Source View Info View Image (velociraptor.gif) Set As Wallpaper Add Bookmark Create Shortcut Send Page Save Image As... Copy Image Location
3. From the pop-up Menu, click *View Image* (filename). If the image is not suitable, locate another and repeat Step 2.	3. From the pop-up Menu, click *View Image* (filename). If the image is not suitable, locate another and repeat Step 2

cont.

4. If the image is acceptable, return to the Web page by clicking the **Back** icon. *Right-click* the image again. This time, however, select *Save Image As . . .*	4. If the image is acceptable, return to the Web page by clicking the **Back** icon. *Click and hold* the image again. This time, however, select *Save Image As . . .*

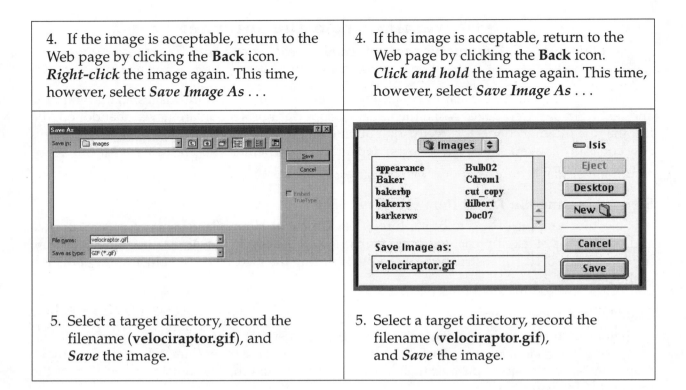

5. Select a target directory, record the filename (**velociraptor.gif**), and *Save* the image.	5. Select a target directory, record the filename (**velociraptor.gif**), and *Save* the image.

Step 3. Capturing Text

Capturing text is even easier than downloading images. Farther down the **Dinosaur Home Page** are lesson objectives for the unit of instruction. *Click and drag the mouse* to highlight the text of Objective I. It will look like this:

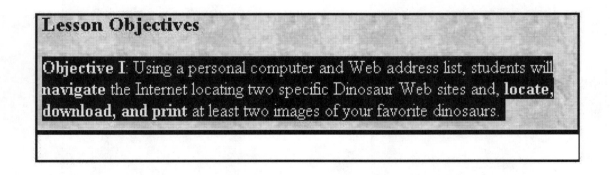

Click the Edit → *Copy pop-down menu* sending the text to the clipboard, then *Edit* → *Paste* to place the text into another document.

Conclusion

Using the built-in features of Netscape's browser software, educators are able to harvest a seemingly infinite cache of instructional resources from the Internet. Images and text may be downloaded, validated, and saved to disk with the click of the mouse button.

Keep in mind the imperative to act responsibly when dealing with copyright and Fair Use laws. Be wary of what is available on the Internet. A pre-service teacher naively boasted that every possible content area is represented by excellent lesson plans, student handouts, and assessment materials just waiting for taking. Experienced teachers, however, know the folly of such a boast. Finding material is only the first step; the remaining chapters discuss how to validate that information and revise it to fit the instructional needs of students.

Bibliography

Books and Publications

December, J. (1997) *The World Wide Web 1997 Unleashed*, 4th ed. Indianapolis, IN: Sams.net Publishing.

Murray, W. H., & Pappas, C. H. (1998). *HTML 4.0 User's Resource.* Upper Saddle River, NJ: Prentice Hall.

Musciano, C., & Kennedy, W. (1998). *HTML The definitive guide, 2nd ed.* Cambridge, MA: O'Reilly Publishers.

Shelly, G. B., Cashman, T. J., Gunter, R. E., & Gunter, G. A. (1999). *Teachers discovering computers.* Cambridge, MA: Course technology.

Smith, R. J., & Gibbs, M. (1994). *Navigating the Internet,* Deluxe Edition. Indianapolis, IN: Sams.net Publishing.

Related Links

http://www.w3.org/History.html *A little history of the World Wide Web.*

http://www.w3.org/People/Berners-Lee/1996/ppf.html *The World Wide Web: Past, present and future.*

http://www.mensdata.nl/seminar97/Internet/History.html *A brief history of the Internet* by Barry M. Leiner, Vinton G. Cerf, David D. Clark, Robert E. Kahn, Leonard Kleinrock, Daniel C. Lynch, Jon Postel, Larry G. Roberts, Stephen Wolff

http://www.internetvalley.com/intval-zagotovka3-0327-25.htm *History of the Internet and World Wide Web.*

http://www.loc.gov/copyright U.S. Copyright Office, Washington, DC.

Appendix

THE DINOSAUR HOME PAGE

Dinosaurs of North America

<u>Go Directly to Dinosaur Web Sites</u>

Introduction

Millions of years ago, long before there were any people, there were dinosaurs. Dinosaurs were one of several kinds of prehistoric reptiles that lived during the Mesozoic Era, the "Age of Reptiles."

The largest dinosaurs were over 100 feet (30 m) long and up to 50 feet (15 m) tall (like Argentinosaurus, Seismosaurus, Ultrasauros, Brachiosaurus, and Supersaurus). The smallest dinosaurs, like Compsognathus, were about the size of a chicken. Most dinosaurs were in-between.

It is very difficult to figure out how the dinosaurs sounded, how they behaved, how they mated, what color they were, or even how to tell whether a fossil was male or female.

There were lots of different kinds of dinosaurs that lived at different times. Some walked on two legs (they were bipedal), some walked on four (they were quadrupedal). Some could do both. Some were speedy, and some were slow and lumbering. Some were armor-plated, some had horns, crests, spikes, or frills. Some had thick, bumpy skin, and some even had primitive feathers.

The dinosaurs dominated the Earth for over 165 million years during the Mesozoic Era, but mysteriously went extinct 65 million years ago. Paleontologists study their fossil remains to learn about the amazing prehistoric world of dinosaurs.

Although dinosaurs' fossils have been known since at least 1818, the term dinosaur (deinos means terrifying; sauros means lizard) was coined by the English anatomist Sir Richard Owen in 1842.

Instructions

 Read the instructions for completing this lesson and the companion Workbook and Slide Presentation by **clicking on this icon**.

Lesson Objectives

Objective I: Using a personal computer and Web address list, students will **navigate** the Internet locating two specific Dinosaur Web sites and, **locate, download, and print** at least two images of their favorite dinosaurs.

Objective II: After locating a given **Web** site, a student will review the information and answer the questions in the **Workbook**: *"What is the difference between an Omnivores and a Carnivore? When did the Dinosaurs Live? And, What Were the Most Common Dinosaurs in North America?"*

Objective III: Given a Web address, students will click on a dinosaur's name to go to a simple black-and-white print-out and color, cut out, and mount their favorite Dinosaur. Students will share a **3-5 minute presentation** on their Favorite Dinosaur and discuss Why the Dinosaur is their favorite and WHY this lesson was important to them.

Web Sites for Student Exploration

The following Web Sites have been selected for this course. Examine each of the sites—in order. If you have any trouble locating a site, please ask for assistance from your instructor.

Jason's Dinosaur Site

Dinosaur Classroom Activities

Dinosaur Information Sheets and Print Outs

Honolulu Community College Dinosaur Exhibit

Student Assessment. You will receive a grade for this lesson based on the following criteria:

Assessment	Possible Points	Percent of Points
Attendance and Participation	100 points	10%
Web Site Navigation	500 points	50%
Workbook	100 points	10%
Presentation	300 points	30%
Total Possible	**1000 points**	**100%**

Created and Maintained by Miss Tammy Brown
Email Address: <u>brown@schoolwise.edu</u>
5th Grade Science Teacher
Schoolwise Elementary School
Email Address: <u>schoolwise@schoolwise.edu</u>

Fair Use Statement

Permission is granted for unrestricted use of the materials found on this Web Page. Author requests that any materials (text or images) acquired from these pages for inclusion in related resources carry a citation of the author as indicated above.

Created: 10/01/99
Revised: 01/01/00

Chapter 4

TEXT MATERIALS
FOR THE CLASSROOM

Teachers often find that concrete, hard copy resources make very effective learning tools for the classroom. Student handouts serve as assessment instruments, remedial content material, and enrichment activities. Study guides offer targeted instruction in the form of guiding questions for discovery learning and additional reading material for test preparation. No matter how much high technology resources are available to the classroom instructor, sometimes text-based material is still the best way to teach a lesson objective. Chapter 4 presents the following major learning objectives:

- **Word Processing Fundamentals.** Objective 4.1: Demonstrate a mastery of word processing fundamentals.

- **Preparing Text-Based Handouts and Study Guides.** Objective 4.2: Demonstrate a grasp of text-based design along with a mastery of enhanced word processing features. Combine these skills with the use of technology resources harvested from the Internet to produce text-based materials for teaching.

Word Processing Fundamentals

Objective 4.1: Demonstrate a mastery of word processing fundamentals.

Microsoft Office includes a robust suite of office productivity tools including the word processing package Word, the graphics presentation system Power Point, spreadsheet application Excel, database application Access, and desktop publishing capability Publisher. Microsoft Office runs equally as well on both the Macintosh and Windows platforms with minimal differences reflecting primarily mouse functions. Microsoft Word employs many of the commands, options, and menus of a full-featured word processor and is the tool of choice for designing, developing, creating, and implementing text-based educational resources.

Launching Word

Microsoft Word contains hundreds of commands, options, and menus. To learn all of the features would require many hours of training. Fortunately, the software is so powerful that it provides shortcuts even for the novice user. Access to the single most frequently used application is facilitated with a Windows shortcut or Macintosh alias. To create these icons on the desktop, follow the procedures found in chapter 2. If a shortcut or alias is available on the desktop, *double click the Word icon* to launch the application. If not, follow the appropriate step.

- For Windows users, *click the Start Button* on the Task Bar, scroll to *Programs* then *Microsoft Word*.
- For Macintosh users, *click on the Apple Menu*, scroll to *Recent Applications* then *Microsoft Word*.

Opening a Document

Word opens with a New Document window named "Document1." Text may be entered directly into this new document and saved to a hard disk, floppy disk, or zip disk. However, it is easier to discuss editing, moving, inserting, and printing features with a completed document on the screen. So, the new document will be ignored for the moment in favor of a CDROM exercise.

The Dinosaur Handouts are a series of one-page introductions to some of these most popular prehistoric creatures. They are provided on the accompanying CDROM. Follow **Best Practices #7** to locate this resource and follow these steps to open the document in Microsoft Word. **A copy of the handout is also available in appendix 1.**

Best Practices #7
On the CDROM locate the folder entitled Dinosaur_Handout. In this folder find the material "Dinosaur Handouts." The file name is dinohandout.doc and contains pages of the five most popular prehistoric creatures including their anatomy, size, behavior, and other interesting facts.

Accessing the CDROM.
- Ensure that the *CDROM* is in the drive.
- On the Menu Bar at the top of the screen, click *File* → *Open* or click the *Open* button icon 🗁 on the Toolbar.
- Access the appropriate media.
    - Windows systems, *double click My Computer, then the CDROM Drive*.
    - Macintosh systems, *double click the Desktop CDROM icon*.
- *Locate the Dinosaur_Handout folder and double-click the file: dinohandouts.doc.* Use the *Slide Bar* to scroll through the document and examine the contents.

Editing Text

Dinosaur Handouts should remain on the screen as each of the basic editing features of Microsoft Word are introduced. Practice each skill, keeping in mind that the original document was opened from the read-only CDROM and remains unaffected by any revisions. **None of the changes made during this exercise affect the original** *dinohandouts.doc,* **so do not be afraid to attempt any of the edits recommended.**

Selecting (Highlighting) Text. Very few features come standard on most word processors. One such feature, however, is highlighting text. Before editing, the text to be modified must first be highlighted or "selected" as it is referred to in word processing parlance. To select

- **A word**, position the cursor on the desired *word* and *double-click* the mouse button.
- **A sentence or line**, place the cursor anywhere in the middle of a sentence or line.
    - Windows machines, hold the *Control* key and *click once.*
    - Macintosh systems, hold the *Command* key and *click once.*
- **A paragraph**, position the cursor within the paragraph and *triple-click* the mouse.

Changing the Appearance of Text. Scroll down page 1 of **The Dinosaur Handouts** and locate the sub-title, "Dinosaurs of North America." Use the mouse and the directions above to *select the entire line*. The highlighted text looks like this:

- **B** *I* **U** **Bold, Underline, and Italics.** Once the text is selected, several editing commands are available to change the look of the line. The three most common editing commands control the appearance of the text. Click on the **Bold** icon, then **Italics**, then **Underline** to affect the look of the selected text. The buttons change appearance when clicked to indicate the feature is ON. A second click toggles the feature OFF..

- **Left, Center, Right, and Justify.** To the right of the BIU icons are four alignment functions. **Left** alignments line the text along the left margin while **Centering** is easily accomplished by clicking the second icon. A **Right** alignment is appropriate for address lines and dates; **Justify** aligns text against both the left and right margins and is appropriate only within paragraphs.

- Times New Roman ▼ 10 ▼ **Changing Fonts and Font Size.** On the same menu line as the BIU icons are pop-down menus for changing Fonts and Font Size. Click the down arrow next to the **Font** window to view the various formats available. The same procedure sets a new Font Size—the larger the number, the larger the size of the type.

Moving Text. With the line still highlighted, try the Cut, Copy, and Paste commands to move text to another location in the document. Take a look at the following icons.

- ✂ 📄 📋 **Cut, Copy, and Paste**. Find the set of icons that look like a pair of scissors, two identical documents, and a clipboard. The scissors **Cut**, or delete the selected text. The twin documents **Copy** text or images. And, the clipboard **Pastes** the text into a new location.
- *Click the scissors* and watch how the **Cut** text disappears from the body of the document.
- The **Copy** command is identical to the Cut command except that the text is duplicated to an area of memory called the "clipboard."
- The text may be **Pasted** to another location elsewhere in the document.

The Undo Command. After any change such as deleting text or bolding an entire paragraph, a simple click of the Undo button on the Toolbar reverses the operation and returns the text to its former appearance.

- ↶ ▾ ↷ ▾ *Click Undo to reverse the last action*. To undo an action, click the left arrow icon. Undo is an important feature that saves time and recovers user mistakes.

Saving a Document. A good rule of thumb is to save a document after composing each paragraph. The process takes only a single mouse click but saves considerable time in the event of a power outage, mechanical failure, or computer virus.

- 💾 To Save the document, *click the Save icon* on the Toolbar or select *File →
  Save* from the menu. If the file has never been saved, the **Save As** dialog box appears.
- Set the location by *clicking the Save In box* until the correct folder appears. *Enter a new File Name* for the document, then *click the Save button or the OK button* (see Figure 4-1 or Figure 4-2).

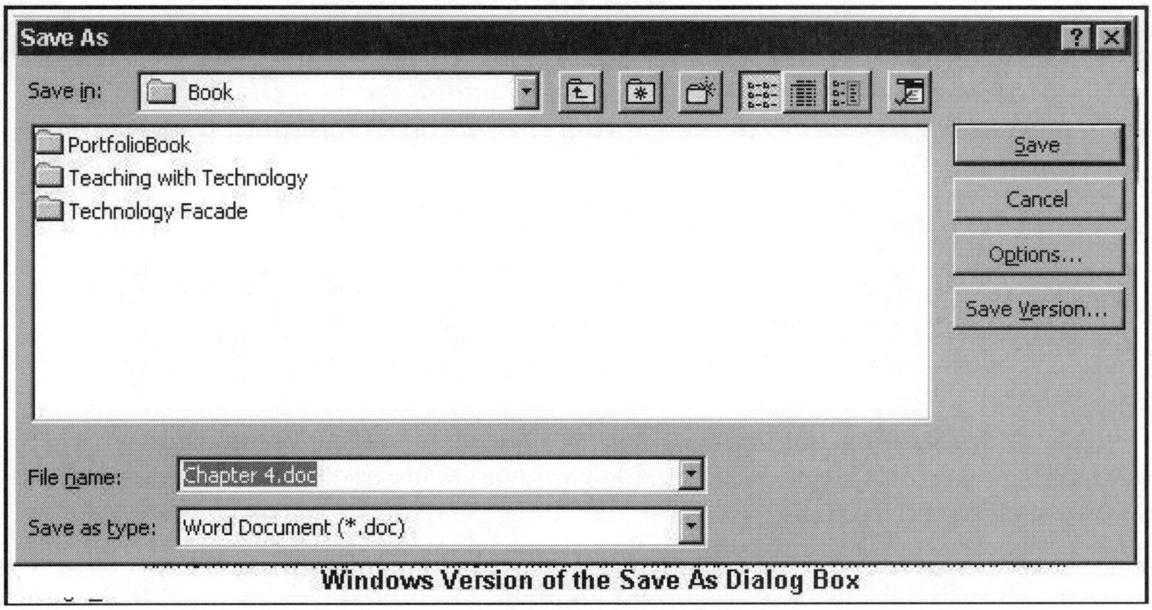

Figure 4-I. Windows Version of the Save As Dialog Box

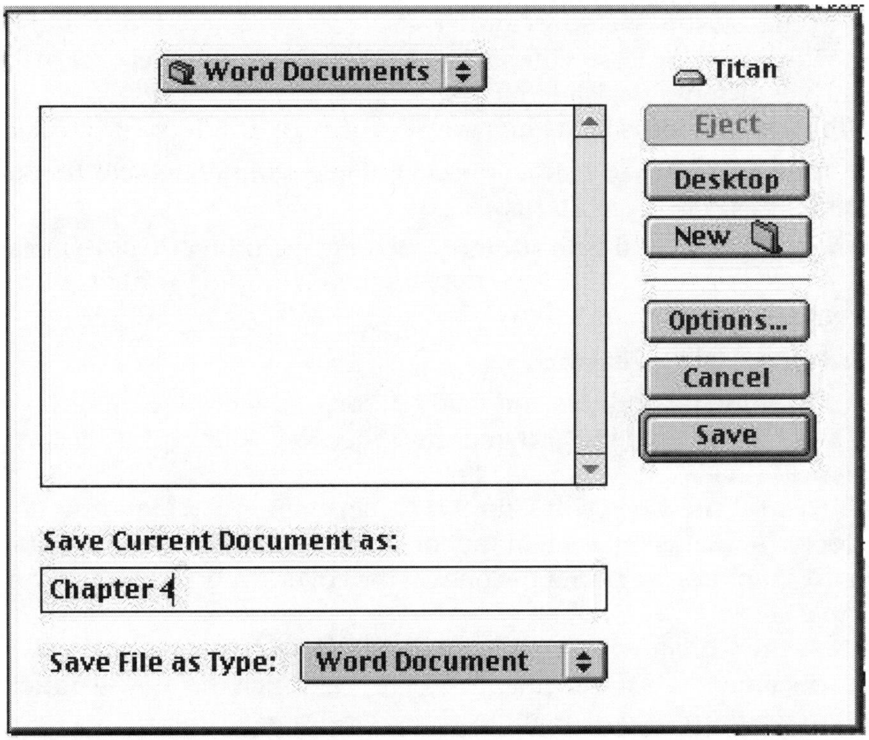

Figure 4-2. Macintosh Version of the Save As Dialog Box

Preparing Text-Based Handouts and Study Guides

Objective 4.2: Demonstrate a grasp of text-based design along with a mastery of enhanced word processing features. Combine these skills with the use of technology resources harvested from the Internet to produce text-based materials for teaching.

Designing Text-Based Materials

The two primary **formats** for text-based materials include handouts and study guides.

Classroom Handouts. These are concise, one or two-page documents that focus on a specific learning objective. Handouts provide specific instructional steps, student materials, procedures for learning, and a short assessment. They are typically completed within a single learning class period.

Study Guides. Study guides focus on one or more lesson objectives. While a study guide might address several objectives, it is limited to a single instructional strategy appropriate for a majority of classroom students. Handout and study guide materials are constructed with a common set of components. As a minimum, they should contain

- **Title of the Lesson** and a graphic or image appropriate for the content material contained in the resource.

- **Student Name**—Materials to be used by learning groups would offer room to identify all students participating in the experience.

- **Date of the Lesson/Section Number**—Successful materials are used year after year. The date of the lesson identifies use in multiple sessions over the course of a semester or multiple academic years.

- **Teacher's Name**—Self explanatory.

- **Page Numbers**—Sequential numbering of pages eliminates student confusion and enhances classroom discussion.

- **A variety of sensory aids to student learning**, including **Clip Art, images, and text.**

Enhanced Word Processing Features

When preparing student handouts and study guides, advanced features involve the integration of graphics and clip art, spelling and grammar checking, and capturing and printing professional classroom products.

Inserting Clip Art—The Microsoft Clip Art Gallery offers a wide array of pictures, photographs, and cartoons for inclusion in a handout or study guide. The **Dinosaur Handouts** incorporate several clip art graphics, including the one on the cover. To **Insert Clip Art** into a document, follow these simple steps:

- **Position the Cursor**—Before inserting clip art, the cursor must be at the point in the document where the image is to appear. Click the mouse button once to position the flashing cursor at the desired location.

Figure 4-3. Clip Art Example

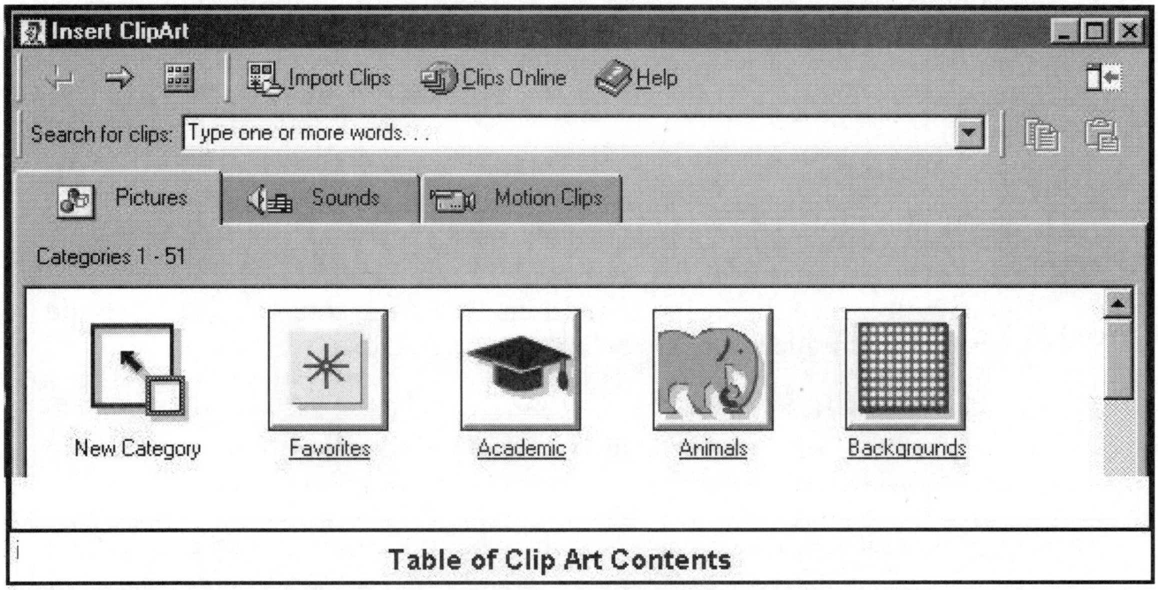

Figure 4-4. Clip Art Gallery

-  **View the Clip Art Gallery**—The clip art icon is found on the Drawing Menu at the bottom of the screen. Or, to use the pop-down menu, click *Insert → Picture → Clip Art.* Either procedure loads a gallery of images from which to choose (see Figure 4-4).

- **Select a Category**—Click an icon to display the contents of images available in each category. Scroll through the available images and locate one appropriate for the instructional material under consideration.

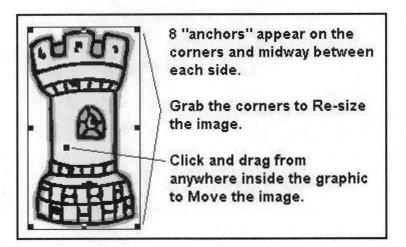

Figure 4-5. Procedures for Resizing and Moving a Clip Art Image

- **Select the Image**—Click the **Insert button** to insert the image into the body of the document. Once there, the image may be resized or moved as desired (see Figure 4-5).

- **To Resize Clip Art**—Click anywhere on the image to activate the "anchors"—little square boxes which appear on the perimeter of the image. Place the cursor on one of the four *corner* anchors to transform the cursor from a pointer to a diagonal arrow. Hold the mouse button and drag diagonally to resize the image proportionally. The anchors appearing in the mid-perimeter locations stretch the image horizontally or vertically.

- **To Move Clip Art**—Move the mouse anywhere inside the target image. The cursor becomes a four-way arrow. Hold the mouse button and drag the image to a new location.

- **Cut, Copy, and Paste**—To the word processor, clip art and text are handled exactly the same. Select the clip art by clicking the image. Click the **Cut** (scissors) icon to delete it, **Copy** the image to the clipboard, or **Paste** it to a new location.

- **Left, Center, Right, and Justify**—These functions operate to align an image as well as text.

Figure 4-6. Image Example

Inserting Pictures from the Internet. Digitized pictures are inserted into a document as easily as clip art. The **Dinosaur Handouts** contain several pictures such as the Tyrannosaurus Rex (see Figure 4-6) that were downloaded from the Internet using the harvesting principles described in a previous chapter. To **Insert Pictures** into a document, follow these steps:

- **Position the Cursor**—Before inserting a picture, the cursor must be moved to the location in the document where the image is to appear. Click the mouse button once to position the flashing cursor at the desired position.

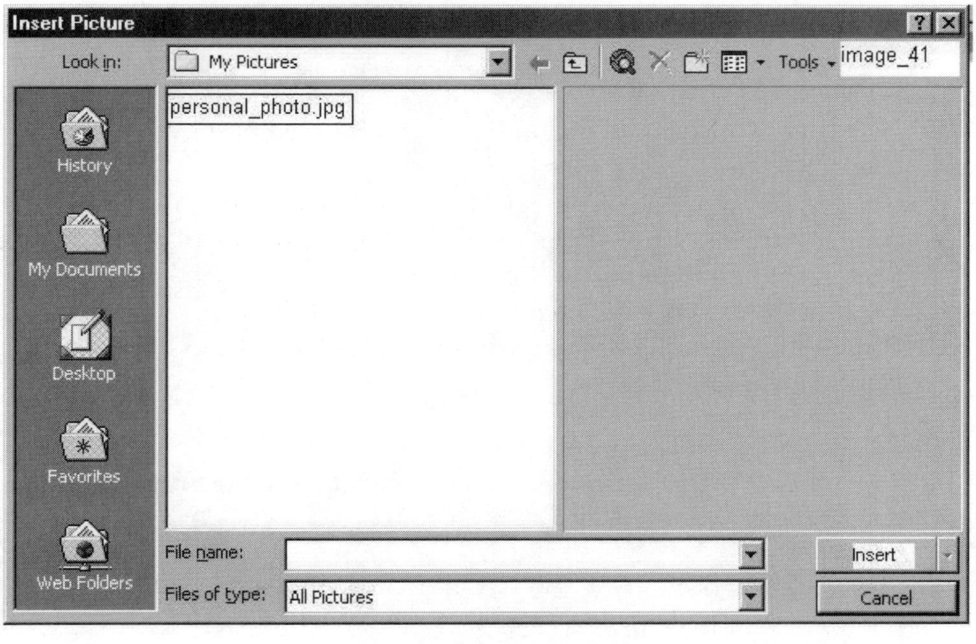

Figure 4-7. Locating a Picture on Disk

- **View the Contents of the Storage Media**—From the pop-down menu, click *Insert → Picture → From File* (see Figure 4-7).
- **Select the File**—Double-click the file name, then the **Insert button** located at the bottom right of the dialog box. The image appears in the body of the document.

Once inserted into a document, the picture may be resized, moved, copied, pasted, or deleted exactly as clip art.

Inserting Text from the Internet. So far, images have been the primary focus of the enhanced features of word processing. To be sure, **Dinosaur Handouts** contain numerous examples, most of them taken from actual Internet explorations. However, textual content, too, may be harvested directly from web sites. To insert text, the easiest method is to cut and paste directly from the web into an awaiting document by following these steps:

- **Position the Cursor**—The cursor must be at the point in the document where the text is to appear. Click the mouse button once to position the flashing cursor at the desired position.

- **Minimize Microsoft Word**—Recall from chapter 2 that minimizing a window is performed differently for Macintosh and Windows systems. Macintosh uses the **Collapse** icon on the Title Bar while Windows uses the boxed underline icon to **Minimize** the application and place it on the Task Bar. *Minimize Microsoft Word now*.

- **Open a Netscape Session**—*Launch Netscape and locate an appropriate web site containing lesson content text.* Identify several sentences or even an entire paragraph appropriate for the target document.

- **Select the Desired Text**—Position the cursor to the left of the desired body of text to be captured. *Click and drag the cursor down and to the right* until all the desire text has been highlighted. Practice selecting text until the movement of the mouse becomes second nature.

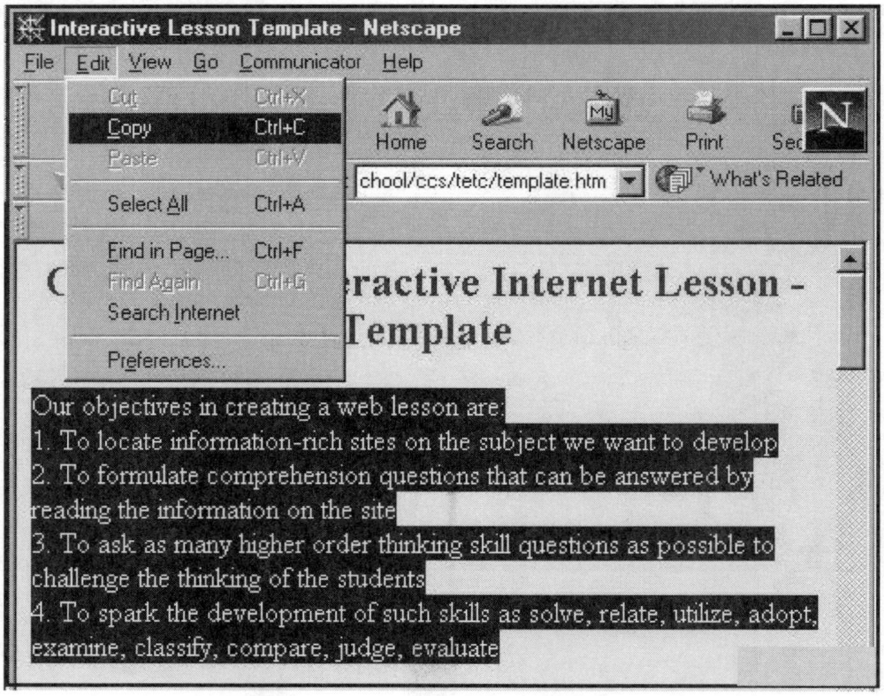

Figure 4-8. Copying Text to the Clipboard

- **Copy the Text to the Clipboard**—Copy the desired text onto the clipboard (see Figure 4-8) using the *Edit → Copy* pop-down menu. Keep in mind that clicking the Copy icon results in no visible action on the screen.

- **Maximize/Restore Microsoft Word**—Return to the document by reversing the minimize/collapse process. For Macintosh machines, a second click of the Collapse button on the Title Bar. For Windows machines, locate the application on the Task Bar at the bottom of the screen and double-click to restore the screen.

- **Paste the Text into the Document**—Click *Edit → Paste* from the pop-down menu to insert the text into the document. Online web pages usually require some formatting changes to make the text presentable. For example, the font size of the copied text may be too big or too small. Simply use the features learned earlier in the chapter to make these changes.

Save the Document. After inserting text, images, or clip art, save the document. There are simply too many steps to risk a loss of power or disk errors. From the *File → Save* pop-down menu, enter an appropriate name—short and free of special characters.

Spell Checking A Document. Microsoft Word automatically checks spelling and grammar and corrections are easily made. Follow these steps

- **Automatic spelling and grammar correction**—The AutoCorrect feature is accessed from the **Tools → AutoCorrect** pop-down menu. It finds and replaces spelling and grammatical errors each time an unrecognized word is entered. For example, "**definately**" is replaced with "definitely." AutoCorrect uses the spelling checker's main dictionary along with a list of personalized entries easily appended to the dictionary.

-  **Check spelling and grammar on demand**—Spelling and grammatical errors may be checked any time by clicking the **Spell Check** icon. This method is most useful when proofing an entire document.

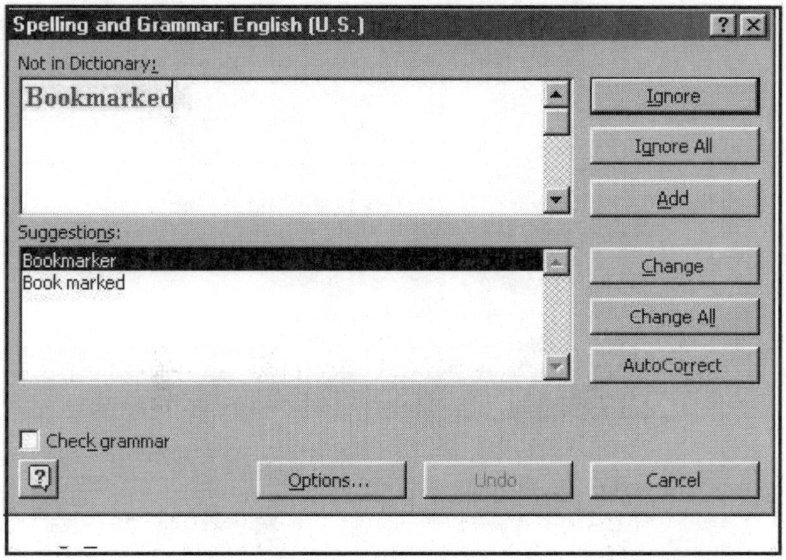

Figure 4-9. The Spell and Grammar Check Window

- **Making Corrections**—The Spelling and Grammar dialog box contains two windows (see Figure 4-9). The top window identifies unrecognized words. The word may even be spelled correctly, but the Spell Checker simply does not recognize the word and therefore highlights it for action. The bottom window is the software's attempt to suggest the correct spelling. Usually its guesses are right on the mark. Other times, however, the suggested change may be wrong and even slightly humorous. There still remains some things a computer cannot do as well as a human—second guessing misspelled words is one of them. If the choices offered are inappropriate, there are two options:

- First, ignore the choices. **Ignore All** disregards all "misspellings" of the highlighted word for the remainder of the document.
- Second, **Add** the new word to the personalized custom dictionary so that all further encounters with the same word will be considered correct.
- If one of the choices offered is suitable, click the desired **Suggestions** in the bottom window, then the **Change** button. **Change All** finds and replaces the word whenever it is encountered throughout the remainder of the document.

Grammar Checking a Document. Selecting the **Check Grammar** box verifies the grammatical structure of each sentence. The most common grammatical errors made by users are subject/verb agreements, passive voice, punctuation, and repeated words.

Printing the Document. After editing is complete, the document is ready for hard copy. Before sending the document to the printer, Word has a feature called the **Print Preview** that is highly recommended.

- **Print Preview**—To view the document as it will look when printed, click **Print Preview** on the Tool Bar. Editing is not permitted while in the print preview mode. To exit Print Preview and return to the document, click **Close**.

Figure 4-10. The Print Menu

- **Print**—Click the **Print** icon at the top of the Menu Bar or the *File → Print* pop-down menu to produce the dialog box shown in Figure 4-10. The two most common options used to print a document are the **Print Range** and **Number of Copies**.

- **Print Range**—**All** prints every page in the document, **Current Page** prints only the page on which the cursor is presently positioned, and **Pages** allows the user to enter a range of pages.

- **Copies**—Enter the **Number of Copies** to be printed. Requesting **Collate** prints each copy from first to last page, then repeats the process for additional copies keeping all the pages in order.

Conclusion

Chapter 4 introduced the first of three media formats for the preparation of technology-based instructional resources. Text-based materials at this level may seem elementary, especially to the more experienced reader. Take heart, the more complicated elements of instructional technology are waiting in the following chapters.

Chapter 4 also provided a primer on the essential elements of word processing including opening documents; editing, moving, and manipulating text; and, saving the results. Student handouts and study guides were introduced along with the components that support text-based learning. Next, some advanced features of word processing provided a look at inserting Clip Art, images, and text harvested from the Internet.

If you followed the exercises and examples, you should be able to meet the two primary objectives established for this chapter. Additional work may be needed before feeling totally comfortable with word processing as a tool for preparing text-based materials.

If remedial instruction is desired, examine **Technology Burst #3** which warehouses a number of the best text-based materials prepared by fellow educators and offered with their permission. Identify resources that may be appropriate for your classroom, and revise these materials while practicing the skills offered in this chapter.

Technology Burst #3

On the CDROM, locate the folder entitled Example_Text. In this folder locate the "List of Example Text-Based Materials." The file name is text.htm and contains excellent examples of handouts and study guides designed by practicing teachers.

Appendix

DINOSAUR HANDOUTS
Dinosaurs of North America

Student Name: _____

Date of the Lesson: _____ **Teacher:** _____

DINOPAGE

Tyrannosaurus rex
the "Tyrant lizard king"

ANATOMY

Tyrannosaurus rex was a fierce predator that walked on two powerful legs in Cretaceous period forests. This meat-eater had a huge head with large, pointed, replaceable teeth and well-developed jaw muscles. It had tiny arms, each with two fingers. Each bird-like foot had three large toes, all equipped with claws. T. rex had a slim, stiff, pointed tail that provided balance and allowed quick turns while running. T. rex's neck was short and muscular. Its body was solidly built but its bones were hollow. T. rex's jaws were up to 4 feet (1.2 m) long and had 50 to 60 thick, conical, bone-crunching teeth that were up to 9 inches (23 cm) long. T. rex could eat 500 pounds (230 kg) of meat and bones in one bite! T. rex had a wrap-around overbite; when T. rex closed its mouth, the upper parts of the lower jaw's teeth fit inside the lower jaw.

SIZE

Tyrannosaurus rex was up to 40 feet (12.4 m) long, about 15 to 20 feet (4.6 to 6 m) tall. It was roughly 5 to 7 tons in weight. T. rex left footprints 1.55 feet (46 cm) long (although its feet were much longer, about 3.3 feet (1 m) long, T. rex, like other dinosaurs walked on its toes).

OTHER HUGE MEAT-EATING DINOSAURS

Although not the biggest meat-eating dinosaur ever discovered, Tyrannosaurus rex was certainly one of the largest terrestrial carnivores of all time. The recently discovered Giganotosaurus carolinii and Carcharodontosaurus may have been even more enormous.

DINOPAGE

VELOCIRAPTOR
"Speedy Thief"

ANATOMY

Velociraptor was a speedy, bipedal carnivore. It had about 30 very sharp, curved teeth in a long, flat snout, an s-shaped neck, long thin legs, arms with three-fingered clawed hands and four-toed clawed feet. Velociraptor may have been able to run up to roughly 40 mph (60 km/hr) for short bursts. Velociraptor was about 6 feet long (2 m), and 3 feet tall (1 m). It may have weighed about 15 to 33 pounds (7 to 15 kg). It had a stiff tail that worked as a counterbalance and let it make very quick turns. One 7 inch (18 cm) long, sickle-like, retractable claw was on the middle toes of each foot. This claw was its main weapon, and could probably kill most of its prey easily. Velociraptor brains were very large in comparison to their body size (this is true for all the Dromaeosaurid dinosaurs, who were the most intelligent dinosaurs).

BEHAVIOR

Velociraptor may have hunted in packs, attacking even very large animals. In 1971, fossils of a Velociraptor and a Protoceratops were found together. They died together; the Velociraptor was attacking the Protoceratops with its claws and the armored head of the Protoceratops had apparently pierced the chest of the Velociraptor. Velociraptor, along with the other Dromaeosaurids, were the smartest dinosaurs, as calculated from their brain:body weight ratio. This made them very deadly predators.

DINOPAGE

Allosaurus and Apatosaurus

ANATOMY

Allosaurus was a powerful predator that walked on two powerful legs, had a strong, s-shaped neck, and had vertebrae that were different from those of other dinosaurs (hence its name, the "different lizard"). It had a massive tail, a bulky body, and heavy bones. Its arms were short and had three-fingered hands with sharp claws that were up to 6 inches (15 cm) long.

SIZE

Allosaurus was up to 38 feet long (12 m) and 16.5 feet tall (5 m). It weighed about 1400 kg. It had a 3 feet long (90 cm) skull with two short brow-horns and bony knobs and ridges above its eyes and on the top of the head. It had large, powerful jaws with long, sharp, serrated teeth 2 to 4 inches (5 to 10 cm) long.

BEHAVIOR

Allosaurus may have hunted in groups. In groups, Allosaurus could ambush even the very large sauropods (like Diplodocus and Camarasaurus). It probably also preyed upon Stegosaurs and Iguanodonts. Allosaurus was the most abundant predator in late Jurassic North America. Allosaurus was a carnosaur, whose intelligence (as measured by its relative brain to body weight) was high among the dinosaurs.

DINOPAGE

Triceratops

Triceratops

ANATOMY

Triceratops was an herbivore, a plant eater (a primary consumer). It probably ate cycads, palms, and other low-lying plants with its tough, toothed beak. Triceratops could chew well with its cheek teeth (like other Ceratopsians, but unlike most other dinosaurs).

SIZE

Triceratops walked on four short legs; it was a relatively slow dinosaur. Dinosaur speeds are estimated using their morphology (characteristics like leg length and estimated body mass) and fossilized trackways.

DINOPAGE

Brachiosaurus

ANATOMY

Brachiosaurus was one of the tallest and largest dinosaurs yet found. It had a long neck, small head, and relatively short, thick tail. It walked on four legs and, like the other Brachiosaurids and unlike most dinosaurs, its front legs were longer than its hind legs. These unusual front legs together with its very long neck gave Brachiosaurus a giraffe-like stance and great height, up to 40-50 feet tall (12-16 m).

SIZE

Brachiosaurus was about 85 feet long (26 m), and weighed about 50-80 tons. Like other Brachiosaurids, it had chisel-like teeth, its nostrils were on the top of its head, and it had large nasal openings indicating that it may have had a good sense of smell. Brachiosaurus had 26 teeth on top jaw and 26 on the bottom for a total of 52 teeth. It had a claw on the first toe of each front foot and claws on the first three toes of each rear foot (each foot had five toes with fleshy pads).

BLOOD PRESSURE PROBLEMS

Brachiosaurus and some of the other large sauropods (the huge long-necked plant-eaters) needed to have large, powerful hearts and very high blood pressure in order to pump blood up the long neck to the head and brain. The heads (and brains) of Brachiosaurus was held high (many meters) above its heart. This presents a problem in blood-flow engineering. In order to pump enough oxygenated blood to the head to operate Brachiosaurus' brain (even its tiny sauropod brain) would require a large, powerful heart, tremendously high blood pressure, and wide, muscular blood vessels with many valves (to prevent the back-flow of blood).

Chapter 5

VISUAL PRESENTATIONS
FOR THE CLASSROOM

The previous chapter discussed the use of word processing to create handouts and study guides that foster student understanding and learning. Of equal importance is the use of classroom presentations to meet the needs of the more visual learner. Towards that goal, chapter 5 offers the following major learning objectives:

- **Graphics Presentation Fundamentals.** Objective 5.1: Demonstrate a mastery of graphics presentation fundamentals.

- **Preparing Visual-Based Presentations for the Classroom.** Objective 5.2: Demonstrate a grasp of visual-based design along with a mastery of enhanced graphics presentation features. Combine these skills with the use of technology resources harvested from the Internet to produce visual-based materials for teaching.

Graphics Presentation Fundamentals
Objective 5.1: Demonstrate a mastery of graphics presentation fundamentals.

Research has found that students learn better when they are permitted to rely on the instructional strategy best suited to their own particular learning style (Fitzsimmons, 1996). While concrete learners depend on the text-based workbook for reinforcement, abstract learners find the visual media of a classroom presentation more to their style of learning.

Visual Fundamentals

Microsoft Power Point creates presentations suitable for the classroom by offering a multimedia environment for concepts and ideas important for student understanding. It provides a suite of tools to create powerful slide shows incorporating bulleted lists and numbered text; multimedia Clip Art, pictures, sounds, and movies; links to teacher-validated Web sites, programs, and documents; colorful charts and graphs; and a choice of output options tailored to individual learning styles. Power Point offers an extensive fare of commands, options, and menus. With the advanced features of AutoContent Wizard, hyperlinks, and printing alternatives, it also provides an array of all the tools necessary to build exciting instructional materials.

Launching AutoContent Wizard

Access to Power Point is made easier with a Windows shortcut or Macintosh alias. To create these icons on the desktop, follow the procedures for Making an Alias or Creating a Shortcut found in chapter 2. If a shortcut or alias is available on the desktop, ***double click the Power Point icon*** to launch the application. If not, follow the appropriate step:

- For Windows users, ***click the Start Button*** on the Task Bar, scroll to ***Programs*** then ***Microsoft Power Point***.
- For Macintosh users, ***click on the Apple Menu***, scroll to ***Recent Applications*** then ***Microsoft Power Point***.

Figure 5-I. Opening Power Point Screen

Creating a Presentation Using AutoContent Wizard. The opening Power Point screen is shown in Figure 5-1. Inside the dialog box are four options. To follow the instructions presented in the next several paragraphs, click the small circle to select ***AutoContent Wizard*** and ***click OK***.

Opening Screen. The opening screen explains that AutoContent Wizard starts by providing ideas and an organization for the presentation and Step One is complete. ***Click the NEXT button*** to proceed.

Presentation Type. Wizard provides several types of presentation formats: Generic, Corporate, Projects, Sales/Marketing, Carnegie Coach, and Selling a Product to name just a few. To view the available types, select the **All** category. Each type is different. The Generic presentation, for example, might include nine slides while the Projects type only three or four. One type might have a red and white color scheme while another uses blue and gold. Scroll through the list of styles and ***select the Training presentation*** type, then ***click NEXT***.

Presentation Style. The program offers a choice of output. On-screen presentations display slides on the computer monitor or projection system. Web presentations assist in the design of

Internet-ready slides. Black and white overheads and color overheads are used with overhead projectors and transparency film. The 35mm slide option formats the screen image to match the dimensions of a camera attached directly to the computer screen. For exercise purposes, *retain On-Screen Presentations* and *click NEXT.*

Presentation Title. This step supplies user information for the first slide in the presentation. Click once inside the *Presentation Title text window* to *enter a title for this lesson.* Enter the author's name in the second box and any additional information such as school, class period, and so forth in the third. *Click NEXT* when the entries are complete.

Finishing the Wizard. The necessary steps to create a Power Point presentation are complete. To view the results, *select FINISH.*

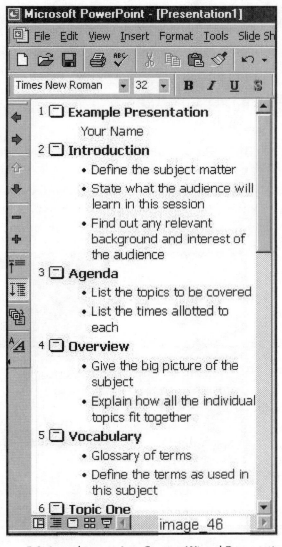

Figure 5-2. Launching an AutoContent Wizard Presentation

AutoContent Wizard results in a new presentation resembling Figure 5-2. Power Point automatically launches into the Outline View. Use the mouse to *scroll through the outline* to view the results of selecting the training presentation type.

Viewing a Power Point Presentation

Power Point uses a series of five view modes which appear at the bottom of the screen. From left to right, the views include:

- **Normal View** provides the outline of the presentation in the left frame and the slide view on the right.

- **Outline View** is for editing the content of presentation rather than its graphic elements.

- **Slide View** must be selected to insert Clip Art, Pictures, and Text as well as centering, background color, text size and color, and drawing.

- **Slide Sorter View** offers a handy, user friendly feature to assist in building transition effects and rearranging slides.

- **Slide Show View** displays the actual presentation on-screen.

For practice, *click the Slide Show View* and follow these steps to advance through the presentation.

- **Advance to the next slide**—Click the mouse, press the space bar, use the Up (Forward) and Down (Back) arrows, or press the Page Up (Forward) or Page Down (Back) keys to move through the slide presentation.

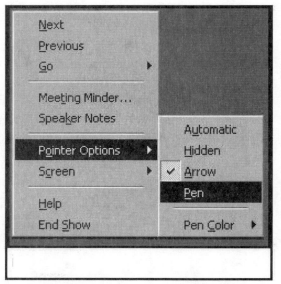

Figure 5-3. Use of the On-Screen Pen Pointer

- **Use the Pointer**—One of the most popular features of the Slide Show is the use of an on-screen pointer. Drag the mouse across a slide until the action button appears on the bottom left of the screen. Click the Action Button then

Pointer Options → *Pen* (see Figure 5-3). The cursor changes from the arrow to a pen. *Click and drag* the mouse around the screen underlining important words, circling key phrases, or drawing arrows to critical bullets. The drawing is temporary and disappears with the next slide.

- **End Show**—After viewing the final slide in the show, Power Point ends the presentation and restores the screen to the previous view mode. A show may also be terminated at any time by pressing the escape key or click End Show from the Action Button.

Editing the Presentation

The newly created presentation should remain on the screen as the basic editing features are introduced. Practice each skill. NOTE: You must be in the **Outline View** before continuing with this exercise.

Selecting Text. Before editing, text must be highlighted or "selected." To select

- ⬚ **A slide,** position the cursor on the slide icon next to the slide number and click the mouse button to select all the text on that slide.
- **A bullet**, place the cursor anywhere in the middle of the bullet sentence and:
  - Windows machines, hold the *Control* key and *click once*.
  - Macintosh systems, hold the *Command* key and *click once*.
- **A word**, position the cursor on the desired word and *double-click* the mouse button.

Bold, Underline, Italics, and Shadow. Power Point includes the option of **Appearance** commands.

- **B** *I* **U** **S**   Click the **Bold** icon, **Italics**, and **Underline** to see how they affect the look of the selected bullet. Power Point also provides a **Shadow** command. Notice that the buttons change appearance to indicate that the feature is ON. A second click toggles the feature OFF.

Left, Center, and Right. To the right of the BIU icons are the **Alignment** functions.

- **Left** alignments line the text along the left margin. **Centering** is accomplished by clicking the middle icon, and the **Right** alignment moves text to the outside margin.

Changing Fonts and Font Size. Fonts and font size have an important role in visual material. Some presentations are designed with so much information they are difficult, if not impossible, to read. Others use font sizes that demand the eye of an eagle to read from a distance. While 10 and 12 pitch is acceptable for hard copy documents, 24 to 36 pitch is more appropriate for visual presentations.

-  The pop-down menus for changing Fonts and Font Size appear on the Tool Bar. Click the down arrow next to the **Font** window to view the available formats and follow the same procedure to set a new **Font Size**.

Moving Text. Practice the **Cut, Copy, and Paste** commands to move text to other locations in the presentation.

- [icon] **Cut, Copy, and Paste**—Find the icons that look like a pair of scissors, two identical documents, and a clipboard. They are in the same location as in the word processor and, of course, have the same purpose. The scissors **Cut** or delete the selected text. The twin documents **Copy** text or images, and the clipboard **Pastes** the text into a new location.

The Undo Command. After any editing changes, a click of the Undo button on the toolbar reverses the operation and returns the text to its former appearance.

- [icon] Click the icon to *Undo the last action.* To undo an action, click the left arrow icon. Undo is an important feature that saves time and recovers user mistakes.

Adding a New Bullet/Sub-Bullet. To add a new bullet, place the cursor immediately following the preceding bullet. For example, to add another agenda item to the third slide (refer to Figure 5-3), position the cursor after the word *"each."* Hit the Enter (Windows) or Return (Macintosh) key. Power Point assumes that another bullet is to be added at this location. For now, oblige the system and *enter a suitable third agenda item*.

Promoting/Demoting Bullets. *Highlight the new bullet* and locate the icons that Promote/Demote text.

- [icon] Click on the right arrow to **Demote** the bullet, effectively creating a **sub-bullet** up to five levels deep.

- [icon] The left arrow **Promotes** each bullet until it reaches the status of the highest level of a new slide.

Saving a Power Point Presentation

Presentations should be saved after each slide is created or modified. The process takes only a single mouse click and saves considerable time in the event of a power outage, mechanical failure, or computer virus.

- [icon] To Save the document, *click the Save icon* on the Toolbar or select the *File → Save* pop-down menu. If the file has never been saved, the **Save As** dialog box appears.
- Set the location by *clicking the Save In box* until the correct folder appears and *enter a new File Name* for the presentation. *Click the Save button* (see Figure 5-4 or Figure 5-5).

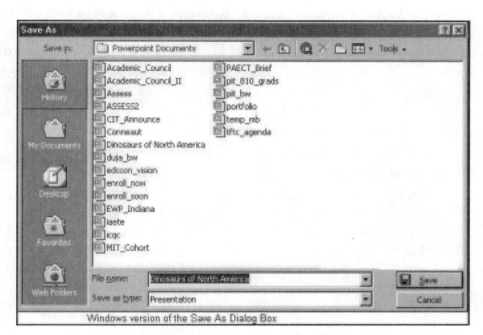

Figure 5-4. Windows Version of the Save As Dialog Box

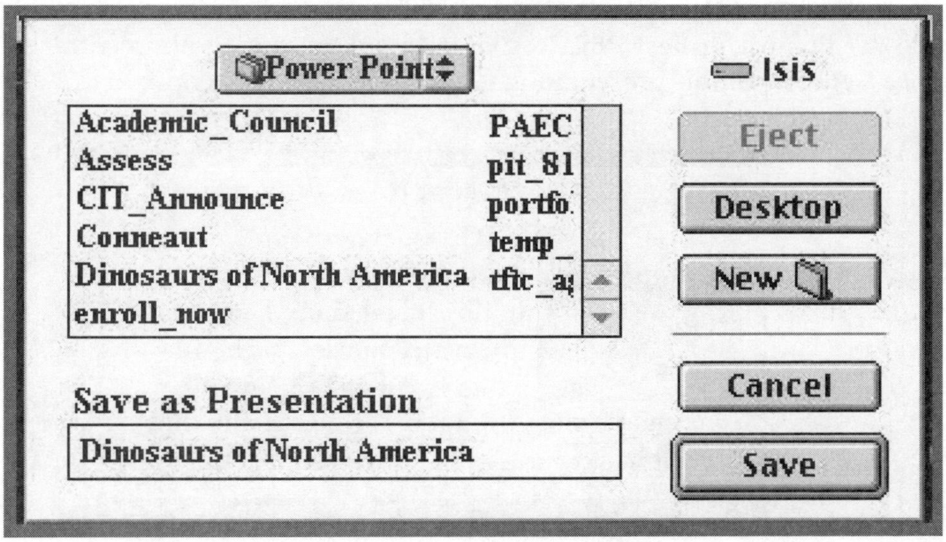

Figure 5-5. Macintosh Version of the Save As Dialog Box

Preparing Visual-Based Presentations

Objective 4.2: Demonstrate a grasp of visual-based design along with a mastery of enhanced graphics presentation features. Combine these skills with the use of technology resources harvested from the Internet to produce visual-based materials for teaching.

Designing Visual-Based Classroom Presentations

Visual-based presentations consist of 12–15 slides with the following elements:

- **Slides 1 and 2** introduce the lesson.
- **Slide 3** delivers the learning objectives. This initial orientation to the presentation helps eliminate misconceptions and establishes prior student knowledge of the content area.
- **Slides 4 through 9** confer the content material of the lesson. Images are offered to students who learn best visually and slides are reinforced with textual material to support the lesson.
- **Slides 10 to 11** define vocabulary words and offer an assessment opportunity to ensure that student understanding has occurred.
- **Slide 12** links the students to information in the form of pre-selected Web sites, workbook material, and outside research to further explore the topic.

Enhanced Graphics Presentation Features

Actually revising an existing presentation is the easiest method of practicing the enhanced features of Power Point. Use **Best Practices #8** to locate the presentation entitled "Dinosaurs of North America." A copy of this presentation is available in the appendix to this chapter.

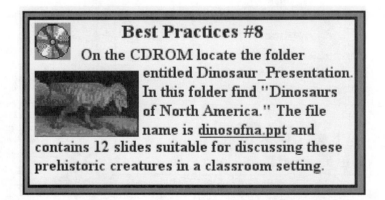

Best Practices #8
On the CDROM locate the folder entitled Dinosaur_Presentation. In this folder find "Dinosaurs of North America." The file name is dinosofna.ppt and contains 12 slides suitable for discussing these prehistoric creatures in a classroom setting.

Inserting Clip Art. The Clip Art Gallery offers a variety of pictures, photographs, sounds, and video clips (see Figure 5-6). To insert clip art into a presentation

-  **Enter the Slide View**—Before inserting clip art, *Power Point must be in the Slide View mode.*

- **Select the Slide**—Move to the slide where the image is to appear. Unlike documents, the flashing cursor may be placed anywhere on the selected slide.

- 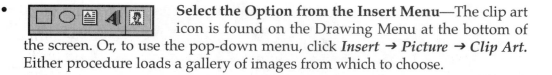 **Select the Option from the Insert Menu**—The clip art icon is found on the Drawing Menu at the bottom of the screen. Or, to use the pop-down menu, click *Insert → Picture → Clip Art.* Either procedure loads a gallery of images from which to choose.

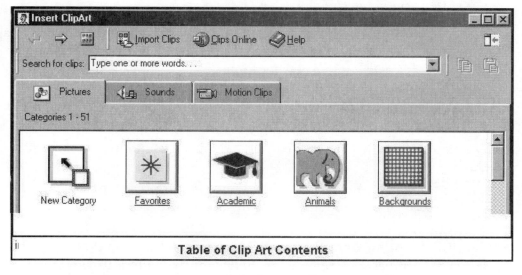

Figure 5-6. Clip Art Gallery

- **Select a Category**—Click an icon to display the contents of images available in each category. Scroll through the available images and locate one appropriate for the instructional material under consideration.

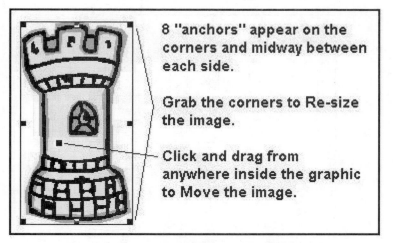

Figure 5-7. Procedures for Resizing and Moving a Clip Art Image

- **Select the Image**—Click the **Insert button** to insert the image into the body of the document. Once there, the image may be resized or moved as desired (see Figure 5-7).

- **To Resize Clip Art**—Click anywhere on the image to activate the "anchors"—little square boxes which appear on the perimeter of the image. Place the cursor on one of the four *corner* anchors to transform the cursor from a pointer to a diagonal arrow. Hold the mouse button and drag diagonally to resize the image proportionally. The anchors appearing in the mid-perimeter locations stretch the image horizontally or vertically.

- **To Move Clip Art**—Move the mouse anywhere inside the desired image. The cursor changes from a pointer to a four-way arrow. Hold the mouse button and drag the image to a new location on the slide.

- **Cut, Copy, and Paste**—Select the clip art by clicking the image. Click the **Cut** (scissors) icon to delete it, **Copy** the image to the clipboard, or **Paste** it into a new location.

- *Run the Slide Show to view the images.*

Inserting Sounds from the Gallery. To insert a digitized sound file into presentations, follow these procedures:

- **Enter the Slide View**—Before inserting sounds, *Power Point must be in the Slide View mode*.
- **Select the Slide**—Place the cursor anywhere on a selected slide.
- **Select the Option from the Insert Menu**—From the pop-down menu, click *Insert → Movies and Sounds → Sounds from Gallery* to view the Gallery contents.

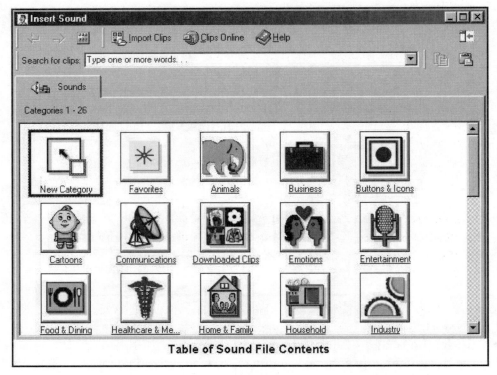

Figure 5-8. Sound Gallery

- **Select the Category**—Click once on an icon to display the sound files available in the category (see figure 5-8). Scroll through the available sounds and locate an appropriate file.

- **Select the Sound**—Double-click the sound icon or *click a sound icon once* then the *Insert button*. An image that looks like a speaker appears on the slide. Move the icon to a desired location on the slide. During the **Slide Show**, the sound file plays when the speaker icon is clicked by the viewer.

- *Run the Slide Show to listen to the sounds.*

Inserting Movies from the Gallery. Inserting a video clip from the Gallery follows the same procedure.

- **Enter the Slide View**—Before inserting movies, *Power Point must be in the Slide View mode.*
- **Select the Slide**—Place the cursor anywhere on a selected slide.
- **Select the Option from the Insert Menu**—From the pop-down menu, click *Insert → Movies and Sounds → Movies from Gallery* to view the movie clip Gallery contents.

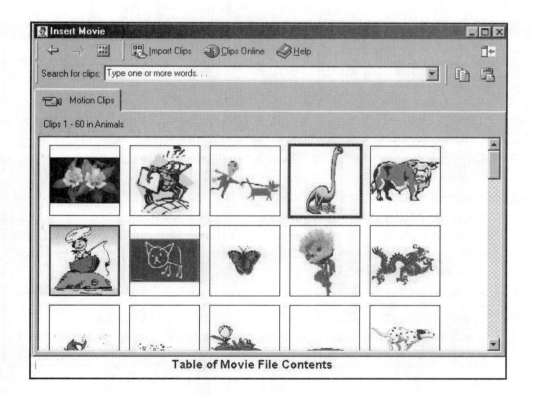

Figure 5-9. Movie Gallery

- **Select the Category**—Click once on an icon to display the animation available in the category (see Figure 5-9). Scroll through the available movies and locate an appropriate file.

-  **Select the Movie**—Double-click the movie icon or *click a movie icon once* then the *Insert button*. An icon appears on the slide depending on the inserted clip. Move the icon to a desired location on the slide. Do not expect feature length movies from the Gallery. Most of the clips are actually "animated gifs," short cartoons lasting barely 2–3 seconds. But they do add motion to a presentation.

- *Run the Slide Show to view the movie.*

Inserting Pictures, Sounds, and Movies from the Internet. Images, sounds, and video clips harvested from the Internet may also be included in a presentation.

- **Enter the Slide View**—*Power Point must be in the Slide View mode.*
- **Select the Slide**—Move to the target slide.
- **Select the Option from the Insert Menu**.
  - To Insert Pictures: *click Insert* → *Picture g From File.*
  - To Insert Sounds: *click Insert* → *Movies and Sounds* → *Sounds from File.*
  - To Insert Movies: *click Insert* → *Movies and Sounds* → *Movies from File.*
- **Select the File**—*Double-click on the file name or click the file icon and Insert.* The image, speaker icon, or video clip icon appears on the selected slide.

- *Run the Slide Show to view the multimedia.*

Inserting Text from the Internet. To insert text, the easiest method is to cut and paste directly from the web into an awaiting document by following these steps:

- **Enter the Slide or Outline View**—The presentation may be in either the Slide or Outline View to accept text.
- **Select the Slide**—Move to the target slide.
- **Minimize Power Point**—Minimizing a window is different for Macintosh and Windows systems. Macintosh uses the **Collapse** icon on the Title Bar to reduce the size of the window while Windows uses the **Minimize** icon to place the application on the Task Bar.

Enter the URL for the following Dinosaur Web Site:

http://www.EnchantedLearning.com/subjects/dinosaurs/classroom/Report.shtml

---

Figure 5-10. Open the URL

- **Open a Netscape Session**—Enter the URL shown in Figure 5-10 to find *"How to Write a Great Dinosaur Report,"* and practice the following exercise:
- **Locate and Select the Desired Text**—*Position the cursor* to the left of the desired body of text. *Click and drag the cursor down and to the right* until all the desired text has been highlighted. Practice selecting text until the movement of the mouse becomes second nature.

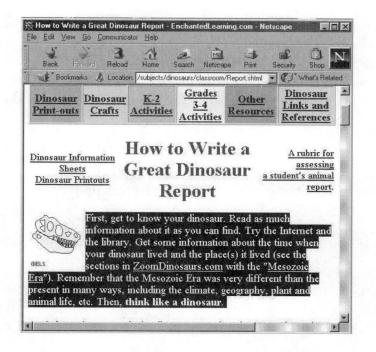

Figure 5-II. Copying Text to the Clipboard

- **Copy the Text to the Clipboard**—Copy the desired text onto the clipboard (see Figure 5-11) using the *Edit → Copy* pop-down menu.
- **Maximize/Restore Power Point**—*Return to Power Point* by reversing the minimize/collapse process. For Macintosh, a click of the **Collapse** button on the Title Bar restores the window. For Windows, locate the application on the **Task Bar** at the bottom of the screen and double-click.
- **Create a Text Box** on the Slide—Using the Drawing menu at the bottom of the screen, *click the Text Box icon*. Move the mouse to the target slide. Click and drag to establish the boundaries for the textual information. A window opens when the mouse button is released.
- **Paste the Text into the Text Box**—Use the *Edit → Paste* pop-down menu to insert text.
- **Reformat the Text**—Make the text fit within the box. Change the font size if it is too big or too small. And, delete any superfluous spaces and line feeds.
- **Save the Presentation**.

Inserting Hyperlinks into a Power Point Slide. Hyperlinks connect the presentation to an Internet site and may be tied to any object on a slide such as text, clip art, and images. Using hyperlinks avoids problems such as sending students to improper sites, avoiding the "dark side" of the Internet, eliminating unproductive searching and surfing, and overcoming obstacles to the discovery process (e.g., typing skills). To insert a Hyperlink

- 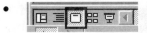 Enter the Slide View—*Power Point must be in the Slide View mode.*
- **Select the Slide**—Move to the target slide. To practice this skill, advance to slide 12 and examine the links provided in the dinosaur presentation.
- **Select the text or image** to serve as the hyperlink—Click on the first bullet, "**Jason's Dinosaur Site**."

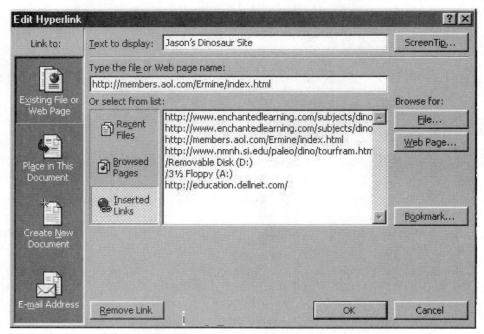

Figure 5-12. Edit Hyperlink Dialog Box

- Click the *Insert → Hyperlink* pop-down menu—If you selected the correct hyperlink, **http://members.aol.com/Ermine/index.html** is displayed (see Figure 5-12). It may be a long address, but this is a great site for elementary school students seeking information about Dinosaurs. *Click OK* to retain the link.

- 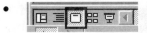 *Run the Slide Show* and click on the link to launch the web browser. Notice that a hyperlink is a different color (usually blue) from the rest of the text.

Spell Checking the Presentation. Power Point checks spelling; however, the options are more limited than the word processor and grammar checking is not yet available.

- **Automatically correct spelling**—The Auto Correct feature, accessed from the *Tools → AutoCorrect* pop-down menu, finds and replaces spelling errors. For example, "definately" is replaced with "definitely." AutoCorrect uses the spell checker's main dictionary along with a list of entries easily appended with personalized words.

-  **Check spelling on Demand**—Spelling errors may be checked at any time by clicking on the Spell Check icon. Spell Check scrolls through every slide to identify errors. This method is useful when proofing an entire presentation.

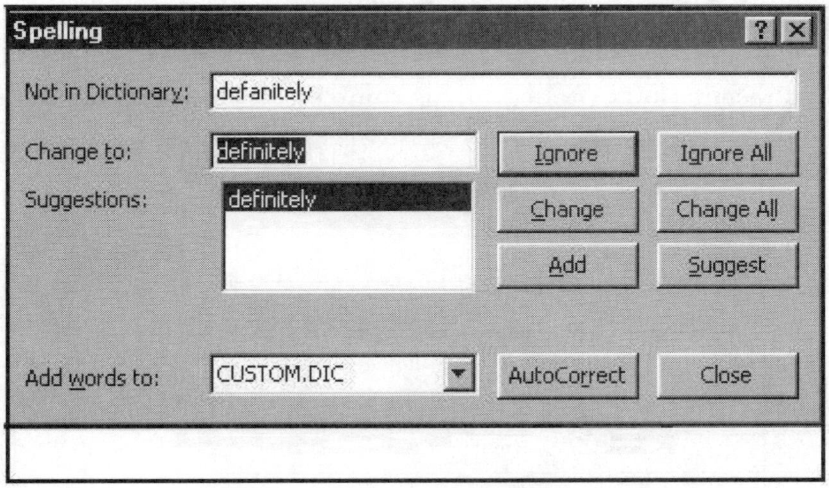

Figure 5-13. Spell Checker Dialog Box

- **Making Corrections**—The Spell Checker dialog box is slightly different than Word (see Figure 5-13); however, the differences are minor.
  - The top window, **Not in Dictionary,** identifies the unrecognized word. Remember, the word may be spelled correctly but Spell Checker simply does not recognize it and therefore highlights it for action.
  - The **Change to** window is the Spell Checker's attempt to suggest the correct spelling from the list that appears in the **Suggestions** window. Usually its guesses are right on the mark. If the choices are inappropriate, there are two options. First, **Ignore** the choices. **Ignore All** disregards the same "misspelling" throughout the remainder of the document. Second, **Add** the new word to the personalized Custom Dictionary and all further encounters with the same word are considered correct.
  - If one of the choices offered is suitable, click the desired **Suggestion,** then the **Change** button. **Change All** finds and replace every occurrence of the word wherever it is encountered throughout the document.

Selecting a New Design Template. Power Point comes with a wide variety of professionally designed templates. When a new template is applied, the background color, font size, and font color may change. Before applying a new template to a presentation, *Save the presentation first* so the original file is available should the results prove unsatisfactory. Change templates early in the design process before a considerable amount of text and images are inserted. To select a new template, follow these instructions:

-  **Enter the Slide View Mode**—A new template may be applied in any mode; however, the Slide View displays the changes immediately.

- Click *Format* → *Apply Design Template* to preview a list of available templates. NOTE: Macintosh users may need to click *Find Files* → *Search Files* → *OK* to locate their templates.
- Locate the desired template and *click Apply*. For practice, *select the Fireball template*; it is one of the most popular.
- *Save the presentation* and *Run the Slide Show* to view the results.

Printing the Presentation. After editing is complete, the presentation is ready to be printed using a few different features than the word processing counterpart.

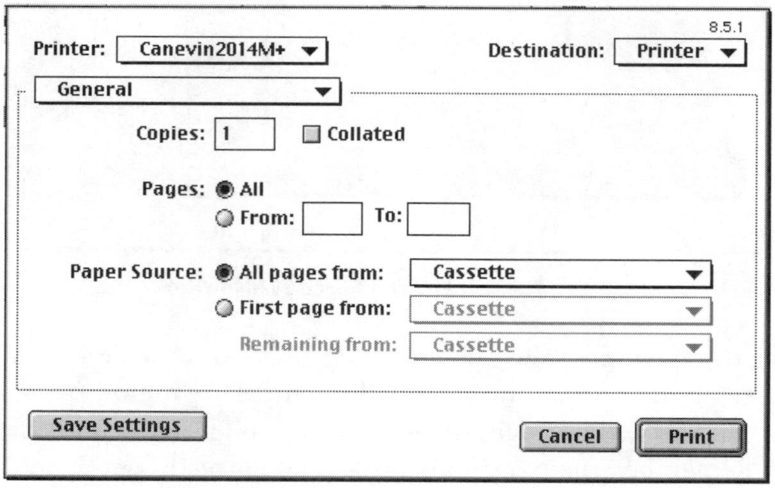

Figure 5-14. Selecting Print Options (Macintosh Version)

- **Selecting Power Point Print Options** (Macintosh Only)—To see a complete list of available options, click the **General** print window of Microsoft Power Point (see Figure 5-14).
- **No Print Preview**—There is no Print Preview; view the Slide Show to display the presentation before printing.
- **Print**—Use the *File* → *Print* pop-down menu to produce the dialog box shown in Figure 5-15.

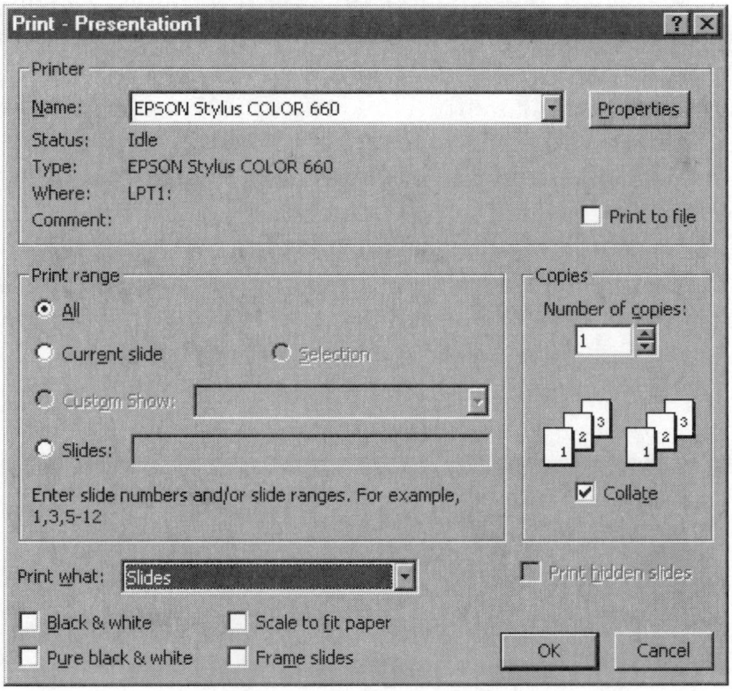

Figure 5-15. The Print Command Dialog Box

- The most common options when printing a presentation include: Print Range, Number of Copies, and Print What.
  - **Print Range**—**All** prints every slide in the presentation, **Current Slide** prints only the single slide presently viewed, and **Slides** allows the user to enter a range of slides.
  - **Number of Copies**—Enter the Number of Copies to be printed. Requesting the copies to be Collated prints them in order from first to last slide, then repeats the process again for additional copies.
  - **Print What**—Another significant feature is the option to print Slides, Handouts, and Outlines. Click on **Slides** to print one slide on a page. Print multiple slides on a page by selecting **Handouts** 2, 3, 4, 6, or 9 slides to a page. The Handouts option is excellent for producing copies of slides for use in classroom situations.

Conclusion

To create a classroom presentation, consider the specific learning objectives before attempting to construct lesson materials. A variety of visual materials, sounds, and video is available. Clip art offers hundreds of graphic images in its gallery. Images may be scanned from a book or downloaded from the Internet to assist learner understanding. Sounds and movies support student learning; however, using too many of these materials distract from an otherwise well-constructed lesson.

Power Point offers a variety of presentation formats. In addition to an on-screen presentation, hard copy reproductions of the presentation facilitate note-taking, student questions, and lesson reviews.

Good design skills are essential to attract, maintain, and direct attention while emphasizing the message. The use of hyperlinks provide teacher-validated Internet sites while helping students eliminate unproductive surfing. Finally, hyperlinks reduce a reliance on typing skills and address technology issues which result in unproductive computer time.

For readers wishing to examine some additional examples of visual-based classroom materials, **Technology Burst #4** provides a number of presentations prepared by fellow educators and offered with their permission. Select presentations that may be appropriate for your classroom and revise them while practicing the skills offered in this chapter.

Technology Burst #4

On the CDROM, locate the folder entitled Example_Visual. In this folder locate the "List of Example Visual-Based Materials." The file name is visual.htm and contains excellent examples of classroom presentations designed by practicing teachers.

Bibliography

Fitzsimmons, B. (1996). *What's your kid's learning style: Auditory, visual, hands-on?* San Francisco: San Francisco Jewish Community Publications.

Appendix

DINOSAURS OF NORTH AMERICA

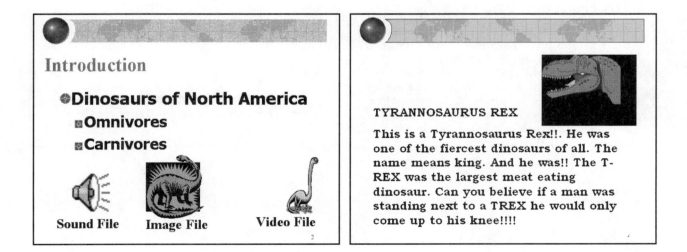

BRONTOSAURUS
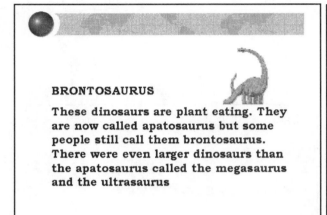

These dinosaurs are plant eating. They are now called apatosaurus but some people still call them brontosaurus. There were even larger dinosaurs than the apatosaurus called the megasaurus and the ultrasaurus

5

VELOCIRAPTOR

These are my favorites!!! They were about the size of a man. They were very very good jumpers. Velociraptors had long claws which they would use to get their prey. They also usually hunted in packs like wolves do. Many people think Deinonychus and velociraptors are the same but they are NOT. They do look and act alike though.   7

VELOCIRAPTOR

These are my favorites!!! They were about the size of a man. They were very very good jumpers. Velociraptors had long claws which they would use to get their prey. They also usually hunted in packs like wolves do. Many people think Deinonychus and velociraptors are the same but they are NOT. They do look and act alike though.   7

PTERODACTYL

This is a pterodactyl, they really are not dinosaurs. They are flying reptiles

8

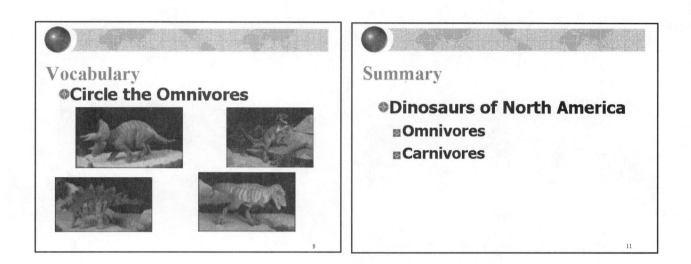

Chapter 6

WEB HOME PAGES
FOR THE CLASSROOM

This chapter examines Netscape Composer and how resources found on the Internet are molded into viable instructional materials matching specific lesson objectives with student learning strategies. In support of those objectives, chapter 6 discusses:

- **Web Page Fundamentals.** Objective 6.1: Demonstrate a mastery of web page fundamentals.

- **Preparing Web-Based Instruction for the Classroom.** Objective 6.2: Demonstrate a grasp of web-based design along with a mastery of enhanced web page features. Combine these skills with the use of technology resources harvested from the Internet to produce web-based materials for teaching.

Web Page Fundamentals

Objective 4.1: Demonstrate a mastery of web page fundamentals.

Whether you prefer handouts, study guides, and workbooks or overheads, 35mm slides, and projected images, the fact remains that the Internet is much too valuable a resource to dismiss as a passing fad. Yet, if the Internet is to reach its full potential as a teaching and learning strategy, educators must come to know and understand not only how to find these resources but how to create them as well.

Composer is most easily accessed from inside Netscape. Chapter 3 presented information about launching Communicator using an alias or shortcut. If they are available on the desktop, *double click the Netscape icon* to launch the application. If a shortcut or alias has not been created, follow the appropriate step below:

- Windows users, *click the Start Button* on the Task Bar, scroll to *Programs* and over to *Netscape Navigator*.

- Macintosh users, *click on the Apple Menu*, scroll to *Recent Applications* and over to *Netscape Navigator*.

Netscape Navigator opens to a pre-selected home page. However, it is Netscape **Composer** that actually edits, moves, and inserts features. Learning the fundamentals of web page development is easier if the **Dinosaur Home Page** again serves as an example. Use **Best Practices #6** (first presented in chapter 3) for practicing the instructions discussed. (A copy of this web site is available at the appendix to chapter 3.)

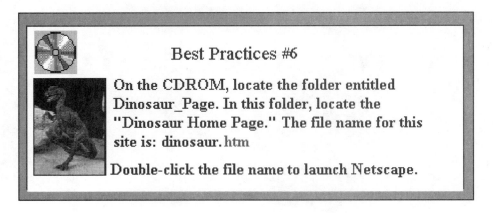

Figure 6-I. Entering Netscape Composer

Launching Netscape Composer. Click the *File → Edit Page* pop-down menu within Navigator to enter Composer (see Figure 6-1).

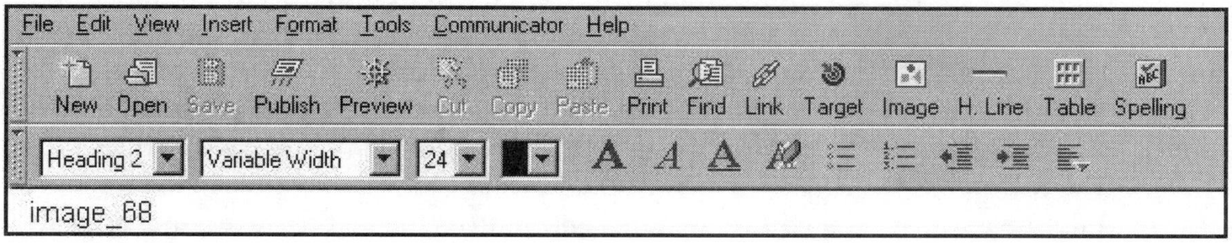

Figure 6-2. The Netscape Composer Tool Bar

Editing Text on a Web Page. The editing features of Composer resemble a word processor. However, Netscape is not affiliated with the Microsoft Corporation; therefore, the icons vary to avoid copyright infringements (see Figure 6-2). There are a few other differences between the software packages reviewed in previous chapters and Netscape Composer.

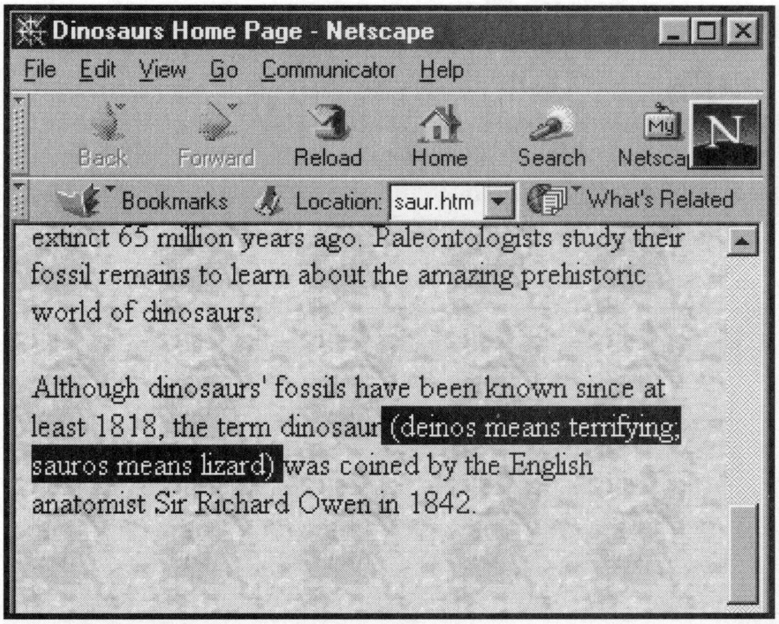

Figure 6-3. Editing Text Using Composer

To practice editing, use the **Dinosaur Home Page** and scroll to the last paragraph under the **Introduction.** Locate the text "**deinos means terrifying; saurus means lizard**" (see Figure 6-3).

- **Selecting Text**—Before editing, text must be highlighted (or "selected"). To select
  - **A word**, position the cursor on the desired word and *double-click* the mouse button.
  - **A sentence or paragraph**, *click and drag* to select a phrase, sentence, or paragraph.

-  **Bold, Underline, Italics, and Remove Style**—Editing commands control the **Appearance** of the text. Click the **Bold** icon, then **Italics**, then **Underline** to see how these commands affect the look of the selected text. Notice that the buttons change their appearance when clicked to indicate that this feature is ON. A second click toggles the feature OFF. There is one additional button, the **Remove Style** icon, which eliminates all special editing features and returns the text to its original appearance. Practice these editing features using the **Dinosaur Home Page**.

- **Left, Center, and Right**—The **Alignment** function is located to the right side of the Tool Bar. Click the pop-down menu to select **Left** alignment which aligns text along the left margin. **Centering** is accomplished by clicking the middle icon, and **Right** alignment moves text to the outside margin.

- **Changing Font and Font Size**—To the left side of the Tool Bar are pop-down menus to change Font and Font Size. Click the down arrow next to the Font window to view the available formats. Use the same procedure to set a new Font Size.

- **Indents Forward and Back**—Use Indent to move text or images across the page. The spacebar will not accomplish the desired effect because Internet browsers ignore blank spaces when displaying the contents of a web page. *Indent the heading Instructions* for practice.

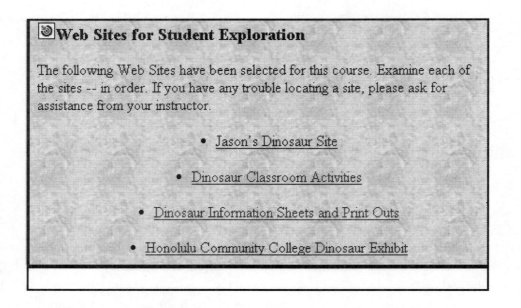

Figure 6-4. Bullets in Netscape Composer

- **Bullets and Numbered List**—The Bullets list icon inserts a bullet on the selected line. The **Numbered List** icon initially inserts a pound sign symbol(#), then substitutes the appropriate number when the Web page is actually viewed. *Locate the Web Sites for Student Exploration and select these four lines of text.* Add *Bullets* to each of the addresses as shown in Figure 6-4.

Moving Text on a Web Page. Cut, Copy, and Paste commands move text within the page. Practice using the following commands on the **Dinosaur Home Page**. Remember that edits attempted during this exercise do not affect the read-only file on the CDROM.

-  **Cut, Copy, and Paste**—Find the familiar scissors, documents, and clipboard icons. The scissors **Cut**, or delete the selected text. The twin documents **Copy** text or images. And, the clipboard **Pastes** text to a new location.

The Undo Command. The experimental aspect of building an interactive web page is very important. Web browsers "paint" the computer screen based on the background, image location, text placement, and size of the window specified. Sometimes changes produce the desired effects; other times they may not. However, the **Undo Command** is available to reverse any action that produces unacceptable results.

- To reverse a previous action, click the *Edit → Undo* command. There are two differences with Composer: first, there is no Undo icon; and second, only one action (the last action) is reversible.

Saving a Web Page. When creating or revising Web pages, save after each element is created or modified. The process takes only a single mouse click and saves considerable time in the event of a power outage, mechanical failure, or computer virus.

- To Save a Web page, click the **Save** icon on the Toolbar or select *File → Save* from the File menu. If the file has never been saved, the **Save As** dialog box appears.
- Set the location by *clicking the Save In box* until the correct folder appears and *enter a new File Name* for the page. Click the *Save button* (Windows) *or OK button* (Macintosh).

Previewing a Web Page. Following each save, **Preview** the changes before going further.

-  *Click the Preview* icon to open Netscape Navigator and display the current version of the changes. Composer remains open for continued editing.

Preparing Web-Based Presentations

Objective 6.2: Demonstrate a grasp of web-based design along with a mastery of enhanced web page features. Combine these skills with the use of technology resources harvested from the Internet to produce web-based materials for teaching.

Designing Web-Based Instruction

A successful instructional web page consists of the following elements:

- **Banner Title and Image** to lead into the topic of the lesson and confirm the location of the page. It is highly recommended that the image appearing on the banner also be provided the student in a handout, study guide, or classroom presentation introducing the web page.

- **Introduction**—Targeted specifically on the content of the lesson, the Introduction provides a brief explanation of the topic and the key elements to be covered on the page.

- **Instructions**—There should be no misunderstanding about what is to be accomplished and how the learning is to be evidenced after completing the web-based materials. The instructions should describe which questions must be completed in a handout. The instructions should present any outside readings required before or after the web page is viewed. The instructions should spell out any special sequencing of materials (for example, discussing a classroom presentation before exploring the web page).

- **Lesson Objectives**—Teachers should share expectations for learning with their students. Let them see the actual learning objectives that will be used to evaluate their understanding. Except for the very youngest of students, this section of the web page reduces confusion and focuses student attention on the important aspects of the lesson.

- **Web Sites for Student Exploration**—Include internal as well as external links to other web pages. An internal link ties teacher-made web pages to other teacher-made web pages or to online handouts and classroom presentations. An external link provides access to other pages on the World Wide Web validated for their academic content and application to the lesson at hand.

- **Student Assessment Information**—Students should be in possession of all the facts related to learning. Provide the criteria for grading in this section of the web page.

- **Address Block**—The Address Block furnishes the policies regarding use of web-based materials including author citation (with name, affiliation, and email address), copyright and Fair Use statement, and a created and revised on date.

Enhanced Features of Netscape Composer

Images, text, and hyperlinks downloaded from Internet sites spark student interest to support the learning objectives of the teacher. Hyperlinks, in particular, connect to sites appropriate for remedial and enrichment activities and offer new venues for student research and exploration.

(

Inserting Images from the Internet. Digitized pictures may be inserted onto a web page using the Main menu bar after positioning the cursor at a desired location.

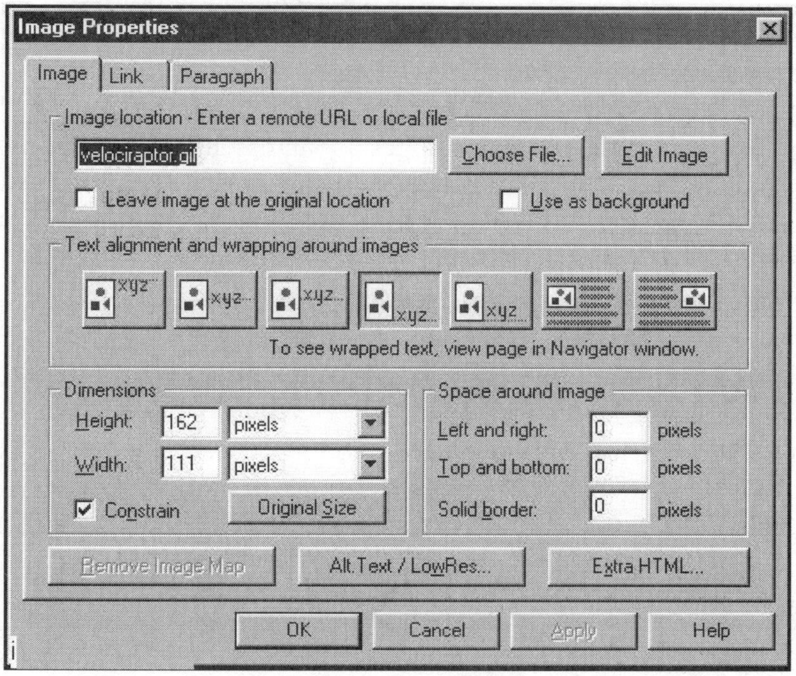

Figure 6-5. Image Properties

- To **Insert Images**, *Click the Image* icon or *Insert → Image* from the pop-down menu. For practice, *scroll to the top of the Dinosaur Home Page and click the image of the velociraptor* to launch the **Image Properties** dialog box (see Figure 6-5).
- **Choose File**—The dialog box displays the Image name and Location; in this case, **velociraptor.gif**. To change an image, double-click *Choose File* to select another image.
- **Text Alignment and Wrapping**—The first five text alignment icons from left to right place text at the top, center, or bottom of the image. Text may also be wrapped around an image by selecting one of the final two icons.
- **Dimensions**—The original size of the image is provided in the **Dimensions** windows and may be resized by entering a new **Height** or **Width** value. Always *click the Constrain* box (shown checked in Figure 6-5) to recalculate the new dimensions. Click **Original Size** to return the initial image dimensions.
- *Click OK* to insert the Image.

Moving an Image on a Web Page. Click anywhere inside the image to change the cursor from a pointer to a hand. *Hold the mouse button and drag the image* to its new location.

Other Image Commands. The **Cut, Copy, and Paste** commands act the same for images as textual material.

- Select the image and use the *Edit* → *Cut* menu to delete the picture.
- *Click Edit* → *Copy* to send the image to the clipboard followed by *Edit* → *Paste* to copy the image to a new location.
- **Save the page**. *File* → *Save* the Web Page.

Inserting Text from the Internet. Images are an essential component of a successful web page. After all, multimedia is a key advantage of using the Internet and textual information has retained its rightful place in the online teaching and learning experience. To **Insert Text**, the easiest method is to **Cut and Paste** directly into an awaiting web page by following these steps:

- **Move** the cursor to the desired location.
- **Minimize Netscape Composer**—Minimizing a window is different for Macintosh and Windows systems. Macintosh uses the **Collapse** icon on the Title Bar to reduce the size of the window, while Windows uses the **Minimize** icon to place the application on the Task Bar.

Enter the URL for the following Dinosaur Web Site:

http://www.EnchantedLearning.com/subjects/dinosaurs/classroom/Report.shtml

---

Figure 6-6. Open the URL

- **Open a Netscape Session**—Enter the URL shown in Figure 6-6 to find *"How to Write a Great Dinosaur Report"* and practice the following exercise:

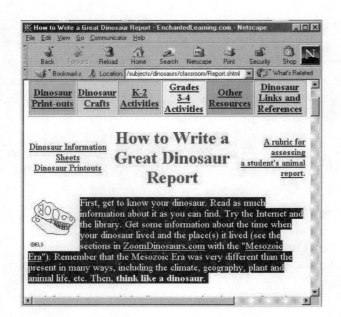

Figure 6-7. Copying Text to the Clipboard

- **Locate and Select the Desired Text**—*Position the cursor* to the left of the desired body of text and *click and drag the cursor* down and to the right until all the desire text has been highlighted. Practice selecting text until the movement of the mouse becomes second nature.

- **Copy the Text to the Clipboard**—Copy the desired text onto the clipboard (see Figure 6-7) using the *Edit → Copy* pop-down menu.

- **Maximizes/Restore Netscape Composer**—*Return to Composer* by reversing the minimize/collapse process. For Macintosh, a click of the **Collapse** button on the Title Bar restores the window. For Windows, locate the application on the **Task Bar** at the bottom of the screen and double-click.

- **Paste the Text onto the Web Page**—Use the *Edit → Paste* pop-down menu to insert the text into the desired location.

- **Reformat the Text**—Make the text fit within the box. Change the font size if it is too big or too small. And, delete any superfluous spaces and line feeds.

- **Save** the web page.

Inserting Hyperlinks onto a Web Page. Hyperlinks connect web pages to other instructionally-rich Internet sites. The use of hyperlinks avoid many of the problems associated with the World Wide Web, such as sending students to invalid sites, avoiding the "dark side" of the Internet, eliminating unproductive searching and surfing, and overcoming obstacles to the discovery process (e.g., typing skills). To insert a Hyperlink

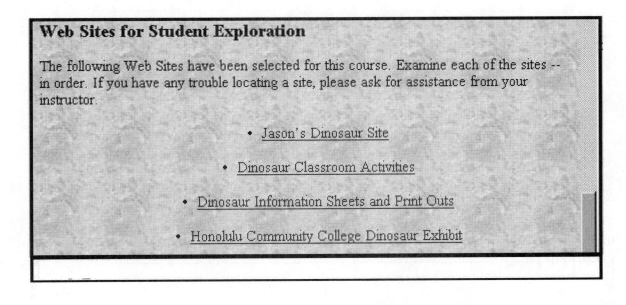

Figure 6-8. Adding a Text Hyperlink

- **Create the text link**—For this exercise, *add the text "Honolulu Community College Dinosaur Exhibit"* to the current list of **Web Sites for Student Exploration** (see Figure 6-8). For appearances, *click the Bullet icon* and *Center alignment* so that it looks like the other links in the list.

- **Select the text** to serve as the hyperlink. Click and drag to highlight the entire string of text as the hyperlink.

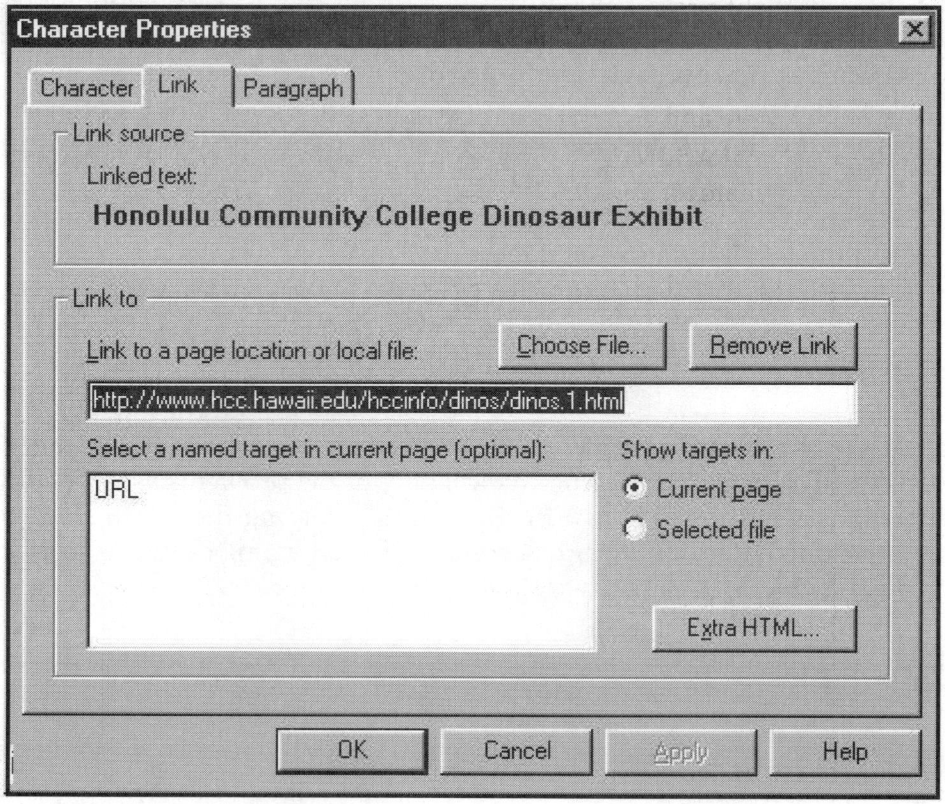

![Character Properties Dialog Box screenshot showing the Link tab with Linked text "Honolulu Community College Dinosaur Exhibit" and Link to a page location or local file field containing http://www.hcc.hawaii.edu/hccinfo/dinos/dinos.1.html]

Figure 6-9. Character Properties Dialog Box

-   **Inserting the Link**—Click the *Link* icon from the Menu bar or the *Insert → Link* pop-down menu. In the dialog box, locate **Link to a page location or local file** and enter the URL: **http://www.hcc.hawaii.edu/ hccinfo/dinos/dinos.1.html.** Notice that the text link changes from black to blue indicating a hyperlink (see Figure 6-9).

- 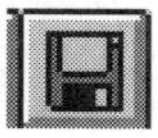 **Save** the web page.

- **Preview** the link in Navigator and test the connectivity to the selected site.

Preparing the Address Block

The Address Block informs viewers of the policies regarding use of the Web-based material and should include the following elements:

- **Author Citation**—Regardless of whether or not the material on the Web page is to be copyright protected, providing an Author Citation offers immediate access for those viewers who wish to contact you either for permission, assurances, or comments.

- **Author's Name and Affiliation**—Self-explanatory.

- **Author's Email Address**—Move to the address block area at the **bottom** of the web page. Create an email link by following these instructions:

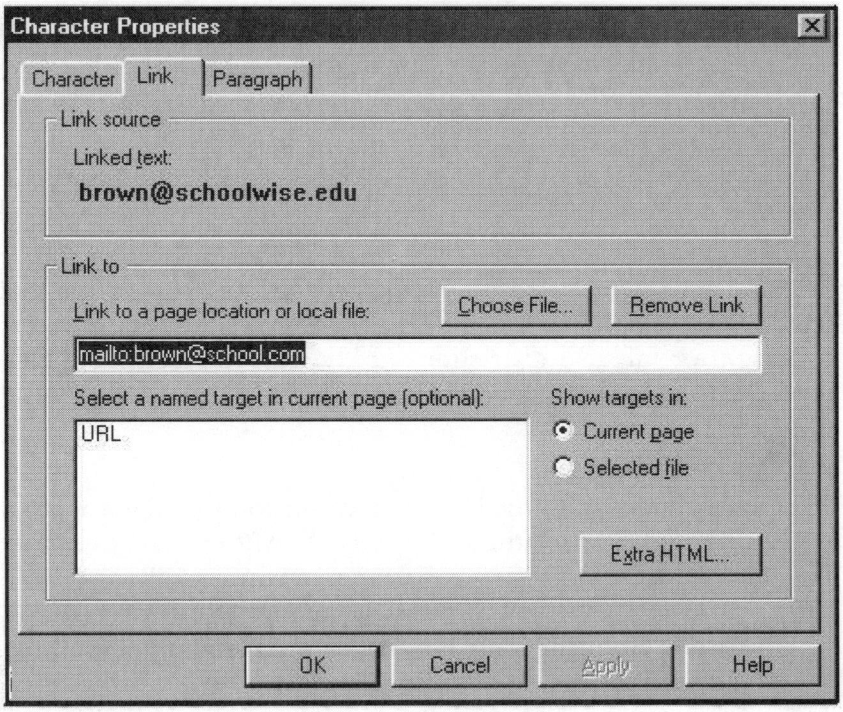

Figure 6-10. Creating an Email Link

- **[Link icon]** *Click the Link icon* from the tool bar or the *Insert → Link* pop-down menu. In the dialog box, locate the window entitled **Link to a page location or local file**. Enter the tag "**mailto://**" (mailto is all one word—no spaces) followed by the email address. Figure 6-10 shows **brown@school.com** as the text link. The resulting text link on the web page changes color indicating a hyperlink.

Affiliation's Name and Email Address. This is important information in the event the link is removed. With this data, chances are you will be able to contact the author and request assistance.

Copyright or Fair Use Statement. Some teachers upload their materials with the expressed intent that they be used by their peers and colleagues. In either case, a Copyright Restriction or Fair Use Statement is appropriate in the Address Block. Two examples are shown below.

> **Copyright Restriction**. *Permission is granted to make copies for department/school use and to excerpt material for local newsletters. All other use (print or electronic) requires the express permission of the Author (Email address provided below).*

> **Fair Use Statement**. *Permission is granted for unrestricted use of the materials found on this Web Page. Author requests that any materials (text or images) acquired from these pages for inclusion in related resources carry a citation of the Author as indicated below.*

Created And Revised Date. For copyright protection, it is imperative that both dates be included. The **Created Date** establishes the initial publication of the page and confirms the first date under which copyright or fair use restrictions apply. The **Revised Date** alerts the viewer that changes have been made to a previous version.

Spell Checking the Web Page

Netscape Composer checks spelling; however, when compared to the previous applications, its features are very limited. For example, there is no Auto Correct feature and no grammar checking.

- **Check Spelling and Grammar on Demand**—Spelling errors are checked by clicking the **Spelling** icon. Each word added to the web page is examined in an attempt to locate and identify errors.

- **Making the Corrections**—The Spelling dialog box for Composer is slightly different that the Microsoft version; however, those differences are minor.

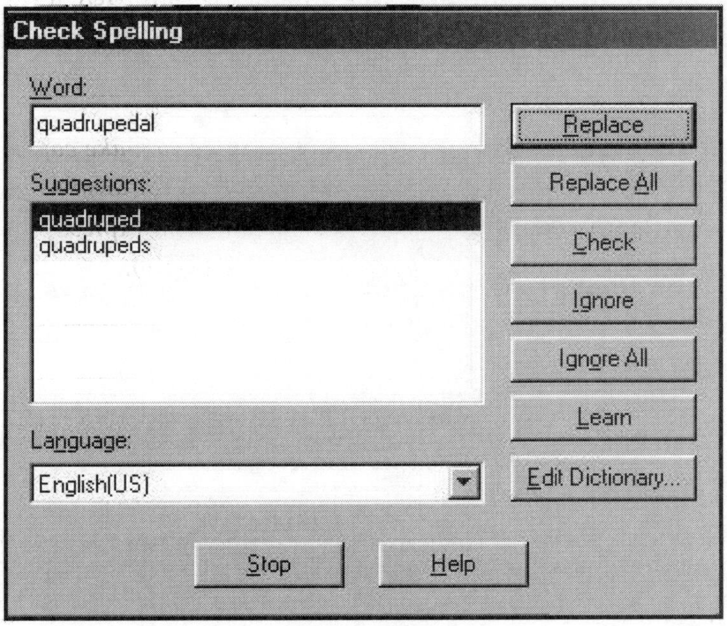

Figure 6-11. Check Spelling Dialog Box

- The top window identifies the item that was not found in the dictionary. The word may be spelled correctly or it may be a word derivative preferred for instructional emphasis. The spell checker simply does not recognize the word and therefore highlights it for action.
- The **Suggestions** window attempts to recommend the correct spelling from a list of possible words. Usually its guesses are right on the mark. If the choices are inappropriate, there are two options. First, **Ignore** the choices. **Ignore All** disregards the same "misspelling" throughout the remainder of the document. Second, add the new word to the personalized dictionary by clicking **Learn** and all further encounters with the same word are considered correct (see Figure 6-11).
- If the choices offered are inappropriate, there are two options. First, **Ignore** the choices. **Ignore All** disregards the same "misspelling" throughout the remainder of the document. Second, **Learn** adds the word to the personalized Custom Dictionary and all further encounters are considered correct.
- If one of the choices offered is suitable, ensure that the correct suggestion is highlighted. Click the desired **Suggestions**, then click the **Replace** button. **Replace All** finds and replaces the word whenever it is encountered throughout the remainder of the document.

Printing the Web Page

After editing is complete, the Web Page is ready to be printed. Before sending the page to the printer, Composer has a feature called the **Print Preview** (**Windows Version only**) that is highly recommended.

- **Print Preview**—To display each page as it will look when printed, *click Print Preview* on the Tool Bar. To exit Print Preview and return to the previous view of the document, *click Close*. To Print directly from the Print Preview click the ⎙ **Print** icon.

- ⎙ Print **Print**. *Click the Print icon* or **File** ➜ **Print** pop-down menu to produce the Print dialog box. The two most common options when printing a hard copy document are Print Range and Number of Copies.

    - **Print Range**—**All** prints the entire web page; **Pages** allows the user to enter a range of pages.

    - **Copies**—Enter the Number of Copies to be printed. Collate the copies to print them in order from first to last slide, then repeat the process.

Conclusion

Before concluding this chapter on web pages, here are a few more tips for creating multimedia materials. First, always develop the objectives of the lesson before constructing any instructional materials. Preparing learning objectives ensures that the instructor considers the specific questions, the location or locations for the student research, and the final learning outcomes that are to be generated from the lesson.

When it comes to creating new materials, begin by harvesting files that already verge upon the final desired product. For example, the "Dinosaur Home Page" offers a suitable boilerplate for future web pages. It is far easier to edit an existing page than to design a new one from scratch.

For classroom applications, web sites should be captured onto a floppy diskette for portability and convenience. Diskettes are easy to reproduce for out of class assignments and easily introduced into a computer lab environment without need of a technology coordinator.

When designing a web page, consider centering images and tables on the page to present a tailored appearance and a minimum of scrolling; using bullets, numbered lists, and tables to display data; saving often and previewing immediately; and, using short file names with no special characters and no spaces.

For readers wishing to examine some additional examples of web-based classroom materials, **Technology Burst #5** provides a number of lesson home pages prepared by fellow educators and offered with their permission. Select examples that may be appropriate for your classroom, and revise them while practicing the skills offered in this chapter.

Technology Burst #5

On the CDROM, locate the folder entitled Example_Web. In this folder locate the

"List of Example Web-Based Materials." The file name is web.htm and contains excellent examples of web home pages designed by practicing teachers.

This completes part 2 of *Teaching Digitally in the 21st Century*. Using Microsoft Word and Power Point plus Netscape Composer, you should possess the necessary skills to develop student-centered, lesson-specific text, visual, and web-based instructional *materials*.

Part 3 of the book continues this exploration with a look at the advanced features of these applications to prepare entire instructional *lessons*.

Appendix

Please refer to the appendix for chapter 4 on page 66.

PART 3

PREPARING INSTRUCTIONAL LESSONS

Chapter 7

A MODEL FOR
TECHNOLOGY-BASED LESSONS

Take your students on a tour of prehistoric dinosaur territory. Observe a tyrannosaurus after a fleeing prey. Visit with the skeletal remains of monsters who inhabited the great plains of America. "Can't be done" you say? "Don't have the time or money in the school budget" is your response. Technology provides the avenue for just such real-time, imaginative explorations; actually, it offers the Information Superhighway. An adventurous spirit is required, along with a little technical help to take those first tentative steps in the preparation of classroom lessons using technology-rich resources harvested from the Internet. To develop such complex instructional lessons, this chapter discusses

- **Preparing Lessons: A Technology-Based Model.** Objective 7.1: Adopt a rubric for designing technology-based lessons that ensures the key elements of lesson development are considered and technology is applied when appropriate.

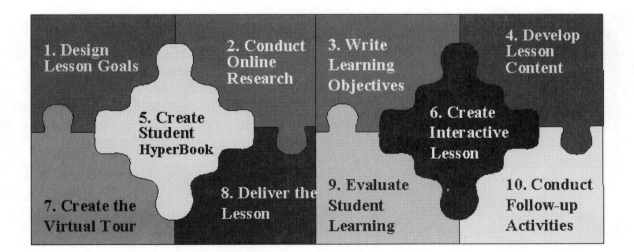

Figure 7-1. The Model for Technology-Based Lessons

Preparing Lessons: A Technology-Based Model

Objective 7.1: Adopt a rubric for designing technology-based lessons that ensures the key elements of lesson development are considered and technology is applied when appropriate.

The "Model for Technology-Based Lessons" is a contemporary rubric especially for teachers interested in preparing their own instructional lessons. It offers a step-by-step rubric for designing, developing, implementing, delivering, and evaluating full-blown technology-based curriculum. Handouts and study guides make way for the more sophisticated HyperBook. Simple visual presentations are replaced with the advanced Interactive Lesson. And, web home pages are exchanged for multifaceted Virtual Tour online explorations.

The Technology-Based Lesson

Step 1: Design the Lesson Goals. Lesson development begins by specifying the overall instructional goals. This step must come before any materials are gathered; even before "surfing" the Web. A technology-based lesson begins with a document containing the following information:

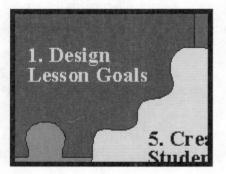

- **Subject Area**
- **Teacher's Name**
- **Grade Level**
- **Description of Student Prior Knowledge**
- **Length of Lesson**
- **Unit of Instruction**
- **Topic Under Exploration**
- **Specific Instructional Goals and Learning Objectives**

Step 2: Conduct Online Research. Once the explicit lesson goals are acknowledged, locating content material is easy. With all this emphasis on technology, teachers must not neglect traditional sources such as the encyclopedia, books and journals, professionals and experts, and the like. However, since this is a text on technology for teaching, *Teaching Digitally in the 21st Century* concentrates on the most productive inquiry tool since the advent of the dictionary; namely, the Internet search engine.

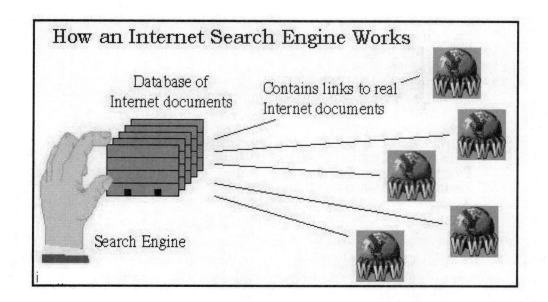

Figure 7-2. Internet Search Engines

A search engine is a software utility that examines selected databases for requested information. Figure 7-2 illustrates how an Internet search engine works. Each time a search is initiated, a query of Internet documents begins. Records in the database contain a link to an actual home page. Contrary to popular belief, search engines do not interrogate every site on the Internet. It would simply take too long.

Search engines differ in how their particular databases are created, either **On-Demand** (machine-generated) or **Pre-Selected** (human-generated). Some engines focus on particular subjects or regional locations while others search for subjects or topical lists. It is often difficult to predict which database might produce the best results; however, here are some important points to keep in mind:

- No search engine is perfect. They are too new to be flawless and many lack the full complement of important search features and options.
- Many engines contain links to web sites that have moved or no longer exist.
- No database is ever complete and no one search engine finds every possible site. One database may support sites that others do not and inquiries often display results very differently.
- No database is ever up to date; some search engines are updated monthly, others semiannually. The content of the Internet changes on a daily basis.
- Search engines often change with upgrades to existing Internet technology. While many features remain the same, others may be added or disappear entirely.

```
Top 20 of 373637 matches.               Show Summaries  View by Web Site

85% Bob Dole's Divorce   [More Like This]
81% This Modern World   [More Like This]
80% Skeleton Closet: All of the Scandals on...   [More Like This]
80% Yahoo! - Government:Politics:Humor:1996 ...   [More Like This]
80% Nerd World : BOB DOLE   [More Like This]
79% newt   [More Like This]
79% Re: Let's all stay friends   [More Like This]
79% Dole's Cash Crunch   [More Like This]
78% Dole Watch   [More Like This]
78% Presidential Primaries   [More Like This]
```

Figure 7-3. On-Demand Search Engine Summary Viewed by Web Site

On-Demand Search Engines. Search engines continuously update their databases by locating documents and capturing selected text from home pages. The process is completed by adding links to the text to summarize the contents of the page. The results of a typical on-demand search is shown in Figure 7-3.

Most machine-generated databases rank the resulting web documents. Rankings are based on a mathematical formula that takes into account how the web page was created. For instance, a site might receive a higher ranking if the search words are found in the title or header than at the bottom of the page. Still, there is a significant difference between what mathematical formulas deem relevant and what a human would consider important.

Pre-Selected Search Engines. Human-generated databases contain sites which have been reviewed by people. A machine-generated search engine might initially explore the web pages, but humans choose what will and will not be included in the final results. The quality of these sites is typically higher; however, they often include far fewer sites.

Metasearch Engines. The metasearch engine represents the newest trend in Internet technology. Rather than compiling their own database, they rely on other Internet search engines to do the work for them. Each metasearch examines multiple databases before retrieving any results, thus saving time by investigating a variety of search engines without connecting separately to each one.

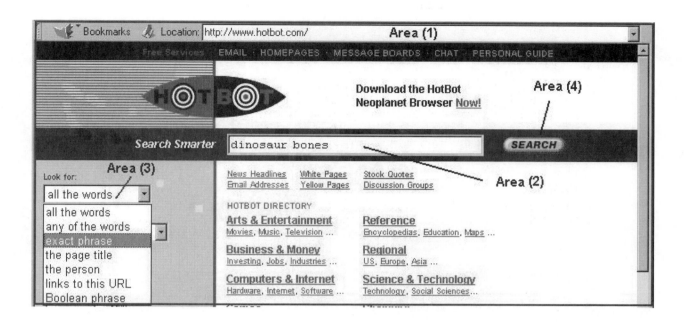

Figure 7-4. Search Engine Home Page

Using an Internet Search Engine. Most search engines include a text box window followed by a start button. The example engine in Figure 7-4 displays four typical areas:

- **Location Window (Area 1)**—The URL **http:www.hotbot.com** in the location window represents the Internet address of this particular search engine.

- **Inquiry Text Window (Area 2)**—Search engines provide a text window for entering one or more of the words. The example shows the words "dinosaur" and "bones" with one space between the words.

- **Query Instructions (Area 3)**—Most engines attempt to locate *any* of the words included in the text window. However, some search and retrieve documents containing *all* the words entered, but not necessarily in any particular order. The task of sifting through sites addressing "dinosaur bones" quickly becomes tedious. To avoid this problem, some search engines allow the user to specify an *exact phrase* (see the highlighted selection in Area 3) to retrieve only those sites containing the two words found in order.

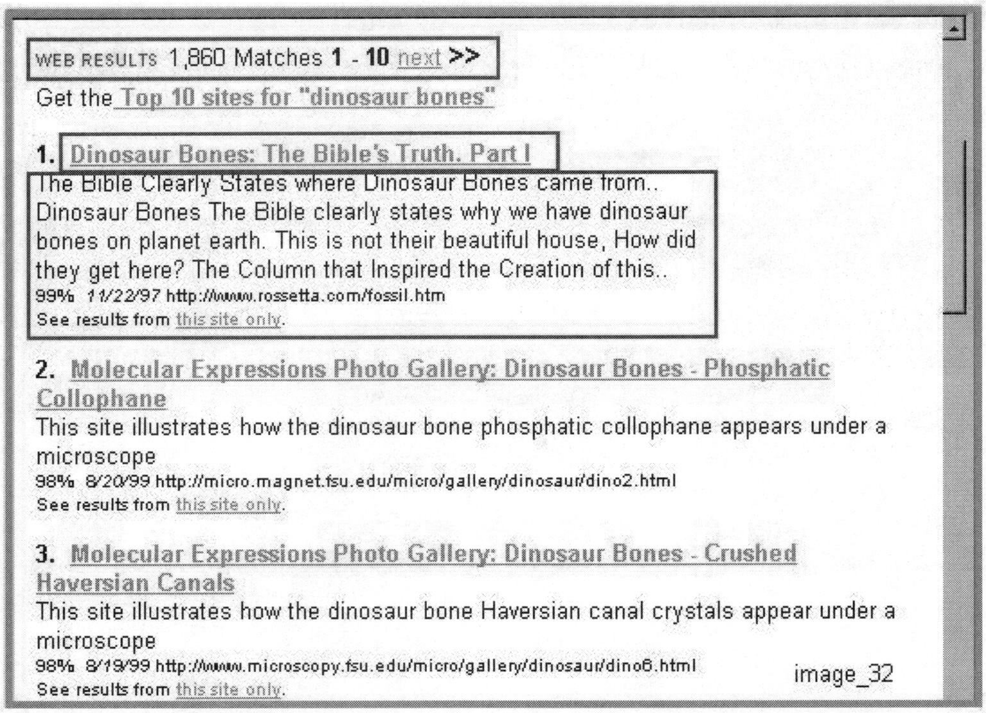

WEB RESULTS 1,860 Matches **1 - 10** next **>>**

Get the Top 10 sites for "dinosaur bones"

1. Dinosaur Bones: The Bible's Truth. Part I

The Bible Clearly States where Dinosaur Bones came from..
Dinosaur Bones The Bible clearly states why we have dinosaur
bones on planet earth. This is not their beautiful house, How did
they get here? The Column that Inspired the Creation of this..
99% 11/22/97 http://www.rossetta.com/fossil.htm
See results from this site only.

2. Molecular Expressions Photo Gallery: Dinosaur Bones - Phosphatic
Collophane

This site illustrates how the dinosaur bone phosphatic collophane appears under a
microscope
98% 8/20/99 http://micro.magnet.fsu.edu/micro/gallery/dinosaur/dino2.html
See results from this site only.

3. Molecular Expressions Photo Gallery: Dinosaur Bones - Crushed
Haversian Canals

This site illustrates how the dinosaur bone Haversian canal crystals appear under a
microscope
98% 8/19/99 http://www.microscopy.fsu.edu/micro/gallery/dinosaur/dino6.html
See results from this site only.   image_32

Figure 7-5. Results of a Search Engine Inquiry

- **Search Command (Area 4)**—All search engines provide an action button to initiate the inquiry. Some refer to the button as SEARCH, others use FIND IT, GO, or OK. The product of the search is typically returned in a matter of moments and displayed in a general format such as that shown in Figure 7-5.

Interpreting an Internet Search. The initial statistics labeled "Web Results" in the example identified 1,860 matches. Links are presented according to an internal reliability index. "Dinosaur Bones: The Bible's Truth," generated a 99% reliability score and is displayed first. The blue title provides a direct hyperlink to the site where its contents are researched to determine whether it satisfies lesson objectives.

Step 3: Write Learning Objectives

Benjamin Bloom created what is considered by many as the most famous classification for educators with his *Taxonomy of Educational Objectives* (Krathwohl & Bloom, 1984). In his landmark exposition, Bloom developed a theory of six progressively complex steps of cognitive development. In that single manuscript, he offered classroom teachers a rubric for developing instructional objectives at increasingly advanced levels of higher order thinking. Knowledge, comprehension, application, analysis, synthesis, and evaluation place among the most practical theories of teaching and learning. But, perhaps the most appealing aspect of Bloom's taxonomy is the subsequent research resulting in a list of action verbs representing intellectual activity on each level. Table 7-1 presents this list for the cognitive domain.

Taxonomy Classification	Action Verbs that represent intellectual activity on this level
Knowledge	Arrange, define, duplicate, label, list, memorize, name, order, recognize, relate, recall, repeat, reproduce, state
Comprehension	Classify, describe, discuss, explain, express, identify, indicate, locate, recognize, report, restate, review, select, translate
Application	Apply, choose, demonstrate, dramatize, employ, illustrate, interpret, operate, practice, schedule, sketch, solve, use, write
Analysis	Analyze, appraise, calculate, categorize, compare, contrast, criticize, differentiate, discriminate, distinguish, examine, experiment, question, test
Synthesis	Arrange, assemble, collect, compose, construct, create, design, develop, formulate, manage, organize, plan, prepare, propose, set up, write
Evaluation	Appraise, argue, assess, attach, choose, compare, defend, estimate, judge, predict, rate, core, select, support, value, evaluate

Table 7-I. The Cognitive Domain

How Does a Taxonomy Work? Classifying thinking skills is helpful when composing learning objectives. Teachers find a taxonomy useful when acknowledging that learning is best structured from the simple to the more complex, first to last, general to specific. However, the literature has yet to adopt an equivalent taxonomy for technology, although many educators readily accept teaching with technology as perhaps the most important strategy to ever hit the classroom.

To fill this void, a new classification called the "Taxonomy for Instructional Technology" is proposed. Table 7-2 demonstrates a corresponding level of progressive technical complexity from literacy to communications, decision-making, instruction, integration, and acculturation.

Taxonomy Classification	Action Verbs that represent intellectual activity on this level
Literacy Understanding technology and its components	• Apply computer terminology in oral and written communication • Consider the various uses of computers and technology in business, industry, and society • Master keyboarding, and click and drag • Use Web-based search engines • Download information via file transfer protocol • Operate input and output devices
Communications Sharing ideas, working collaboratively, and forming relationships using technology	• Use technology tools for individual writing and personal communications • Share information electronically among students and teachers • Communicate interpersonally using electronic mail
Decision-Making Using technology in new and concrete situations	• Apply electronic tools for research and problem-solving • Design effective instruction • Formulate new ideas with the help of brainstorming software • Prepare an electronic spreadsheet • Create calendars, address books, and class schedules
Instruction Breaking down technology-based instructional material into its components	• Appraise educational software for its pedagogical strengths • Choose developmentally appropriate multimedia resources • Formulate an environment for teaching and learning using technology-based tools • Create teacher and student Web-based materials • Create text-based materials using technology • Create visual-based classroom presentations
Integration Re-assembling technology-based instruction to create new materials	• Assimilate technology into a personal learning style • Facilitate lifelong learning by constructing a personal schemata for using technology • Consider the consequences of inappropriate uses of technology • Enhance personal productivity with technology
Acculturation Judging the value of technology	• Support copyright and Fair Use laws for using technology • Debate the issues surrounding legal/ethical behavior when using technology

Table 7-2. The Taxonomy for Instructional Technology

Level 1: Technology for Literacy. Literacy is defined here as *the minimum level of competency expected of teachers and students with respect to computers, educational programs, office productivity software, and the Internet.* The first rung on the ladder of taxonomy establishes a fundamental level of literacy. At this lowest rung of intellectual activity, learning objectives are steeped in computer skills necessary before students graduate or teachers receive their classroom certification. Literacy involves the recall, consideration, and use of technical skills as well as the ability to bring to mind appropriate information about technology in a timely manner. Here are two example learning objectives grounded in literacy:

> After reviewing a list of selected computer terms, the student will label each of the respective pieces of computer hardware within five minutes.

> Given a series of three keyboard exercises, students will create a word processing document for each exercise without syntax or grammatical error.

Level 2: Technology for Communication. Level two is defined as *the ability to use technology to interact* including written and verbal communication, the professional exchange of information, and interpersonal collaboration. These skills are evidenced by sharing information in written form (word processing, desktop publishing), by participating in and interpreting interpersonal dialog (via newsgroups, list servers, and chat rooms), and by responding to directed interchange (electronic mail). Communication goes one step beyond the mere recall of important material. It requires active participation on the part of the learner and represents the lowest level of authentic technical understanding. An example learning objective in communication might include:

> Using electronic mail, the student will subscribe to a science-related list server and participate by initiating at least 2 original messages and replying to another 4 posted exchanges during the first two weeks of the semester.

Level 3: Technology for Decision-Making. Decision-making is *the ability to use technology in new and concrete problem-solving situations.* Helping students learn demands a mastery of such important tools as spreadsheets, brainstorming software, statistical analysis packages, and gradebook programs. Learning outcomes at this level require a higher degree of understanding. Here is an example objective that reflects the strength of this level:

> After recording the quantitative results of a two-week observation period, students will capture the resulting weather data in electronic format and use the "what if" features of spreadsheets to forecast the next day's weather.

Level 4: Technology for Instruction. Technology is a potent tool for exploring any academic subjects. At this level, learning outcomes center around *identifying instructional materials, analyzing their component parts, integrating these components, and understanding the organizational principles in-*

volved in their application. While teachers are expected to have a firm grasp of their academic discipline, the taxonomy expands these expectations with the use of technology-based instruction including printed materials, audiovisual multimedia, educational software, and web-based materials. Examine two learning objectives that demonstrate technology for instruction:

> Students will locate four Internet sites concerning the Holocaust and select the site that best reflects their feelings and emotions about the Nazi's final solution.

> Using the computer lab, students will create a 5-page portfolio using word processing and graphics presentation software depicting the most important scenes of holocaust atrocities gathered from online material.

Level 5: Technology for Integration. Technology for Integration *acts upon the component parts of content material and re-assembles them for better learner understanding.* The Internet may seem a boundless resource, but oftentimes the information found on these sites is extremely disjointed. Text-based technology captures online text, images, and hyperlinks to bring together a lesson that is specific to the needs of the logical learner. Visual technologies foster lessons which appeal to the learning styles of the visual/spatial learner while web-based instruction focuses on the strengths of interpersonal intelligence. Howard Gardner would be proud. In 1993 and again in 1999, Gardner submitted the notion that there is not a single "intelligence," but seven. He has since added an eighth and is currently working on a ninth. Visual/spatial, musical, verbal, logical/mathematical, interpersonal, intrapersonal, and body/kinesthetic combine with technology to present instruction in a variety of formats that best fit the individual student.

Level 5 moves the individual from user to advocate. The true proponent of technology seeks to improve education by concentrating on its strengths and avoiding any weaknesses. Outcomes at this level represent the highest degree of understanding necessary for classroom learning. Here are three example objectives at the integration level.

> After locating several given Web sites, students will review the information and answer the questions in the *Student HyperBook*: What is the difference between an Omnivores and a Carnivore? When did the dinosaurs live? What were the most common dinosaurs in North America?

> Given an *Interactive Lesson* on dinosaur extinction, students will provide a 3–5 minute presentation explaining one of the three theories of extinction and the research supporting why that theory is the most plausible.

> Given a *Virtual Tour of the Dinosaurs of North America*, students will locate, download, and print at least two images of their favorite dinosaurs; distinguish between the Omnivore and Carnivore; iden-

tify two dinosaurs which lived in each of the four major periods of evolution; and, locate the geographical regions of the world where dinosaurs lived.

Level 6: Technology for Acculturation. Technology for Acculturation concerns itself with *the ability to judge the value of technology*. Many social issues surface when considering the responsible use of technology; for example, the disparity of computer access between the wealthy and poor. Other issues include copyright and fair use laws, censorship on the Internet, and the ethical use of information. Learning outcomes cover a broader range of activities and objectives and at each level contain elements of all previous stages. Here is an example learning objective:

> Students will be provided copies of recent publications, journals, and newspapers. They will locate an article which reflects the legal/ethical use of technology and prepare a grammatically correct, three-page minimum, double-spaced report defending or criticizing the premise of the work.

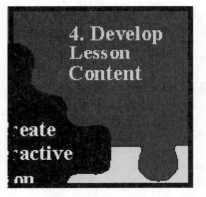

Step 4: Develop Lesson Content. Learning with technology peaks when linked to practical, hands-on activities (Shelly, Cashman, Gunter, 1999). According to the authors, "Teachers have found that using modern computers or computer-related technologies can capture and hold a student's attention, especially when matched to skill-building, real-world, interactive learning situations."

In this step, teachers create three different types of learning activities. *Initiating activities* prepare students to learn by creating interest in the subject matter. *Developing activities* provide the majority of projects in the lesson and present new material for student understanding and learning. Selection of appropriate activities is based on student needs, interests, and lesson objectives. *Concluding activities* offer closure by allowing students an opportunity to apply what they have learned. Not all initiating, developing, or concluding activities must include technology. Table 7-3 presents some example activities in each category.

Initiating Activities
Purchase three to four medium-sized watermelons and paint them white. Hide them in a "dinosaur nest" somewhere on the playground before the start of the lesson. Tell the students they must find the dinosaur's nest to begin the dinosaur unit. Once they find the "eggs," cut them open and share them with the group. After returning to the classroom have the students draw pictures of imaginary creatures that may have laid those "eggs."
Developing Activities
Scientists have proposed several reasons for the dinosaurs' disappearance (the earth became too cold, there wasn't enough food, etc.). Have students research these reasons and then divide them into groups, each group supporting one of the reasons. Provide time for them to discuss and defend their positions (**History Application**).
Ask the students to pretend they must convince their parents that they want a dinosaur as a pet. Ask them to identify the dinosaur they would want and tell how they would capture and tame it (**Affective Home/Family Application**).
Ask students to create riddles about dinosaurs (e.g., What is the best way to get a piece of paper out from under a dinosaur? Wait until it moves.) Compile these riddles into a class booklet, "Dinosaur Riddles" (**Language Application**).
Concluding Activities

Provide students with plastic dinosaur figures, clay, dinosaur model sets, and so on. As a class, create a display that depicts a prehistoric time when dinosaurs roamed the world. Discussion Questions for the end of the lesson:
 	
    Why do you think dinosaurs became extinct?
 	
    What problems would we have if dinosaurs were still living today? Explain.
 	
    What are some of the ancestors of dinosaurs that still live today?

Table 7-3. Developing Lesson Content in the Form of Classroom Activities

Step 5: Create the Student HyperBook. Student workbooks contribute to learning. Exercises and activities incorporated into a workbook guide students through the lesson objectives. Chapter 8 introduces the HyperBook along with its components, construction, and the advanced features of Microsoft Word necessary for its creation.

Step 6: Create the Interactive Lesson. Interactive lessons provide self-paced, highly visual instruction with built-in student assessment. They are offered for those who need individualized instruction, additional practice, or enrichment activities. Chapter 9 discusses the advanced features of Power Point necessary to effectively create an interactive lesson.

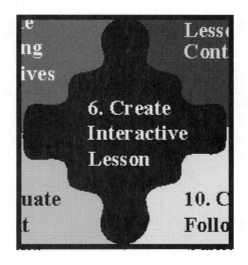

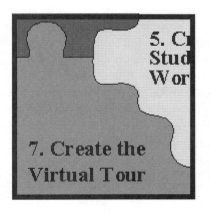

Step 7: Create the Virtual Tour. The Virtual Tour is a web-based teaching strategy for presenting multi-sensory, multimedia instruction. It employs "Front Doors" and "amplified sites" to present highly focused content material appropriate for learners who benefit from a humanistic teaching strategy. The Virtual Tour expands the walls of the classroom, opens students to new perspectives, enhances curriculum with real-life experiences, provides authentic learning opportunities, motivates the learner, and breaks down barriers to student understanding. Chapter 10 guides teachers in the choice of a format appropriate for their technical skills and matches technology to individual student learning styles.

Step 8: Deliver the Lesson. Presentation of the instruction depends on many factors including the technology incorporated into the lesson, the nature of the content material, the learning styles to be implemented, and the technical competency of the designer.

The Technology. *Teaching Digitally in the 21st Century* offers three innovative formats for delivering technology-based lessons:

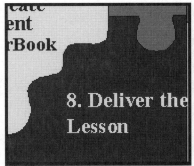

- The **HyperBook** is a text-based instructional resource combining word processing skills with practical exercises and activities to guide the student through a *cognitive* learning experience.
- The **Interactive Lesson** favors a *behavioral* learning experience using the strengths of visual-based classroom presentations with the teacher controlling the sequence of the instruction while the student controls the pace.
- The **Virtual Tour** concentrates on the strengths of the *humanistic* approach to learning by integrating Internet sites specifically selected to focus attention on content important to the learner.

The Nature of the Content Material. Piaget, Gruber, and Voneche (1995) isolated the formation of concrete thinking beginning at age 7 and abstract thinking at age 11. Understanding the importance of these gateways to higher order thinking is critical to the success of any technology-based lesson. *Concrete* instruction is characterized as sequential, highly teacher-controlled, containing as many hands-on exercises as technically possible. *Abstract* learning, on the other hand, thrives in a less structured environment with more student control and personal exploration. Technology offers effective formats for both types of learning.

Competency. Designer skill and technical experience is the final factor in the delivery of the lesson. A technically *easy* lesson might involve text-based material, perhaps a few visual-based slides in a classroom presentation, and a minimal number of Internet sites for student exploration. A more technically *challenging* lesson incorporates imbedded hyperlinks, software utilities for modifying images and graphics, a growing numbers of web sites. A technically *difficult* lesson requires skill in creating bitmapped images, complex charts and tables, and multimedia web sites.

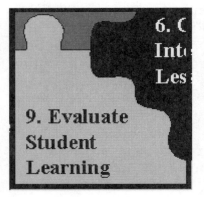

Step 9: Evaluate Student Learning. Proper assessment of student learning is critical because of technology's fairly recent adoption as an instructional strategy. The HyperBook, interactive lesson, and virtual tour each offer its own effective brand of evaluating students. Watch for the uses of self-assessment, traditional and authentic assessment in the following chapters.

Step 10: Conduct Follow-up Activities. Follow-up activities provide an opportunity to integrate additional resources into a lesson such as videotape, film, white boards, calculators, scanners, digital cameras, video conferencing, and electronic mail.

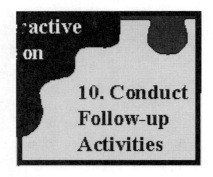

Conclusion

The Model for Technology-Based Lessons is an easy-to-follow rubric for analyzing, designing, developing, implementing, evaluating, and revising a unit of instruction in which technology is to play a key role. Steps 1–4 guide the construction of lesson goals, learning objectives, and lesson content. Steps 5–7 incorporate teacher-developed materials and lay the foundation for the HyperBook, interactive lesson, and virtual tour described in the following chapters. And, Steps 8–10 complete the process by considering lesson delivery, assessment, and follow-up activities to ensure student understanding.

The model presented in this Chapter is used throughout the remainder of *Teaching Digitally in the 21st Century* as the governing rubric for developing advanced technical lesson materials. Refer to these steps often to ensure all the pertinent elements of lesson design, development, and implementation are considered.

Bibliography

Dembo, M. (1991). *Applying educational psychology, 4th ed.* Needham Heights, MA: Allyn & Bacon.

Krathwohl, D., & Bloom, B. S. (1984). *Taxonomy of educational objectives, Handbook 1: Cognitive domain.* New York: Addison-Wesley.

Gardner, H. (1993). *Multiple intelligences: The theory in practice.* New York: Basic Books.

Gardner, H. (1999). *Intelligence reframed: Multiple intelligences for the 21st century.* New York: Basic Books.

Shelly, G. B., Cashman, T. J., & Gunter, R. E. (1999). *Teachers discovering computers: A link to the future.* Cambridge, MA: Course Technology Publishers.

Piaget, J., with Gruber, H. E., & Voneche, J. J. (Eds.). (1995). *The essential Piaget.* Northvale, NJ: Jason Aronson Publishers.

Chapter 8

THE HYPERBOOK LESSON

Microsoft Office is arguably becoming the integrated software package of choice for many schools and school districts while Internet Explorer and Netscape Communicator offer access to the World Wide Web. The HyperBook is the first manifestation of technology integrated specifically for the purpose of teaching and learning.

> A HyperBook is a text-based, workbook-centered teaching strategy integrating images, real-world exercises, visual aids, and real-time links appropriate for learning and assessment.

To be successful, the HyperBook is created in an environment rich in word processing, graphics, and the Internet. However, its implementation does not depend on sophisticated equipment or even a state-of-the-art classroom computer. For these reasons, the HyperBook is introduced first among the models of technology-based instruction. Chapter 8 addresses the following objectives:

- **Advanced Word Processing Features.** Objective 8.1: Demonstrate a mastery of the advanced features of word processing.
- **Preparing the HyperBook Lesson.** Objective 8.2: Demonstrate a knowledge of text-based design along with a mastery of advanced word processing features. Combine these skills with the use of technology resources harvested from the Internet to produce the HyperBook lesson.

Advanced Word Processing Features

Objective 8.1: Demonstrate a mastery of the advanced features of word processing.

The additional word processing features necessary to create the HyperBook format include Word Art, text color, tables and columns, and hyperlinks. Open a handout or study guide document created during chapter 4 to practice the skills presented below. The previous convention of using *bold, italicized text to indicate practice exercises* continues.

WordArt

WordArt combines the features of simple text with the graphic effects of color, size, and shape while offering more sophisticated and visually appealing hard copy for classroom applications. WordArt produces a graphic-like image in effect making pictures from words. WordArt is especially appropriate for cover pages and illustrations.

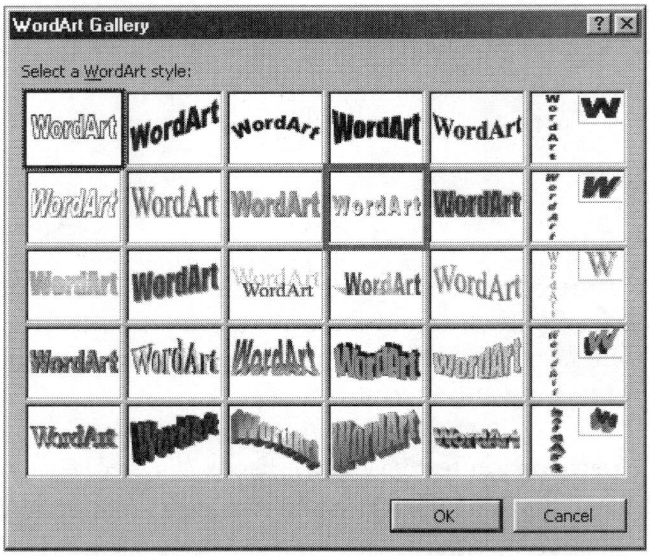

Figure 8-I. WordArt Gallery

-  To create WordArt, ***click the WordArt icon*** on the **Drawing** tool bar to open the gallery or click the ***Insert → Picture → WordArt*** pop-down menu. Choose from among the 24 available styles offering various colors, sizes, and shapes (see Figure 8-1). Highlight the selected box, then ***click OK.***

- In the **Edit WordArt Text** dialog box, ***enter the desired text.*** Also, select the Font, Font Size, or Appearance options and ***click OK*** to place the text on the slide. The same rules to resize, move, and edit apply to WordArt as they did to images and clip art and may be reviewed in chapter 4 if necessary.

-  After the text is inserted into the document, the WordArt menu bar is displayed for additional editing and formatting. Click the menu to revise the contents, access the gallery, change colors and format, integrate basic shapes, rotate the text on the page, wrap the WordArt within regular text, or align WordArt on the page.

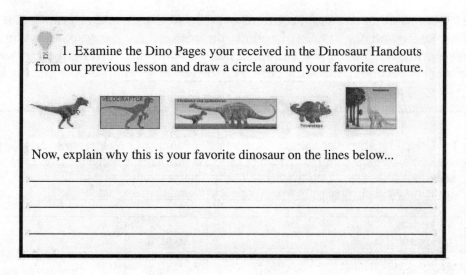

Figure 8-2. Text Color

Text Color

Another simple but effective visual enhancement is the use of text color. Student instructions in the HyperBook are generally displayed in blue (see Figure 8-2). Once students grasp this visual clue, they are on the lookout for elements within a workbook exercise requiring a response. To change the color of text, highlight the target words with a mouse click and drag.

- 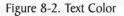 Click the *Font Color* icon on the Drawing tool bar located at the bottom of the window. To use the color currently shown under the "A," simply click the icon. To change to another color, click the down arrow and select from among 40 primary colors or click *More Colors* to select from the rainbow. Text color may be edited for appearance (bold, italics, or underline) and its font or font size changed to suit the designer.

Tables

A table is composed of rows and columns of cells filled with text or graphics. It organizes and presents information and has a variety of other applications. Tables are excellent for aligning numbers within columns, creating individualized page layouts, and arranging text and graphics. To create a table in HyperBook, move the cursor to the target location within the document.

2. Find two dinosaurs that are not in this Workbook by accessing the following Web Site. When you decide on which creatures you like the best, **complete the information below**. Your teacher will help you use the computer to find the site. [http://www.enchantedlearning.com/subjects/dinosaurs/dinos/dinolist.html]

What was the Name of your Dinosaur?	Describe the Dinosaur Here (Anatomy, Size, etc.)	Carnivore or Omnivore?	Draw a picture of the Dinosaur Here

Figure 8-3. Tables

 Click *Insert Table* on the Standard tool bar at the top of the window. Click and drag the mouse to select the desired number of rows and columns. A cell holds either text or images and may be accessed using the mouse or Tab key to move from one cell to the next.

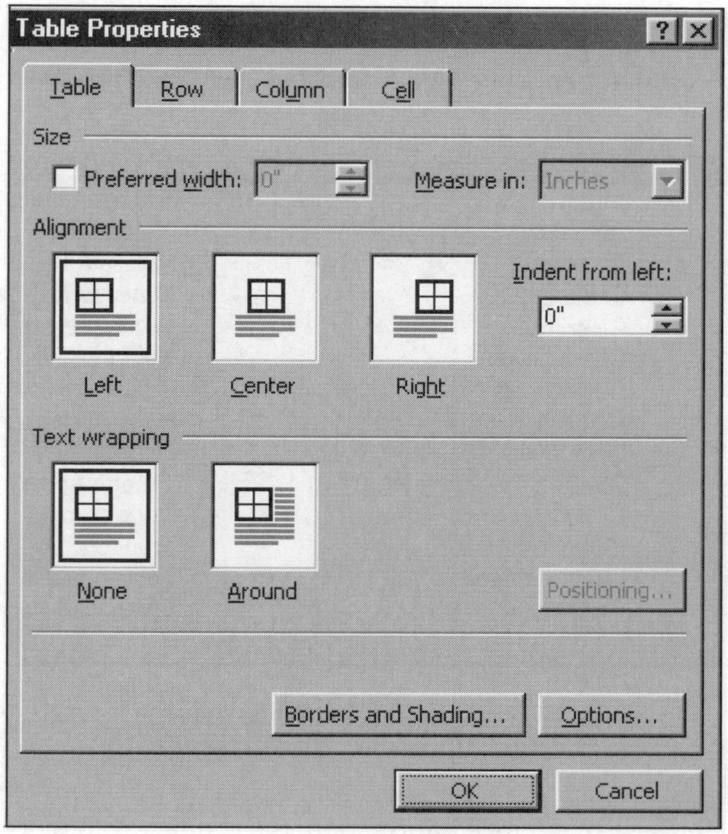

Figure 8-4. Table Properties

- *Table Properties* presents options for alignment and text wrapping for the entire table or any of its component rows, columns, and cells. Use the ***right mouse button*** (Windows) or ***click and hold the mouse*** (Macintosh) to access the dialog box (see Figure 8-4).

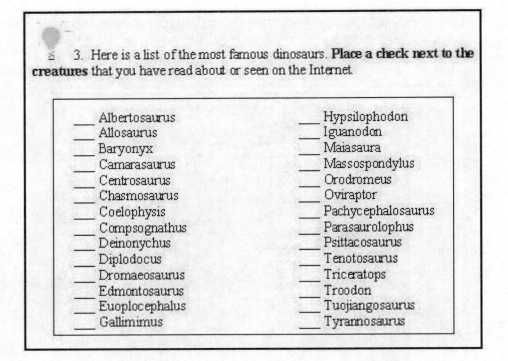

Figure 8-5. Columnar Text

Columns

Columns, like tables, also organize information; the primary difference is the flow of the text. While tables present information horizontally in blocks, columns align text vertically across the page (see Figure 8-5). Newspaper articles are examples of text presented in columnar format. To create Columns, enter the text initially in typical linear format. After completing data entry, select and highlight the text to be placed into columns.

-  On the **Standard** tool bar, *click Columns.* Select the desired number of columns. For HyperBook applications, two or three columns is recommended. The selected text is immediately reformatted. Use the Undo command if the results are unacceptable.

Hyperlinks

A "hyperlink" connects users to other documents, presentations, and web sites. Hyperlinks assumes that the document is online; otherwise, there is no reason to include this feature. To insert a hyperlink, enter and select the text to serve as the link.

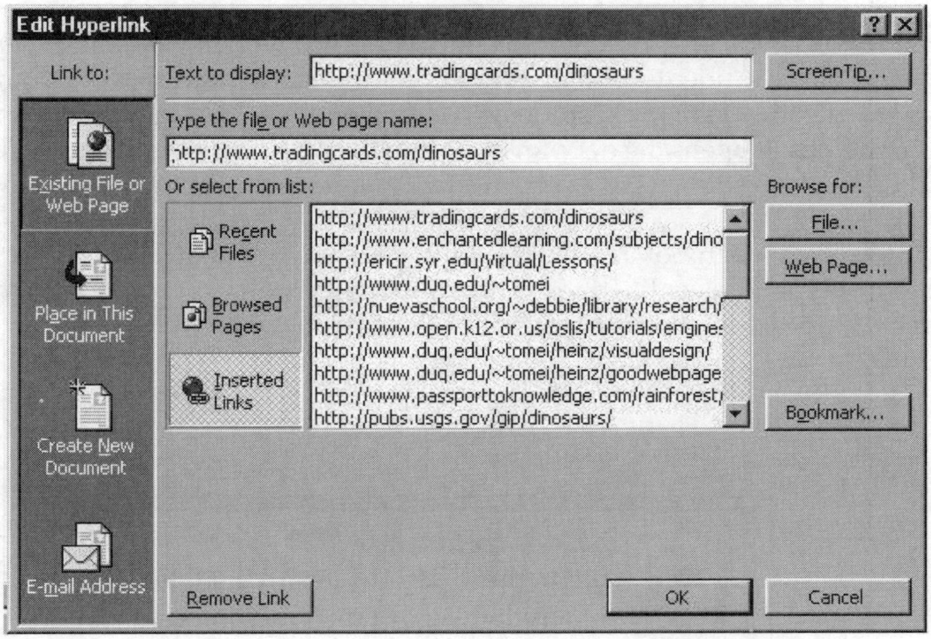

Figure 8-6. Insert/Edit Hyperlink

-  On the **Standard** tool bar, click the *Insert Hyperlink* icon or select *Insert* → *Hyperlink* from the pop-down menu.

- To link to an Internet site, *enter the Web page name* and prefix the URL with **http://**. *Click OK* (see Figure 8-6). Typically, the hyperlink displays as blue text. To link to a file (another document, presentation, etc.) enter the **Web page name** as a file name without a prefix or use the *Browse for:* → *File* button to locate the target file.

- *Save* the document.

Preparing the HyperBook Lesson

Objective 8.2: Demonstrate a knowledge of text-based design along with a mastery of advanced word processing features. Combine these skills with the use of technology resources harvested from the Internet to produce the HyperBook lesson.

The HyperBook lesson offers students an opportunity to work together in groups and encourages teachers to match students who own home computers with those who do not. Text-based material is very effective in helping students comprehend new concepts with its diagrams, outlines, and summaries. It opens the door for individualized discovery and inquiry learning opportunities and encourages students to make intuitive guesses using guided questions to keep them on task.

An example of a HyperBook is available on the accompanying CDROM. Use **Best Practices #10** to locate the HyperBook entitled the "Dinosaur HyperBook." A copy of the workbook is also available in the Appendix to this chapter.

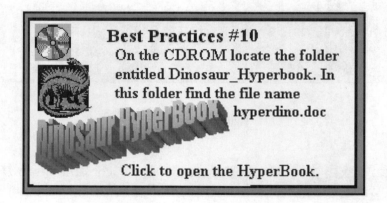

Best Practices #10
On the CDROM locate the folder entitled Dinosaur_Hyperbook. In this folder find the file name hyperdino.doc

Click to open the HyperBook.

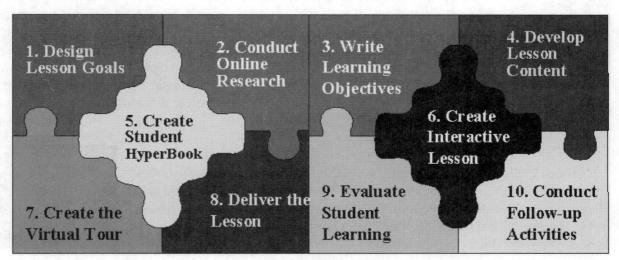

Figure 8-7. Model for Technology-Based Lessons

Creating a HyperBook Lesson

Many teachers prefer to combine text-based workbooks with web-based lessons. Some use the workbook to encourage parents to assist their child with online research. Others find the HyperBook useful in verifying that students personally accomplished the assigned exercises. Designing, developing, implementing, and evaluating the HyperBook follows the "Model for Technology-Based Lessons" (Figure 8-7) presented in the previous chapter.

Step 1: Design the Lesson Goals. The HyperBook provides a series of instructional exercises to help students acquire basic knowledge of the content material. Since introductory information is often found in books, encyclopedias, and the Internet, teachers are encouraged to continue identifying materials from a variety of sources, selecting those which specifically address their own learning objectives. Throughout the development of this lesson, keep in mind that the HyperBook is ideal for group learning, homework assignments, and individualized instruction. To satisfy the demands of the HyperBook format, lesson goals should include:

- **Indicative Information** such as student name, date of the lesson, and the teacher's name.
- **Introduction** to the topic written at the student's level. (Note: For early childhood lessons, this may mean pictures rather than words.)
- **Instructions** for completing the HyperBook. Students should understand what is required to complete the lesson.
- **Allotted Time**—The lesson goals should clearly state the amount of time available and how much of that time is allotted to the completion of the HyperBook.
- **Lesson Goals**—The following goals were identified for the HyperBook lesson: select a favorite dinosaur, distinguish between carnivores and omnivores, identify dinosaurs by sight and features, share ideas about dinosaurs, and learn about dinosaurs outside the classroom.

Step 2: Conduct Online Research. This step focuses on locating material that addresses each of the specific lesson goals. Chapter 3 discussed the process of exploring the Internet, evaluating content material, and harvesting text, graphics, and files. Search engines are an excellent way of locating resources, especially if the researcher has no idea where to start. An online review of dinosaurs found over 50,000 sites with information about dinosaur habitats and their physical characteristics. The best sites were included in the HyperBook and highlighted in red to make them readily identifiable to students.

Step 3: Write Learning Objectives. In this step, specific learning objectives are created along with a statement of prior student knowledge and classroom assignments. It is perhaps the most important phase of lesson development as learning objectives are closely matched with the established goals of the lesson (see Table 8-1).

Lesson Goal: Select a favorite dinosaur. Prior Knowledge: Students are familiar with dinosaurs from television, books, etc.	**Learning Objective 1: Students will examine the Dino Cards provided in the HyperBook, draw a circle around their favorite dinosaur, and explain why this is their favorite.**
	Assignment: Students will compose a paragraph in the HyperBook explaining their favorite dinosaur.
Lesson Goal: Distinguish between carnivores and omnivores. Prior Knowledge: Students' working use of computers, mouse, and Internet navigation.	**Learning Objective 2: Students will locate another dinosaur by searching provided Web sites and complete information describing the creature.**
	Assignment: Students will draw a picture of the selected dinosaur in the HyperBook.
Lesson Goal: Identify dinosaurs by sight and features. Prior Knowledge: Student knowledge of dinosaurs from television, books, or movies.	**Learning Objective 3: Students will identify any dinosaurs they already know from a list of dinosaurs.**
	Assignments: None.
Lesson Goal: Share your ideas about dinosaurs. Prior Knowledge: Student experience and practice with group learning and sharing situations.	**Learning Objective 4: Students will cut out "trading cards." Not all cards are provided to each student. Students will identify duplicate cards and trade with classmates to obtain desired cards.**
	Assignments: Students may print out additional cards to complete their collection.
Lesson Goal: Learn about dinosaurs on your own. Prior Knowledge: Students familiarity with previous portions of the HyperBook.	**Learning Objective 5: Students will complete three questions to evaluate the success of this lesson and their use of computers to learn.**
	Assignments: None.

Table 8-1. Learning Objectives for the HyperBook

Step 4: Develop Lesson Content. The primary task in this step of lesson development is to decide on the instructional content of the HyperBook by connecting learning objectives with content material as outlined in Table 8-2.

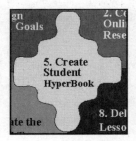

Step 5: Create the Student HyperBook. The HyperBook is a combination of images, charts and graphs, tables, and Web site links. While text remains its primary format, there is the option of providing students with an electronic version containing active hyperlinks to the selected Web sites. The HyperBook is shown in its entirety at the appendix to this chapter. Examine it closely to identify the key elements required for an effective resource. A summary of the key components of a successful HyperBook lesson include:

- **The Lesson Overview Page** containing, as a minimum
  - **Indicative Information**
  - **Introduction to the Topic**
  - **Instructions**
  - **Allotted Time**
  - **Lesson Goals**
- **Exercise Pages**. Components of these pages include
  - **Learning Objectives**
  - **Student Exercises**
  - **Student Assignment**
  - **Student Evaluation and Feedback**
- **Follow-on Activities** with additional information for remedial students and enrichment activities.
- **Additional Resources** such as videotapes, audiocassettes, and publications.
- **Student Materials**

Learning Objective	HyperBook Lesson Content
Learning Objective 1: Students will examine the Dino Cards provided in the HyperBook, draw a circle around their favorite dinosaur, and explain why this is their favorite.	1. Select from among images of the: • T-rex • Raptor • Brontosaurus • Triceratops • Gallimimus 2. Explanations should include information about the dinosaur's anatomy, size, and behavior along with affective statements of value, likes, and fears.
Learning Objective 2: Students will locate another dinosaur by searching provided Web sites and complete information describing the creature.	1. Access **www.enchantedlearning.com/dinosaurs** to locate additional dinosaurs. 2. Provide the following information: • Name of the dinosaur • Physical description to include anatomy, size, and behavior • Identify the dinosaur as a carnivore or omnivore 3. Draw a picture of the animal in the HyperBook.
Learning Objective 3: Students will identify any dinosaurs they already know from a list of dinosaurs.	1. Use **www.arts-letters.com/dinosaur** to identify the most famous dinosaurs from among: • Albertosaurus, Allosaurus, Baryonyx, Camarasaurus, Centrosaurus, Chasmosaurus, Coelophysis, Compsognathus, Deinonychus, Diplodocus, Dromaeosaurus, Edmontosaurus, Euoplocephalus, Gallimimus, Hypsilophodon, Iguanodon, Maiasaura, Massospondylus, Orodromeus, Oviraptor, Pachycephalosaurus, Parasaurolophus, Psittacosaurus, Tenotosaurus, Triceratops, Troodon, Tuojiangosaurus, Tyrannosaurus
Learning Objective 4: Students will cut out "trading cards." Not all cards are provided to each student. Students will identify duplicate cards and trade with classmates to obtain desired cards.	1. Cut out the dinosaur trading cards provided at the end of the HyperBook. 2. Determine which creatures are needed to complete the collection. 3. Trade with fellow classmates to complete the collection. 4. Use **www.tradingcards.com/dinosaurs** to locate additional cards to complete the collection.
Learning Objective 5: Students will complete three questions to evaluate the success of this lesson and their use of computers to learn.	Questions include: 1. Did you enjoy using computers to find dinosaurs? 2. What did you discover about dinosaurs from the HyperBook that you did not know before? 3. What is your experience as a computer user? (Note: This question is appropriate for HyperBooks to determine the status of student technology training).

Table 8-2. HyperBook Content Material

Step 6: Create the Interactive Lesson is discussed in detail in chapter 9.

Step 7: Create the Virtual Tour is discussed in detail in chapter 10.

Step 8: Deliver the Lesson. The HyperBook lesson is most often delivered in its text-based format as a hard copy workbook printed for each student. A variety of graphics and visual materials aid in student learning. Clip art includes hundreds of graphics. Images, either scanned from textbook pages or downloaded from the Internet, introduce a visual component to materials that teachers expect the student to read and understand.

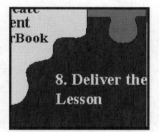

- **The Online HyperBook**—Although text remains the primary media for the HyperBook, there is the option of providing students with an electronic version of the workbook containing active hyperlinks to selected web sites. Offering the HyperBook on diskette, for example, is appropriate when teachers wish to discourage access to unsuitable sites, online hate material, or unauthorized "surfing" in general. For homework assignments, the online HyperBook provides an excellent resource to parents who wish to monitor the Internet explorations of their children. Researched web sites decrease hours of potentially unproductive searching, especially for younger children whose typing skills often result in wasted time in front of a computer. Specific web addresses placed as bookmarks and favorite links speed up the process of locating sites and offers parents some assurance that the teacher and school are aware of the inherent hazards of Internet technology and are taking steps to reduce potential harm to their children.

To produce an online version of the HyperBook, transfer the document as a word processing file to a diskette. Rarely will a HyperBook exceed the 1.4 megabyte capacity of a diskette. Recall the caution noted in earlier chapters that a Macintosh machine reads the DOS format but a Windows machine does not accept a Mac-formatted diskette.

Each student should be provided their own diskette. To complete an online HyperBook lesson, students must also have access to a computer, either in school or at home, with both Microsoft Word and an Internet connection. This version of the HyperBook encourages students in higher grades (probably fifth grade or higher in most schools) to complete the required exercises and assignments online, thereby advancing their own word processing and Internet skills. Students should be encouraged to complete the exercises by deleting the blank lines and filling in the available spaces with their own responses.

- **A Final Consideration**—The format and structure of the HyperBook with its lesson overview page, exercise page, and so forth. is meant to ensure that the teacher considers all aspects of the lesson during its development. Early childhood teachers, for example, may see the folly in preparing such detailed instructions for students who cannot read yet. In such cases, completing the elements of the HyperBook is more for colleagues who may wish to use your materials should you make them available either online or in hard copy form. Consider offering a "Teacher's Only Section" for these potential users and concentrating the student material later in the HyperBook.

Step 9: Evaluate Student Learning. The HyperBook serves as an excellent assessment tool if a few key elements are kept in mind:

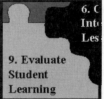

- **Select an Appropriate Format for Student Responses**—A simple question, checklist, or fill-in-the-blank is often appropriate. Activities such as Student Exercise 4 and the dinosaur trading cards provide a forum to guarantee student participation. A properly constructed HyperBook encourages other venues for valid, reliable student assessment as well.

- **Allow Sufficient Time and Space for Student Responses**—The student should use the HyperBook to document answers to the exercise scenarios. Enough time must be allotted for student to think and reflect. The HyperBook offers related topics for individual consideration and contemplation.

- **Involve Behavioral, Cognitive, and Humanistic Exercises**—Behavioral responses, such as the one demonstrated in student Exercise 3, ensure mastery and increase student confidence. Cognitive instruction, like Exercise 2, builds on a student's prior knowledge and adds structure to the particular subject at hand. Humanistic opportunities, such as Exercise 4, assist in making the information important to each student.

- **Include a Section for Personal Self-Evaluation** (by the student) at the end of the workbook. Always seek feedback regarding the lesson, the learning, and the learner. Allowing the student the opportunity to ask questions and express concerns often generates important teaching moments during succeeding classroom discussions.

Step 10: Conduct Follow-up Activities. If possible, integrate a variety of technologies into the HyperBook lesson such as the Internet, videotapes, audio resources, and other text-based materials. Provide a list of additional teacher-validated Internet sites, but do not send a student to a location you have not visited first. Placing additional Web addresses at the end of a HyperBook ensures that students visit sites containing authentic learning information.

Technology is wonderful, but teachers must not forget other medium for instruction. "The Dinosaur HyperBook" references video material readily accessible to the student in the school's library eliminating the risk of offensive or inappropriate material. Audio only resources are being replaced with multimedia materials. However, for many content areas, audio tapes remain a viable instructional resource and should be included in the lesson to benefit the aural learner. Finally, books are a natural for students and should not be overlooked in favor of the more "high tech" resources.

Conclusion

Essential ingredients in the successful implementation of the HyperBook are to form the goals, conduct the research, write the objectives, and develop the lesson content before attempting to construct the text-based materials. To complete a successful HyperBook lesson—the final steps of the "Model for Preparing Technology-Based Lessons"—consider delivery of the lesson, evaluation of student learning, and follow-up activities to make the lesson come alive for the student.

For teachers who find it challenging to create the more technical materials demonstrated in later chapters, the HyperBook offers a word processing-based lesson with a less demanding range of skills and competencies from which the designer may choose. Yet, the more straightforward and uncomplicated HyperBook can ensure just the right combination of technical expertise and student focus to meet the specific learning objectives of the lesson.

Appendix

The Dinosaur HyperBook

Student Name: _____

Date of the Lesson: _____ **Teacher:** _____

Introduction to the Topic. You already know quite a lot about dinosaurs having seen several movies in our classroom and reading the books you checked out of the school library last week. You should know something about the United States as well and the area of the country were dinosaur fossils are most commonly found, since we finished our geography chapter on States of the Mid-West last week. You have also been on the Internet at least three times in computer class, so you should know how to point and click on a link to access a Web site.

Feel free to explore the subject at your own pace and in consonance with your own personal learning goals. The questions being asked are designed to guide you through the lesson objectives to ensure that you experience the full range of goals and performance objectives targeted by your teacher. You do not have to complete the questions in the order they are presented, but you should complete all of the questions.

Instructions. Each **fourth-grade student** will receive their own copy of this Student Workbook. You are encouraged to explore the subject of this lesson with other members of your class. For this particular lesson, group interaction, assistance, and cooperation are at least as important as the material you will be studying. Be sure to turn in all of the material requested to your teacher. If at any time you encounter difficulty, immediately notify your teacher and the facilitator of the Exploration.

Time. Students will have two 40-minute class periods to complete this lesson. Complete the HyperBook as you encounter the answers to the questions throughout the lesson.

Lesson Goals. Your lesson will help you:

- Select a favorite dinosaurs
- Distinguish between carnivores and omnivores
- Identify dinosaurs by sight and features
- Share your ideas about dinosaurs
- Learn about dinosaurs on your own

> *Learning Objective 1: Students will examine the Dino Cards provided in the HyperBook, draw a circle around their favorite dinosaur, and explain why this is their favorite.*

Student Exercise 1: Examine the Dino Cards in the HyperBook and **draw a circle around your favorite creature**.

Student Assignment: Now, **explain why this is your favorite dinosaur** on the lines below.

_____

_____

_____

_____

_____

_____

Learning Objective 2: Students will locate another dinosaur by searching provided web sites and complete information describing the creature.

Student Exercise 2: Find two dinosaurs that are not in this workbook using the following web site. When you decide on which creatures you like the best, **complete the information below**. Your teacher will help you use the computer to find the site. **[http://www.enchantedlearning.com/subjects/dinosaurs/dinos/dinolist.html]**

Student Assignment:

What was the Name of your Dinosaur?	Describe the Dinosaur Here (Anatomy, Size, etc.)	Carnivore or Omnivore?	Draw a Picture of the Dinosaur Here

Learning Objective 3: Students will identify any dinosaurs they already know from a list of dinosaurs.

Student Exercise 3: Here is a list of the most famous dinosaurs. **Place a check next to the creatures** that you have read about or seen on the Internet.

Student Assignment:

___ Albertosaurus   ___ Hypsilophodon

___ Allosaurus   ___ Iguanodon

___ Baryonyx   ___ Maiasaura

___ Camarasaurus   ___ Massospondylus

___ Centrosaurus   ___ Orodromeus

___ Chasmosaurus   ___ Oviraptor

___ Coelophysis   ___ Pachycephalosaurus

___ Compsognathus   ___ Parasaurolophus

___ Deinonychus   ___ Psittacosaurus

___ Diplodocus   ___ Tenotosaurus

___ Dromaeosaurus   ___ Triceratops

___ Edmontosaurus   ___ Troodon

___ Euoplocephalus   ___ Tuojiangosaurus

___ Gallimimus   ___ Tyrannosaurus

Learning Objective 4: Students will cut out "trading cards." Not all cards are provided to each student. Students will identify duplicate cards and trade with classmates to obtain desired cards.

Student Exercise 4. At the end of this Workbook are some Data File cards for the most popular dinosaurs. You do not have ALL the cards, but you do have a couple of the same animals, so you may **trade with your classmates to complete the set**. Or you can print out some of your own cards at: [**http://www.tradingcards.com/dinosaurs**]

Student Assignment: Cut out, collect, and trade with others in your class.

Learning Objective 5: Learning about dinosaurs on your own.

Student Exercise 5: Please evaluate this lesson on dinosaurs. **Circle your answer**, and be sure to **turn in your Workbooks** to the teacher when you are done.

Student Assignment:

Yes / No   a. Did you enjoy using computers to find Dinosaurs?

Yes / No   b. Did you discover information about Dinosaurs that you did not know
                  before? If so, name at least one or two new things you learned.

1. _____

2. _____

            c. What is your experience as a computer user? Check one . . .

____   (1) I have a computer at home and can get to the Internet.

____   (2) I have a computer at home but have never used the Internet.

____   (3) I want one of these for Christmas!

____   (4) I only use a computer at school.

Additional Activities for the HyperBook Lesson

Internet Sites

Rockville's Creative Learning's Science Kit Center
URL: **http://www.sciencekits.com/science.htm**

Dinosaur Poems
URL: **http://www.iup.edu/~njyost/KHI/DINOSO.HTML**

Paper Dinosaurs, 1824-1969
URL: **http://www.lhl.lib.mo.us/pubserv/hos/dino/welcome.htm**

American Museum of Natural History
URL: http://www.amnh.org

National Geographic Dinosaur Eggs
URL: **http://www.nationalgeographic.com/dinoeggs/**

Visit a Dinosaur Dig — The Dinosaur Society
URL: **http://www.webscope.com/webscope/dino/digs.html**

Guide to Dinosaur Sites in Western Colorado and Eastern Utah
URL: **http://www.rmwest.com/dinosaur/guide.htm**

Videotapes

Bill Nye: Dinosaurs, V, TV, 50 minutes, taken from Bill Nye TV Shows: facts, surprise celebrity guests, hot music videos, and fabulous experiments

Dinosaur! V, 60 minutes, Vestron, 1985, 1987, Host Christopher Reeve

Dinosaurs, Fun, Facts, and Fantasy, Volume 1, V, 30 minutes, Diamond Entertainment Corporation Nature Series, 1991

Dinosaurs, Fun, Facts, and Fantasy, Volume 2, V, 30 minutes, Diamond Entertainment Corporation Nature Series, 1991

Whatever Happened to the Dinosaurs? 31 minutes, Golden Book Video, 1992

When Dinosaurs Ruled - a T.L.C. Series - 5 Parts, 1 hour each

Audio resources

Search for the Thunderlizards, Cassette Tape, 58 minutes

Planet of Life — When Dinosaurs Ruled, Cassette Tape, 26 minutes

Return of the Dinosaurs, Cassette Tape, 60 minutes, VideoSaurus/Midwich Entertainment, 1991

Other text-based materials

Attack of the Dinosaurs/With Dinosaur Stickers, Tor Books; ISBN: 0812534921

Dad's Dinosaur Day. By Diane Dawson Hearn; Simon & Schuster (Juv); ISBN: 0027434850

Dinosaur : An Interactive Guide to the Dinosaur World. By Dougal Dixon; Dorling Kindersley; ISBN: 1564586839

The Dinosaur Question and Answer Book. By Sylvia Funston, Dinosaur Project; Little Brown & Co (Juv Pap); ISBN: 0316570214

Dinosaur Worlds: New Dinosaurs New Discoveries. By Don Lessem; Boyds Mills Pr; ISBN: 1563975971

Dinosaur National Monument (New True Books). By David Petersen; Little Brown & Co; ISBN: 0516410741

DINO Cards

Name *Albertosaurus*   **DATA FILE**

Meaning	Alberta lizard
How to say it	al-BERT-oh-saw-russ
Where found	North America
Length	9 m
Height	about 3.5 m
'Weight' (mass)	about 1500 kg
How it walked	walked on 2 legs
Teeth	saw-edged, flesh-slicing teeth
Type of feeder	carnivore (meat-eater)
Food	probably plant-eating dinosaurs
Period	Cretaceous
When it lived	76-74 million years ago
Type of hip	lizard-hipped
Dinosaur group	theropod
Other info	A close relative of *Tyrannosaurus* but smaller and not so heavily built.

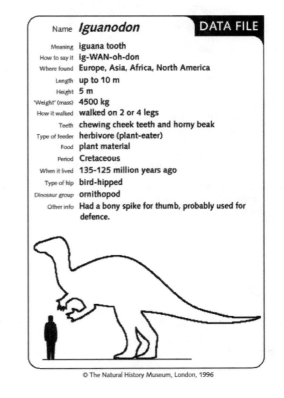

© The Natural History Museum, London, 1996

Name *Diplodocus*   **DATA FILE**

Meaning	double beam
How to say it	dip-lod-OH-kuss
Where found	North America
Length	26 m
Height	about 8 m
'Weight' (mass)	10,000 kg
How it walked	walked on 4 legs
Teeth	rows of teeth like a comb
Type of feeder	herbivore (plant-eater)
Food	leaves from trees and soft plants
Period	Jurassic
When it lived	155-145 million years ago
Type of hip	lizard-hipped
Dinosaur group	sauropod
Other info	Had a hollow backbone, which was light but very strong.

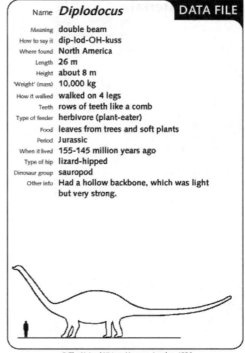

© The Natural History Museum, London, 1996

Name *Gallimimus*   **DATA FILE**

Meaning	fowl mimic
How to say it	gal-i-ME-muss
Where found	Asia
Length	5.6 m
Height	3 m
'Weight' (mass)	about 200 kg
How it walked	walked on 2 legs
Teeth	horny beak, no teeth
Type of feeder	omnivore (eats plants and animals)
Food	plants, insects, lizards
Period	Cretaceous
When it lived	74-70 million years ago
Type of hip	lizard-hipped
Dinosaur group	theropod
Other info	Could run fast (at up to 30 kph) but not over very long distances.

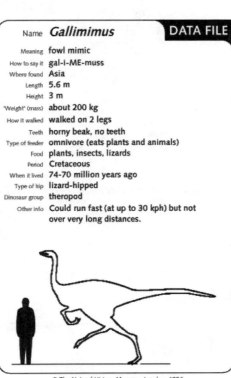

© The Natural History Museum, London, 1996

Name *Iguanodon*   **DATA FILE**

Meaning	iguana tooth
How to say it	ig-WAN-oh-don
Where found	Europe, Asia, Africa, North America
Length	up to 10 m
Height	5 m
'Weight' (mass)	4500 kg
How it walked	walked on 2 or 4 legs
Teeth	chewing cheek teeth and horny beak
Type of feeder	herbivore (plant-eater)
Food	plant material
Period	Cretaceous
When it lived	135-125 million years ago
Type of hip	bird-hipped
Dinosaur group	ornithopod
Other info	Had a bony spike for thumb, probably used for defence.

© The Natural History Museum, London, 1996

DINO Cards

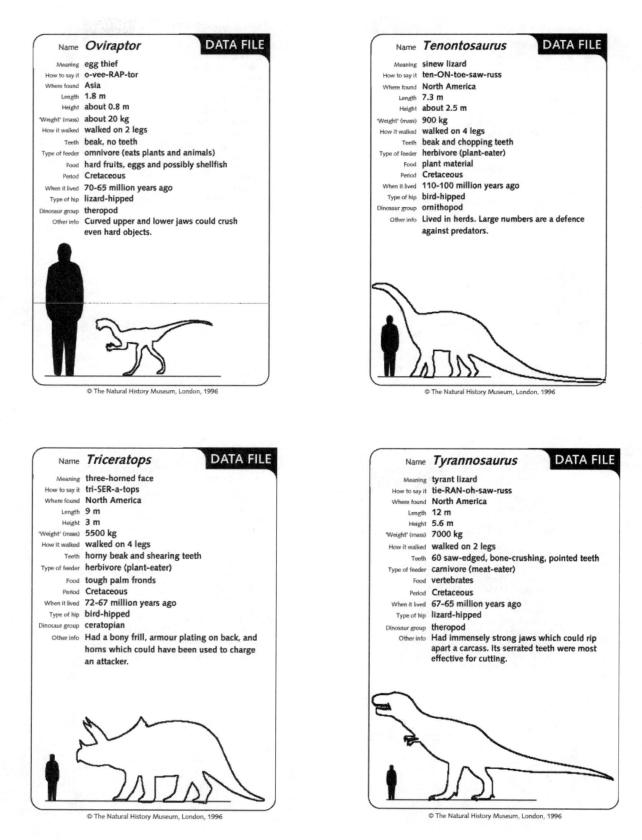

Name *Oviraptor*   DATA FILE

Meaning	egg thief
How to say it	o-vee-RAP-tor
Where found	Asia
Length	1.8 m
Height	about 0.8 m
'Weight' (mass)	about 20 kg
How it walked	walked on 2 legs
Teeth	beak, no teeth
Type of feeder	omnivore (eats plants and animals)
Food	hard fruits, eggs and possibly shellfish
Period	Cretaceous
When it lived	70-65 million years ago
Type of hip	lizard-hipped
Dinosaur group	theropod
Other info	Curved upper and lower jaws could crush even hard objects.

© The Natural History Museum, London, 1996

Name *Tenontosaurus*   DATA FILE

Meaning	sinew lizard
How to say it	ten-ON-toe-saw-russ
Where found	North America
Length	7.3 m
Height	about 2.5 m
'Weight' (mass)	900 kg
How it walked	walked on 4 legs
Teeth	beak and chopping teeth
Type of feeder	herbivore (plant-eater)
Food	plant material
Period	Cretaceous
When it lived	110-100 million years ago
Type of hip	bird-hipped
Dinosaur group	ornithopod
Other info	Lived in herds. Large numbers are a defence against predators.

© The Natural History Museum, London, 1996

Name *Triceratops*   DATA FILE

Meaning	three-horned face
How to say it	tri-SER-a-tops
Where found	North America
Length	9 m
Height	3 m
'Weight' (mass)	5500 kg
How it walked	walked on 4 legs
Teeth	horny beak and shearing teeth
Type of feeder	herbivore (plant-eater)
Food	tough palm fronds
Period	Cretaceous
When it lived	72-67 million years ago
Type of hip	bird-hipped
Dinosaur group	ceratopian
Other info	Had a bony frill, armour plating on back, and horns which could have been used to charge an attacker.

© The Natural History Museum, London, 1996

Name *Tyrannosaurus*   DATA FILE

Meaning	tyrant lizard
How to say it	tie-RAN-oh-saw-russ
Where found	North America
Length	12 m
Height	5.6 m
'Weight' (mass)	7000 kg
How it walked	walked on 2 legs
Teeth	60 saw-edged, bone-crushing, pointed teeth
Type of feeder	carnivore (meat-eater)
Food	vertebrates
Period	Cretaceous
When it lived	67-65 million years ago
Type of hip	lizard-hipped
Dinosaur group	theropod
Other info	Had immensely strong jaws which could rip apart a carcass. Its serrated teeth were most effective for cutting.

© The Natural History Museum, London, 1996

DINO Cards

	Name	**Oviraptor**	**DATA FILE**
	Meaning	egg thief	
	How to say it	o-vee-RAP-tor	
	Where found	Asia	
	Length	1.8 m	
	Height	about 0.8 m	
	'Weight' (mass)	about 20 kg	
	How it walked	walked on 2 legs	
	Teeth	beak, no teeth	
	Type of feeder	omnivore (eats plants and animals)	
	Food	hard fruits, eggs and possibly shellfish	
	Period	Cretaceous	
	When it lived	70-65 million years ago	
	Type of hip	lizard-hipped	
	Dinosaur group	theropod	
	Other info	Curved upper and lower jaws could crush even hard objects.	

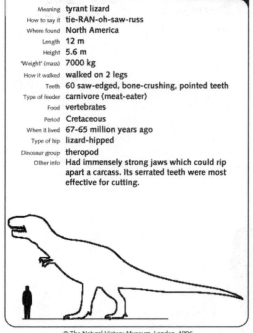

© The Natural History Museum, London, 1996

	Name	**Tyrannosaurus**	**DATA FILE**
	Meaning	tyrant lizard	
	How to say it	tie-RAN-oh-saw-russ	
	Where found	North America	
	Length	12 m	
	Height	5.6 m	
	'Weight' (mass)	7000 kg	
	How it walked	walked on 2 legs	
	Teeth	60 saw-edged, bone-crushing, pointed teeth	
	Type of feeder	carnivore (meat-eater)	
	Food	vertebrates	
	Period	Cretaceous	
	When it lived	67-65 million years ago	
	Type of hip	lizard-hipped	
	Dinosaur group	theropod	
	Other info	Had immensely strong jaws which could rip apart a carcass. Its serrated teeth were most effective for cutting.	

© The Natural History Museum, London, 1996

	Name	**Gallimimus**	**DATA FILE**
	Meaning	fowl mimic	
	How to say it	gal-i-ME-muss	
	Where found	Asia	
	Length	5.6 m	
	Height	3 m	
	'Weight' (mass)	about 200 kg	
	How it walked	walked on 2 legs	
	Teeth	horny beak, no teeth	
	Type of feeder	omnivore (eats plants and animals)	
	Food	plants, insects, lizards	
	Period	Cretaceous	
	When it lived	74-70 million years ago	
	Type of hip	lizard-hipped	
	Dinosaur group	theropod	
	Other info	Could run fast (at up to 30 kph) but not over very long distances.	

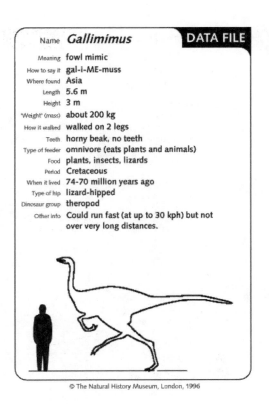

© The Natural History Museum, London, 1996

	Name	**Diplodocus**	**DATA FILE**
	Meaning	double beam	
	How to say it	dip-lod-OH-kuss	
	Where found	North America	
	Length	26 m	
	Height	about 8 m	
	'Weight' (mass)	10,000 kg	
	How it walked	walked on 4 legs	
	Teeth	rows of teeth like a comb	
	Type of feeder	herbivore (plant-eater)	
	Food	leaves from trees and soft plants	
	Period	Jurassic	
	When it lived	155-145 million years ago	
	Type of hip	lizard-hipped	
	Dinosaur group	sauropod	
	Other info	Had a hollow backbone, which was light but very strong.	

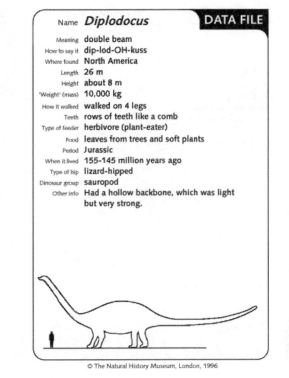

© The Natural History Museum, London, 1996

Chapter 9

THE INTERACTIVE LESSON

Interactive lessons take the form of self-paced, individualized learning opportunities embedded throughout with student assessment.

> An Interactive Lesson is a visual-based, classroom-centered teaching strategy appropriate for learners of all ages who benefit from concrete, sequential instruction imbedded with real-time assessment necessary to assure student learning.

In practice, these lessons are offered to all students but for different reasons. Some students need individualized instruction, others remedial instruction or additional practice, still others only enrichment activities. Chapter 9 submits the following objectives

- **Advanced Graphics Presentation Features.** Objective 9.1: Demonstrate a mastery of the advanced features of graphics presentation.

- **Preparing the Interactive Lesson.** Objective 9.2: Demonstrate a knowledge of visual-base design along with a mastery of advanced graphics presentation features. Combine these skills with the use of technology resources harvested from the Internet to produce the Interactive Lesson.

Advanced Graphics Presentation Features

Objective 9.:1 Demonstrate a mastery of the advanced features of graphics presentation.

Additional Power Point features, over and above those basic features presented in an earlier chapter, are necessary to create the Interactive Lesson. They include the Master Slide, WordArt, text color, drawing tools, slide transitions, and hyperlinks. There are also a few supplementary features introduced later in the chapter.

Creating custom templates is a four-step process. First, the desired image is captured. Second, the image is inserted onto a slide. Third, the image is resized to the maximum dimensions of the slide. Fourth, the image is placed on the Master Slide and sent to the background. In chapter 3, images were captured from the Internet; and in chapter 5, they were insert onto a slide and resized. The only remaining task to learn is how to place an image on the Master Slide so that it appears on every slide in the presentation.

Master Slides

Creating templates from images offers the designer an unlimited number of choices for customizing the interactive lesson. However, the quality of the image, color scheme, and brightness make most images unacceptable as backgrounds. In addition to a background image, the Master Slide formats the titles, main text, and any background items. A change to the Master Slide affects all slides in the presentation. To create a new template, follow these instructions:

Figure 9-I. The Master Slide

- **Attach the Desired Image**—Click the *View → Master → Slide Master* pop-down menu (see Figure 9-1). Notice that the Master Slide contains the primary template for the presentation. *Insert → Picture → From File* selects the desired image for the new background. Resize the image to fill the entire slide.

Figure 9-2. Converting an Image to a Watermark

- **Convert the Image to a Watermark**—Once an image is placed on the Master Slide, it must be converted to a watermark. When an image is selected, the Picture Tool bar appears. From the Image Control icon shown in Figure 9-2, click *Watermark* to soften the image making it suitable as a template background.

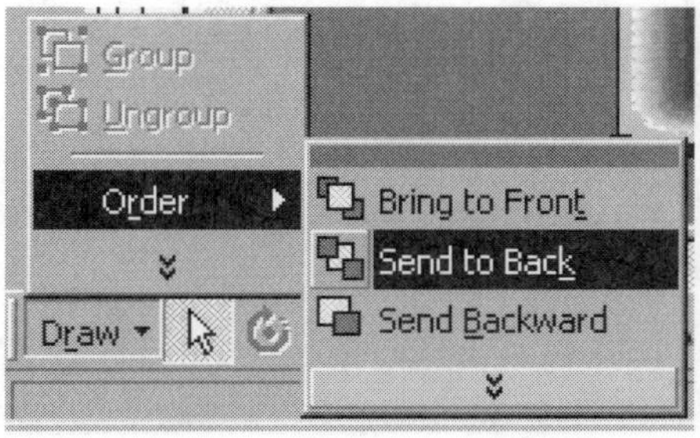

Figure 9-3. Sending an Image to the Background

- **Send the Image to the Background**—Unless the new image is sent to the background, subsequent titles, bullets, and other images remain hidden. To send an image to the background, locate the Draw command at the bottom left of the screen. Click *Draw → Order → Send to Back* (see figure 9-3) to position the image behind other elements on the slide.

- **Close the Master Slide**—To effect the changes on every slide, click any of the View Modes (Slide View, Slide Sorter View, Slide Show View, etc.) to close the Master Slide and complete the modifications.
- **Save the presentation**—*File → Save* the presentation to retain the Master Slide format.

WordArt

Similar to the HyperBook, WordArt in Power Point offers more sophisticated and visually appealing text. Most of the required commands are the same with only a few notable exceptions. To insert WordArt onto a slide, follow these steps:

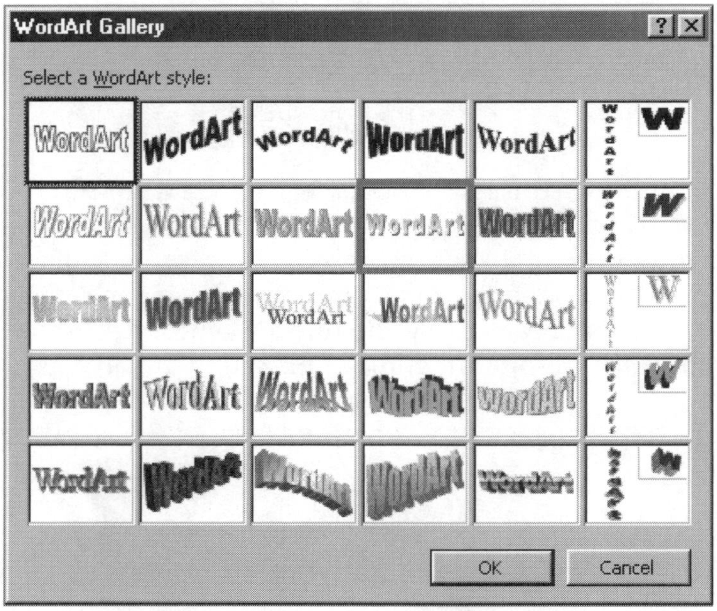

Figure 9-4. WordArt Gallery

- **Select the Slide**—Before inserting WordArt, Power Point *must be in the Slide View*. Move to the target slide using the up and down arrows which appear on the scroll bar on the right side of the screen.

-  On the **Drawing** Tool Bar, click the *WordArt icon* to open the Gallery. Or, click the *Insert → Picture → WordArt* pop-down menu. Choose from among 24 available styles offering various colors, sizes, and shapes (see Figure 9-4). Highlight the selected box and *click OK.*

- In the **Edit WordArt Text** dialog box, *enter the desired text.* Also, select the Font, Font Size, or Appearance options and *click OK* to place the text in the slide. The same rules to resize, move, and edit apply to WordArt as they did to images and clip art in previous chapters.

-  After the text is inserted, the WordArt menu bar is displayed for additional editing and formatting. Click to revise the contents, access the gallery, change colors and format, integrate basic shapes, rotate the text on the slide, or align WordArt.

- **Save the presentation**—*File → Save* the presentation to retain the changes.

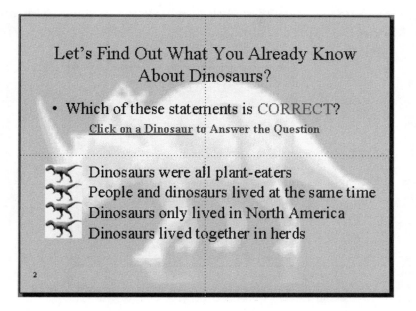

Figure 9-5. Text Color

Text Color

Another simple but effective visual enhancement is the use of text colors. Student instructions throughout the Interactive Lesson are generally displayed in blue (see Figure 9-5). Once students grasp this visual clue, they are on the lookout for elements within the lesson requiring a response. To change the color of text, highlight the target words with a mouse click and drag and follow these steps:

-  Click the *Font Color* icon on the Drawing Toolbar located at the bottom of the document window. To use the color currently shown under the *A*, simply click the icon. To change to another color, click the down arrow and select from among 40 primary colors or click *More Colors* to select from the rainbow. Colorized text may be edited for appearance (bold, italics, or underline) and its font or font size changed to suit the designer.

- **Save the presentation**—*File* → *Save* the presentation to retain the changes.

Drawing Tools

Drawing Tools provide pre-established shapes, patterns (rectangles, arrows, and ovals), and Fill Colors.

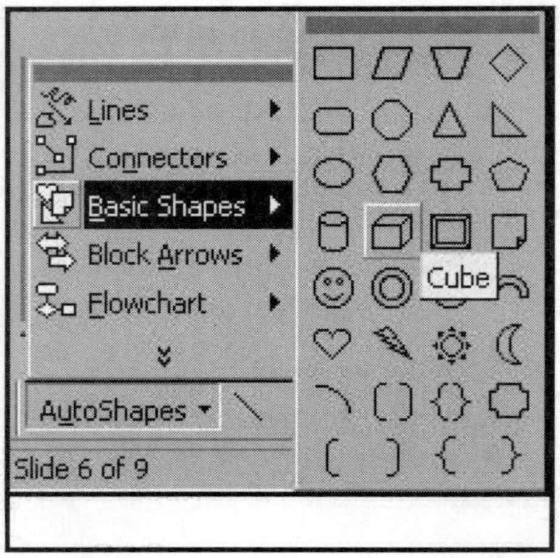

Figure 9-6. AutoShapes

- **AutoShapes**—Power Point comes with a set of ready-made shapes for use in presentations. The shapes may be resized, rotated, flipped, colored, and combined to make even more complex images. The **AutoShapes** menu on the **Drawing** toolbar contains several categories of shapes, including lines, connectors, basic shapes, block arrows, and flowchart symbols (see Figure 9-6). For example, to add a **Cube** to a slide click *AutoShapes → Basic Shapes → Cube*, resize and move the shape to the desired location on the slide.

- 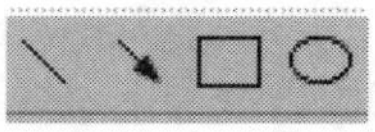 **Pattern Shapes**—To draw a straight line, arrow, circle, or square, click the appropriate pattern icon and resize and move the shape to the desired location on the slide.

-  **Fill Colors**. The paint bucket changes the color of any selected shape or object. Click the bucket icon to use the color displayed. To change the fill color, click the down arrow next to the bucket and select from among several primary colors or click **More Fill Colors** to access the color rainbow. **Automatic** returns the shape back to its pre-set default color.

- **Save the presentation**—*File → Save* the presentation to retain the changes.

Slide Transitions

As each slide is displayed, transition effects provide the look and feel of a professional presentation. For a basic, no frills presentation, transitions are held to a minimum. They may not even be noticeable to the viewer. However, for an Interactive Lesson exact control over the advancement of each slide is necessary.

- **Select the Slide**—To initiate the slide transition, Power Point *must be in the Slide View.* Move to a target slide using the scroll bar on the right side of the screen.

- Enter the transition mode by clicking *Slide Show* → *Slide Transition* (see Figure 9-7). Three options are available. First, the **Effect**—as each new slide is presented, a pattern introduces the contents of the slide at a slow, medium, or fast rate. Second, the slide **Advance** may occur either on a mouse click or after a specified amount of time set by the designer. Third, pre-packaged sounds are available including applause, camera clicks, typewriter keys, and chimes in the **Sound** window of the pop-down menu.

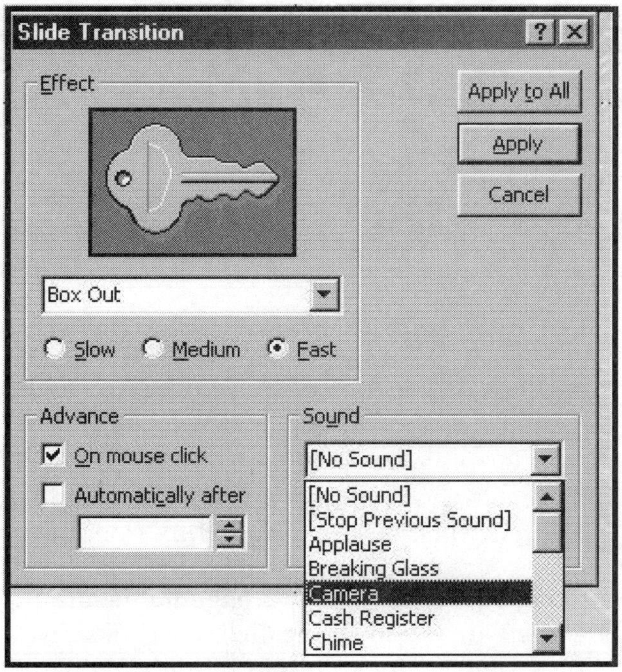

Figure 9-7. Slide Transition Dialog Box

- **Save the presentation**—*File* → *Save* the presentation to retain the changes after adding the transition effects. One word of caution—transitions add life to an otherwise mundane presentation. However, they are easily overdone, making a presentation too flashy and overshadowing the learning objectives. Keep the transition effects, especially sounds, to a minimum.

Hyperlinks.

Use of Hyperlinks assumes that the presentation is online; otherwise, there is no reason to include this feature. To insert a hyperlink, follow these instructions:

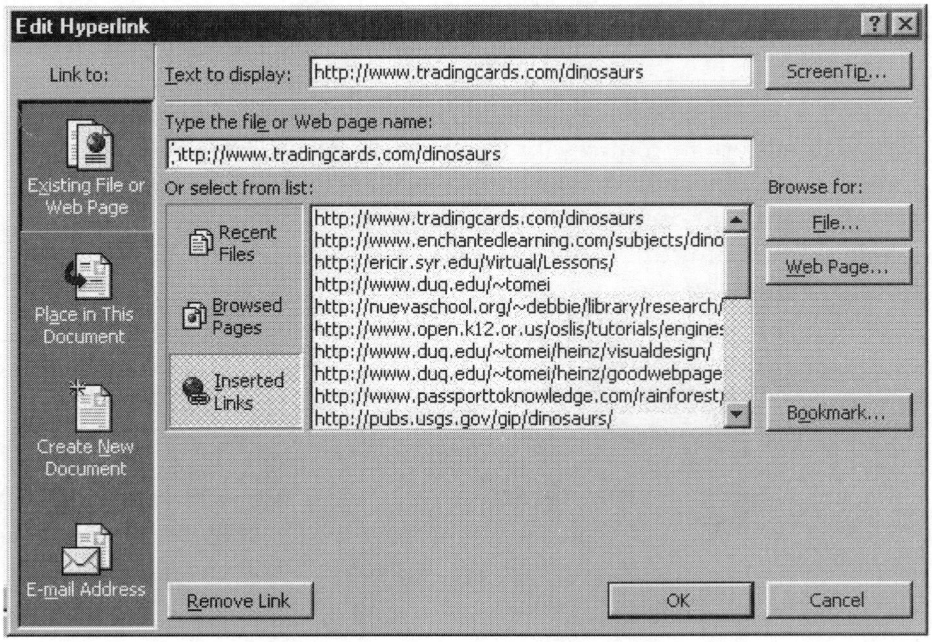

Figure 9-8. Insert/Edit Hyperlink

- **Type the Text**—Move to the target slide where the link is to appear. Enter the text to serve as the link and select the text.

-  On the **Standard** toolbar, click the *Insert Hyperlink* icon or click *Insert → Hyperlink* from the pop-down menu.

- To link to an Internet site, enter the **Web page name** and prefix the URL with **http://**. Click **OK** (see Figure 9-8). Typically, hyperlinks display as blue text. To link to another presentation, for example, enter a file name as the **Web page name** without a prefix or use the *Browse for: → File* button to locate the target file.

- **Save the document.**

Preparing the Interactive Lesson

Objective 9.2: Demonstrate a knowledge of visual-based design along with a mastery of advanced graphics presentation features. Combine these skills with the use of technology resources harvested from the Internet to produce the Interactive Lesson.

Interactive lessons are not new. They have existed almost since the start of instructional technology. However, the "Model for Technology-Based Lessons" offered in chapter 7, combined with the advanced features of Power Point discussed earlier (plus a few more features to be introduced in Steps 8 and 9 in this chapter), make this an unbeatable recipe for developing a successful student-centered presentation.

An example of an Interactive Lesson is available on the accompanying CDROM. Use **Best Practices #11** to locate the Interactive Lesson entitled "Why Did Dinosaurs Become Extinct? An Interactive Lesson." The lesson slides are available in the appendix to this chapter.

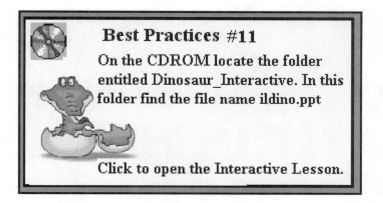

Best Practices #11

On the CDROM locate the folder entitled Dinosaur_Interactive. In this folder find the file name ildino.ppt

Click to open the Interactive Lesson.

Creating an Interactive Lesson

To be successful, the Interactive Lesson integrates self-paced content with specific, logical, systematic instruction that places a good deal of the responsibility for mastering the material directly in the hands of the learner. The Interactive Lesson embraces mastery learning techniques and suggests alternatives for presenting learning objectives, corrective instruction, and enrichment activities.

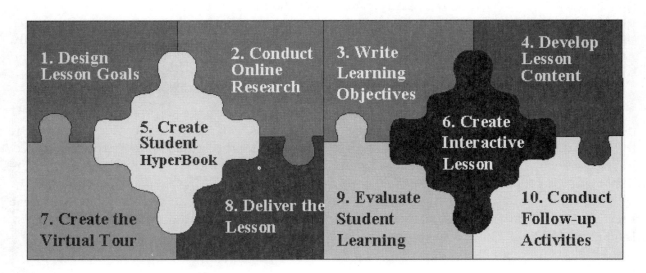

Figure 9-9. The Model for Technology-Based Lessons

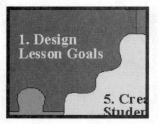

Step 1: Design the Lesson Goals. There are two specific tasks associated with this step: selecting a topic for the Interactive Lesson and identifying the target learners. The topic for the "Dinosaur Interactive Lesson" is "Why did dinosaurs become extinct?" Fourth-grade students are the target learners. To satisfy the Interactive Lesson format, lesson goals include:

- **Introduction** to the topic written at the student's level. (Note: For early childhood lessons, this may mean pictures rather than words.)
- **Instructions** for completing the Interactive Lesson. Students should understand what is required to complete the lesson.
- **Allotted Time**—Lesson goals should clearly state the amount of time available and how much of that time is allotted to the completion of the Interactive Lesson.
- **Lesson Goals**—Students are asked to select an extinction theory they believe is responsible for dinosaurs vanishing from the Earth. They may choose from cosmic collision, global temperature change, or evolution explanations. Follow-on classroom discussions allow students to offer details from the Interactive Lesson to justify their position.

Step 2: Conduct Online Research. Online research provides the specific behavioral-based elements from which the Interactive Lesson is created. An online review of dinosaur sites found several that specifically address prevailing theories of extinction. With research material on the Internet so abundant, the only challenge is in selecting which images, video clips, and other artifacts to incorporate into the Interactive Lesson. With the Interactive Lesson, material from discovered web sites is most often incorporated directly into the lesson (after giving proper credit and copyright permissions) rather than linking directly to the site. In this manner, the material may be validated by the teacher for content and applicability, student online exploration is controlled, and deleted/moved sites are avoided.

Step 3: Write Learning Objectives. The Interactive Lesson is behavioral in nature with lessons constructed sequentially from first to last, easy to difficult. Writing clear, unambiguous learning objectives requires the teacher to understand the "Taxonomy for Instructional Technology" available in chapter 7.

In this step, specific learning objectives are created along with a statement of prior student knowledge and classroom assignments and is the most important phase of lesson development. In this step, learning objectives are closely matched with the established goals of the lesson. See Table 9-1 for an example of the "Dinosaur Interactive Lesson" and its respective learning objectives.

Lesson Goal: Select the theory of dinosaur extinction you think is correct. Prior Knowledge: Students will share their prior knowledge of dinosaurs and comments on any television documentaries or movies they have seen regarding the subject.	**Learning Objective 1. Students will be able to explain the "Death by Cosmic Collision" theory of dinosaur extinction.** **Learning Objective 2. Students will be able to explain the "Global Temperature Change" theory of dinosaur extinction.** **Learning Objective 3. Students will be able to explain the "Evolution" theory of dinosaur extinction.**
	Assignment 1. Students must select one theory as most plausible. Assignment 2. Students must prepare a two paragraph justification supporting their selections. Assignment 3. Students should locate the geographic regions of dinosaur habitat.

Table 9-1. Learning Objectives for the Interactive Lesson

Step 4: Develop Lesson Content. In this step, the instructional sequence of the Interactive Lesson connects each learning objective with specific content material. The content of the "Dinosaur Interactive Lesson" is displayed in Table 9-2 below.

Learning Objective	Interactive Lesson Content
Learning Objective 1: Students will be able to explain the "Death By Cosmic Collision" theory of dinosaur extinction.	The Death By Cosmic Collision Theory a. Large celestial body strikes the Earth b. Asteroid at least Five Miles Across c. The Iridium Anomaly d. The Yucatan Crater e. The Havoc f. Clouds of Darkness
Learning Objective 2: Students will be able to explain the "Global Temperature Change" theory of dinosaur extinction.	The Global Temperature Change Theory a. Slow Decline of Dinosaur Population b. Other Species Unaffected c. The Fossil Record d. Change in Anatomy of Dinosaurs e. Demise of the Cold-Blooded Dinosaur
Learning Objective 3: Students will be able to explain the "Evolution" theory of dinosaur extinction.	The Evolution Theory a. Dinosaurs Evolved Too Large b. Brains made Them Non-Competitive c. Food Sources Were Insufficient d. Smaller Scavengers

Table 9-2. Interactive Lesson Content Material

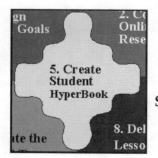

Step 5: Create Student HyperBook. This is discussed in detail in chapter 8.

Step 6: Create the Interactive Lesson. The dinosaur lesson exhibits the best the Interactive Lesson has to offer. Visual and aural classroom presentation remains the primary strength of this format; however, there is the option of providing students with an electronic version containing active hyperlinks to the selected web sites. The Interactive Lesson is shown in its entirety at the appendix to this chapter. Examine it closely to identify the key elements required for an effective resource. A summary of the key components of a successful Interactive Lesson include

- **The Lesson Overview Page** contains, as a minimum
  - **Introduction to the Topic**
  - **Instructions**
  - **Allotted Time**
  - **Lesson Goals**
- **Prior Knowledge Review**—Elements of these first few slides in the lesson include
  - **Selected questions** to arrive at the level of student understanding of the topic
  - **Positive Feedback slide** to reinforce the correct response
  - **Negative Feedback slide** to provide the correct response and encourage further student exploration
- **Transition Slide** moves the learner from the pre-lesson to the body of new material.
- **Learning Objective Component** includes a series of slides containing content material presented in the following sequence
  - **Objective Title** slide
  - **Content** slide(s)
  - **Formative Assessment** slide(s)
- **Summative Assessment slide(s)** recap the lesson goals with a measurement of student learning outcomes over the entire lesson.
- **Follow-on Activities** with additional information (e.g., web sites) for student enrichment activities.
- **Additional Resources** such as videotapes, audiocassettes, and publications.

Step 7: Create the Virtual Tour. This is discussed in detail in chapter 10.

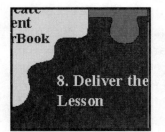

Step 8: Deliver the Lesson Using the Kiosk Browser. Kiosks are self-running audiovisual presentations found at many amusement parks, trade shows, and conventions. The kiosk feature supports unattended slide shows that run continuously, restart automatically, or require the learner to manually advance the slides. It is this last characteristic that makes the Interactive Lesson possible. Each slide in the presentation has its own Next Slide button; otherwise, the presentation would stop dead in its tracks.

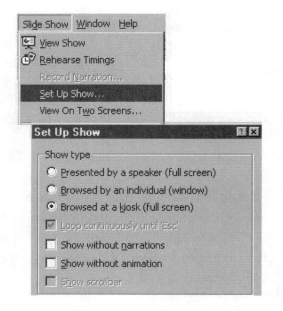

Figure 9-10. Activating the Kiosk Feature

- Creating a kiosk is done by clicking *Slide Show → Set Up Show → Browsed at a Kiosk* (see Figure 9-10). **This feature should remain off during the construction** of the presentation for ease of troubleshooting.
- Each slide must contain a way to advance the presentation, either a button or an icon, otherwise the ESCAPE key is the only way for the instructor to end the show. The Kiosk feature ensures that the student does not skip around the presentation. The teacher controls the sequencing through the Action Buttons and Hide Slides discussed next.

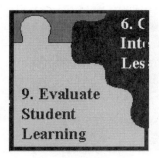

Step 9: Evaluate Student Learning. Earlier in the chapter, the Interactive Lesson was presented as an instructional technique of mastery learning. An important premise with this popular teaching strategy is its underlying dependence on behavioral psychology. To be successful, the Interactive Lesson must follow two basic rules. First, there must be some form of on-going feedback. Mastery learning advocates refer to this as *formative assessment*. Second, there must be a final determination of student learning called the *summative assessment*. The Assessment Slide accomplishes this second task.

- **Action Buttons**—Power Point comes with built-in Action Buttons for Next Slide, Movies and Sound clips, Help or Information. Movement within an Interactive Lesson is critical to its success. Even more important, however, is the use of Action Buttons to assess student understanding. By creating a question with several possible responses, the presentation transfers students to new information if the response was correct or remedial information if more instruction is necessary. To create an Action Button, review these steps:

Figure 9-II. Creating an Action Button

- Click the *Slide Show* → *Action Buttons* menu (see Figure 9-11). Select one of the available buttons and drag the button to a slide. Some of the pre-formatted buttons indicate Home, Questions, Index, Back, Forward, First, Last, Sound, and Video. However, any element in a Power Point slide may serve as an Action Button—text, images, even Clip Art.

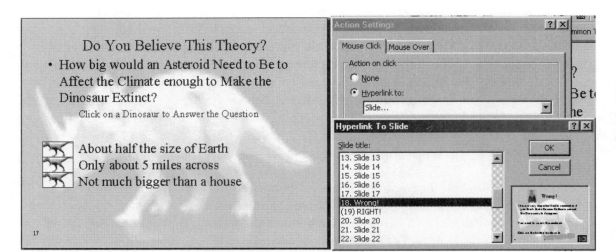

Figure 9-12. Linking an Action Button to Another Slide

In Figure 9-12, the dinosaur icons serve as the Action Buttons. It asks the question, "How big would an asteroid need to be to affect the climate enough to make the dinosaur extinct?" Notice three possible answers. If the student selects either incorrect response, "About half the size of earth" or "Not much bigger than a house," the Interactive Lesson advances to Slide 18 containing the negative feedback "Wrong!" Slide 18 then sends the student back to Slide 12 to reread the original material on Cosmic Collision. A correct response of "only about 5 miles across" triggers the hyperlink which advances to Slide 19 and from there to the rest of the lesson. Action Buttons enable immediate feedback, but they would be confusing to the student without the Hide Slide feature.

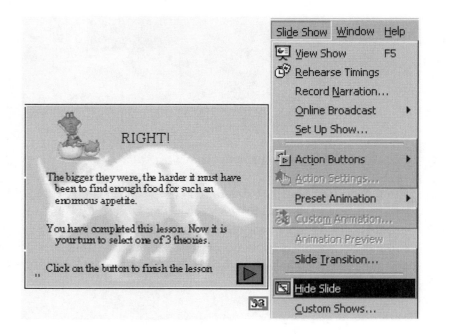

Figure 9-13. Hide Slide

- **Hide Slide**—In a typical presentation, students view slides sequentially from the first slide to the final slide. There are times, however, when the designer wants the individual to see certain slides only under special circumstances. A formative assessment question is a good example. Unless feedback slides are hidden, they will be viewed as the presentation unfolds and cause unnecessary confusion. In the "Interactive Dinosaur Lesson," feedback slides are hidden using the pop-down menu shown in Figure 9-13.

  - Click on *Slide Show g Hide Slide*. Once hidden, the null icon (a diagonal slash through the slide number) appears when viewing the presentation in the Slide Sorter mode. The only way to view this slide during a presentation is to access it using an Action Button and the kiosk browser.

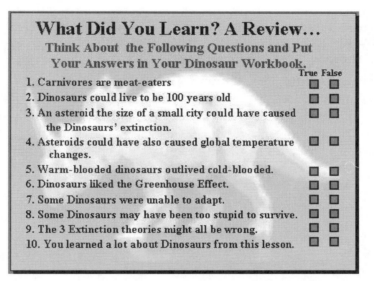

Figure 9-14. The Summative Assessment Slide

- **Summative Assessment Slide**—One of the final slides in an Interactive Lesson meets the requirements for a final, cumulative assessment to ensure students complete the lesson, master the learning objectives, and receive some reward for their efforts. In a computer lab, the Summative Assessment slide, displayed in bold colors on the computer monitor, alerts an observant teacher that the lesson was completed and the student is ready for the next instructional challenge. Notice that the Assessment Slide shown in Figure 9-14 references the Dinosaur HyperBook and instructs the student to answer the final questions in the text-based workbook created in chapter 8.

Step 10: Conduct Follow-up Activities. Concluding activities are in order as the lesson is completed. These culminating projects do not need to involve technology and surely not the same technologies used to present the Interactive Lesson. Films and videos make excellent concluding activities; perhaps "Jurassic Park" would offer a final venue for a classroom discussion of dinosaurs. The Interactive Lesson has many practical applications for content rich subjects and is highly recommended for your next teaching with technology adventure. But, as with all the technologies, it must be properly used in conjunction with a variety of other instructional strategies to produce the desired student learning outcome across a classroom of individual students.

Conclusion

Essential ingredients in the successful implementation of the Interactive Lesson is to form the lesson goals, conduct the research, write the objectives, and develop the lesson content before attempting to construct the visual-based materials. In producing an Interactive Lesson, the tendency is to include as many audiovisual and web-based resources as possible on each and every slide. Such misuse of technology is highly discouraged. Images, hyperlinks, and sounds must be used judiciously throughout the presentation and then only if they contribute to student understanding of the content under exploration.

Teachers find the Interactive Lesson of medium difficulty. Only the HyperBook is less technologically demanding with its word processing-based lessons and hard copy workbook format. On the other hand, web-based materials presented in the next chapter offer many more features but are considerably more demanding.

APPENDIX

WHY DID DINOSAURS BECOME EXTINCT

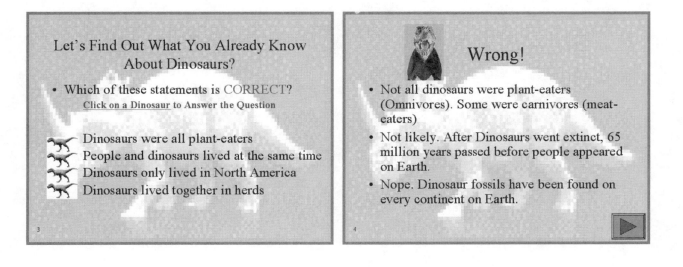

BRONTOSAURUS

These dinosaurs are plant eating. They are now called apatosaurus but some people still call them brontosaurus. There were even larger dinosaurs than the apatosaurus called the megasaurus and the ultrasaurus

5

Let's Find Out What You Already Know About Dinosaurs?

- Which of these statements is CORRECT?
  Click on a Dinosaur to Answer the Question

All fossils are from dinosaurs
Only 100 species of Dinosaurs are named
Some Dinosaurs lived to be 100 years old
Omnivores ate meat

6

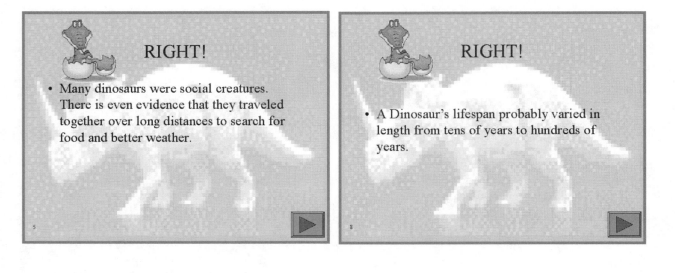

RIGHT!

- Many dinosaurs were social creatures. There is even evidence that they traveled together over long distances to search for food and better weather.

5

RIGHT!

- A Dinosaur's lifespan probably varied in length from tens of years to hundreds of years.

8

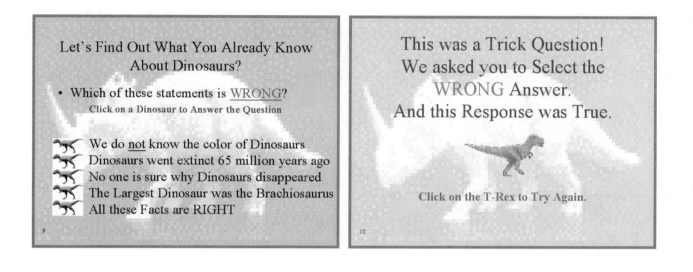

Let's Find Out What You Already Know
About Dinosaurs?

- Which of these statements is <u>WRONG</u>?
  Click on a Dinosaur to Answer the Question

We do <u>not</u> know the color of Dinosaurs
Dinosaurs went extinct 65 million years ago
No one is sure why Dinosaurs disappeared
The Largest Dinosaur was the Brachiosaurus
All these Facts are RIGHT

9

This was a Trick Question!
We asked you to Select the
WRONG Answer.
And this Response was True.

Click on the T-Rex to Try Again.

10

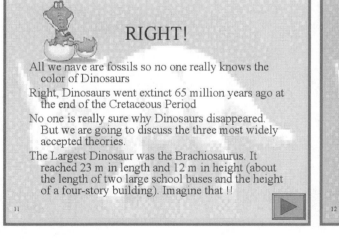

RIGHT!

All we nave are fossils so no one really knows the
color of Dinosaurs

Right, Dinosaurs went extinct 65 million years ago at
the end of the Cretaceous Period

No one is really sure why Dinosaurs disappeared.
But we are going to discuss the three most widely
accepted theories.

The Largest Dinosaur was the Brachiosaurus. It
reached 23 m in length and 12 m in height (about
the length of two large school buses and the height
of a four-story building). Imagine that !!

11

Why Did Dinosaurs Become Extinct?

Now that you some important facts about Dinosaurs,
let's discuss what happened to them. Why are all the
Dinosaurs gone? Why did they become extinct?

The scientists have 3 explanations… they call them
theories… about what happened to the Stegosaurus,
Tyrannosaurus, Brachiosaurus, Triceratops, and the
Velociraptor.

Want to Find Out? Just Click the NEXT Button

12

In 1980, two famous geologists blamed the extinction of the dinosaurs on a large celestial body which hit Earth 65 million years ago.

An asteroid five miles across blasted through Earth's crust, and threw up molten rock, ash, and dust.

14

Some point to craters such as this one on the Yucatan Peninsula to prove that an asteroid only five miles across could have caused extreme and immediate havoc, including, a blast wave which would have set global wildfires, destroying every thing in its path.

15

The impact of the asteroid would cause massive earthquakes all over the Earth, and these earthquakes would increase volcanic activity. The power of the collision would have also caused a cloud of dust and smoke that would have blocked out the sun.

16

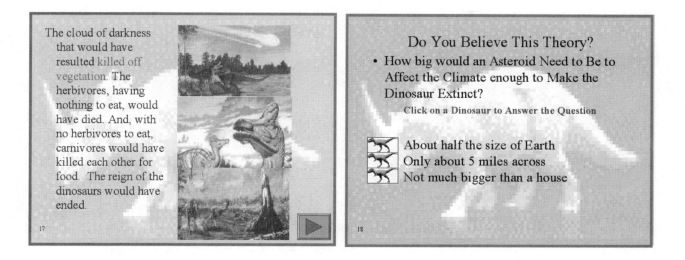

The cloud of darkness that would have resulted killed off vegetation. The herbivores, having nothing to eat, would have died. And, with no herbivores to eat, carnivores would have killed each other for food. The reign of the dinosaurs would have ended.

17

Do You Believe This Theory?

- How big would an Asteroid Need to Be to Affect the Climate enough to Make the Dinosaur Extinct?

Click on a Dinosaur to Answer the Question

About half the size of Earth
Only about 5 miles across
Not much bigger than a house

18

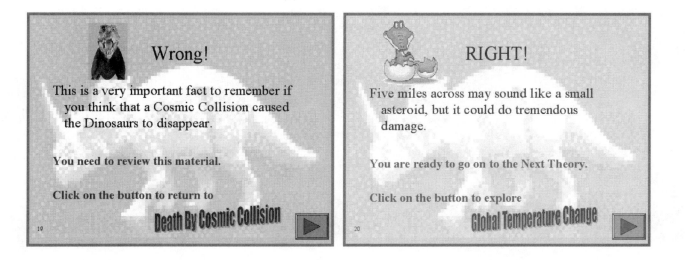

Wrong!

This is a very important fact to remember if you think that a Cosmic Collision caused the Dinosaurs to disappear.

You need to review this material.

Click on the button to return to

Death By Cosmic Collision

19

RIGHT!

Five miles across may sound like a small asteroid, but it could do tremendous damage.

You are ready to go on to the Next Theory.

Click on the button to explore

Global Temperature Change

20

Many paleontologists believe that dinosaurs began a slow subtle decline approximately 100 million years ago with global temperature changes .

Changes killed off the cold-blooded dinosaurs and only the warm-blooded dinosaurs survived.

22

A "greenhouse" effect triggered from volcanoes sent carbon dioxide into the atmosphere where it allowed heat from the sun to enter, but not exit. This destroyed the seasons as we know them, and most of the world became tropical, which well suited the dinosaurs.

23

Eventually, the environment returned to normal; events pushed the carbon dioxide levels in the atmosphere down, causing the return of the seasons. Dinosaurs could not cope with the cold of winter, so they began a slow but steady decline and ending the dinosaurs' great reign.

24

Do You Believe This Theory?

- How did the "Greenhouse Effect" impact the Dinosaur?

  Click on a Dinosaur to Answer the Question

  It killed most of the Dinosaurs that lived
  It happened before Dinosaurs lived
  They thrived in the warm climate

25

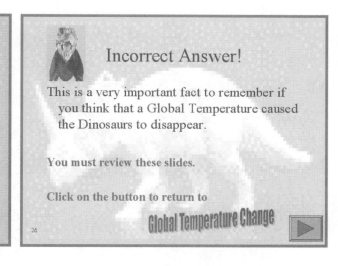

Incorrect Answer!

This is a very important fact to remember if you think that a Global Temperature caused the Dinosaurs to disappear.

You must review these slides.

Click on the button to return to

Global Temperature Change

26

RIGHT!

The hotter, the better for Dinosaurs. Right?

You are ready to go on to the Next Theory.

Click on the button to explore

Evolution Spells Disaster

27

One early theory suggested that as dinosaurs evolved into larger and larger creatures they simply became too stupid to survive.

Perhaps their brains, small to begin with, just did not grow large enough leaving the dinosaurs unable to adapt to the changing environment.

29

Another evolution theory states that dinosaurs simply became too heavy to survive, preventing them from effectively finding enough food.

30

Some scientists believe that small shrew-like and catlike mammals were abundant in the late Cretaceous period. These animals scavenged and ate so many dinosaur eggs that few dinosaur babies were born, dooming the great reptiles to extinction.

31

Do You Believe This Theory?

- If Dinosaurs got too big, how could that cause their extinction?

   Click on a Dinosaur to Answer the Question

They could not find enough food
They would be easy prey for Carnivores
They would be too hot

32

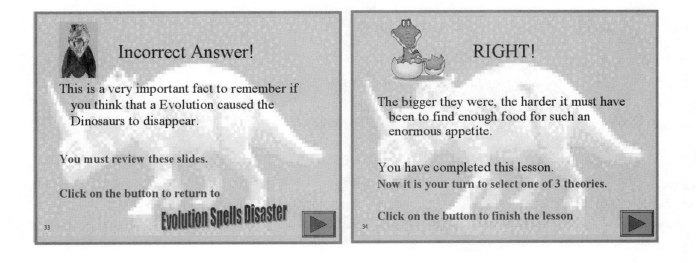

Incorrect Answer!

This is a very important fact to remember if you think that a Evolution caused the Dinosaurs to disappear.

You must review these slides.

Click on the button to return to

Evolution Spells Disaster

33

RIGHT!

The bigger they were, the harder it must have been to find enough food for such an enormous appetite.

You have completed this lesson.
Now it is your turn to select one of 3 theories.

Click on the button to finish the lesson

34

What Did You Learn? A Review...

Think About the Following Questions and Put Your Answers in Your Dinosaur Workbook.

	True	False
1. Carnivores are meat-eaters	☐	☐
2. Dinosaurs could live to be 100 years old	☐	☐
3. An asteroid the size of a small city could have caused the Dinosaurs' extinction.	☐	☐
4. Asteroids could have also caused global temperature changes.	☐	☐
5. Warm-blooded Dinosaurs outlived cold-blooded creatures.	☐	☐
6. Dinosaurs liked the Greenhouse Effect.	☐	☐
7. Some Dinosaurs were unable to adapt.	☐	☐
8. Some Dinosaurs may have been too stupid to survive.	☐	☐
9. The 3 Extinction theories might all be wrong.	☐	☐
10. You learned a lot about Dinosaurs from this lesson.	☐	☐

35

Follow-up Activities

- If you complete the lesson early, check out these terrific dinosaur sites
  - web.syr.edu/~dbgoldma/pictures.html
  - www.dinodon.com
  - www.dinosauria.com

36

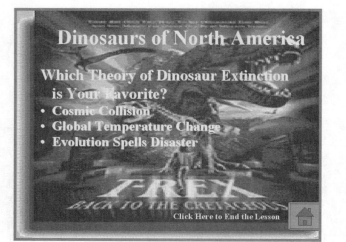

Chapter 10

THE VIRTUAL TOUR LESSON

The number of Internet users in the United States and Canada reached 92 million in 1999. A demographic survey found that access to the Internet was most predominant from home (72 million users), work (46 million users), and school (28 million users) (Network Wizards, 2000). Figure 10-1 demonstrates the phenomenal growth in the number of Internet domains (host computer systems) appearing on the World Wide Web in the period January 1995 through July 1997.

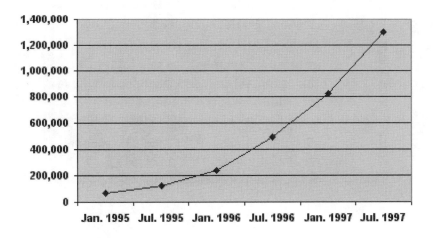

Figure l0-I. Growth in Internet Domains

Both statistics support what educators already know: there is virtually an endless number of Internet resources for teaching and learning. Many sites represent innovative, top-quality, far-reaching thinking; sites that teachers wish to share with their students. Others, unfortunately, constitute petty scholarship at best, some even dangerous. One technologist called the Internet without question, the largest, most inclusive, comprehensive, collection of knowledge while remaining essentially the most unorganized and unsupervised resource ever gathered.

What is the teacher to do with all this information? Perhaps the Virtual Tour is the answer. A *Virtual Tour* is a *"web-based teaching strategy which presents multi-sensory, multimedia instruction appropriate for individual student exploration and group learning experiences."* They offer the learner a host of **Front Doors**—14 in all—each uniquely suited to address a particular learning style and **Amplified Sites** which provide the specific content information. Chapter 10 offers an answer to this question by addressing the following objectives:

- **Advanced Web Page Features.** Objective 10.1: Demonstrate a mastery of the advanced features of web page design.
- **Preparing the Virtual Tour Lesson.** Objective 10.2: Demonstrate a knowledge of web-base design along with a mastery of advanced web page construction features. Combine these skills with the use of technology resources harvested from the Internet to produce the Virtual Tour lesson.

Advanced Web Page Features

Objective 10.1: Demonstrate a mastery of the advanced features of web page design.

Additional features of Netscape Composer required to construct the Virtual Tour include page properties, horizontal lines, tables, image hyperlinks, animated graphics, and targets. A web page is provided on the accompanying CDROM. Follow **Best Practices #12** and look for the folder entitled **"Example"** and locate the file named **page.htm**. Click the file name to launch Netscape and enter Composer using the *File → Edit Page* pop-down menu to practice the instructions for advanced web page design. A copy of this web site is available at the appendix to this chapter.

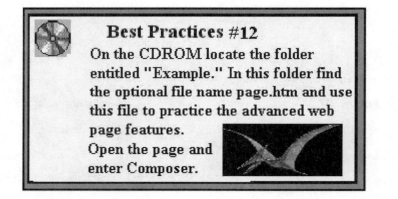

Page Properties

Page Properties address the visual composition of a web page and provides general properties, colors, and background images. Properties add color and increase the appeal to the viewer. To enter Page Properties, click *Format → Page Colors and Properties* from the Tool Bar.

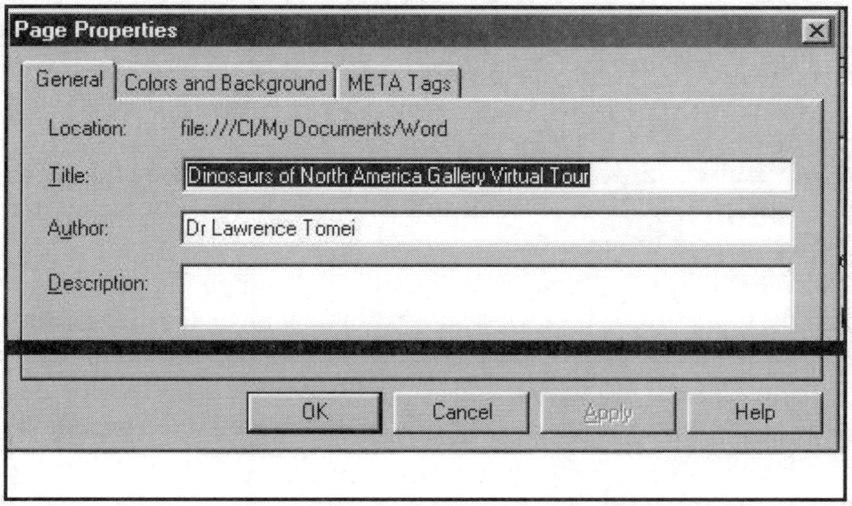

Figure I0-2. Page Properties General Tab

- **General Tab**—Web pages include a title at the top left of the Netscape window that is included whenever the web page is printed. The **General Tab** (see Figure 10-2) adds and revises the **Title** as necessary. Although the **Author** information never really appears, it is included in the page source code and should contain the name of the page designer for security purposes.

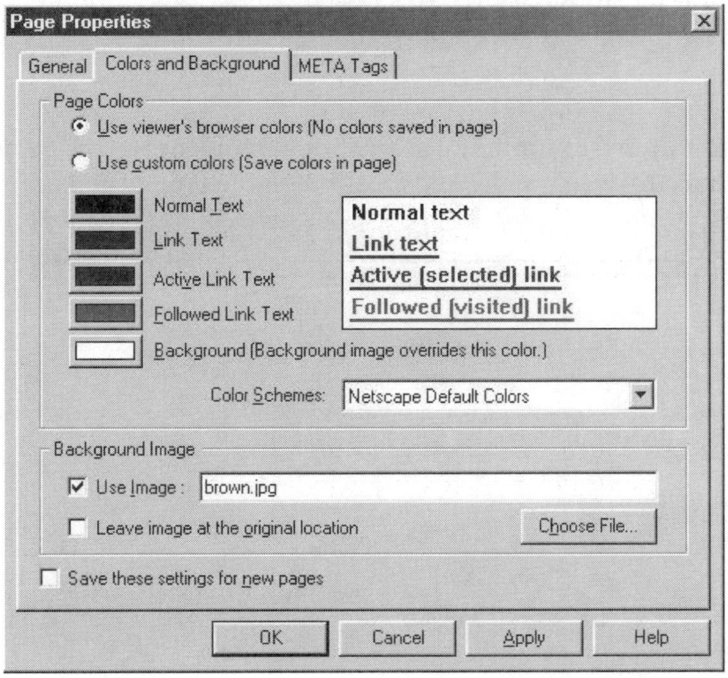

Figure I0-3. Page Properties Colors and Background Tab

- **Colors and Background Tab**—Each type of text is set to a predefined color which may be changed using this tab (see Figure 10-3).

- **Normal Text** is typically viewed in black. To change the default, **click the current color box** and select a new color from the rainbow. Two cautions are in order: First, do not use the same color that is used by another type of text—that causes confusion. Second, do not use a color that blends with the background—that makes the page difficult to read.

- **Link and Active Link Text**—Hyperlinks are displayed in their own unique color—usually blue. The color selection may be changed but keep in mind that most users expect to see blue hyperlinks.

- **Followed Link Text**—Browsers automatically change the color of any visited hyperlinks to distinguish viewed sites from new ones. Do not set this option to the same color as the Active Link. Also, do not set this option to the same color as the page background unless you want the hyperlink to disappear (i.e., blend with the background color making it look as if the link has vanished) after the site is visited.

- **Background Color and Background Image**—To set the background color, click the current color box and select a new color from the rainbow. To place an image on the background, click the *Use Image* option box and *enter the file name* or click the *Choose File* button to locate the file on disk.

- **Save the web page** to retain the changes.

Horizontal Lines

To create a horizontal line for visual separation of content material, position the cursor and click the *H.Line icon* on the Tool Bar. To delete an unwanted horizontal line, click *Edit → Delete* from the pop-down menu. **Save the web page** to retain the changes.

Tables

One of the easiest and most popular organizational tools for web page design is the Table. To insert a table, move the cursor to the desired location on the web page and click the *Table icon* on the Tool Bar or *Insert → Table → Table* from the pop-down menu. The text list of dinosaur names at the bottom of the example demonstrates how tables are used to arrange a series of terms.

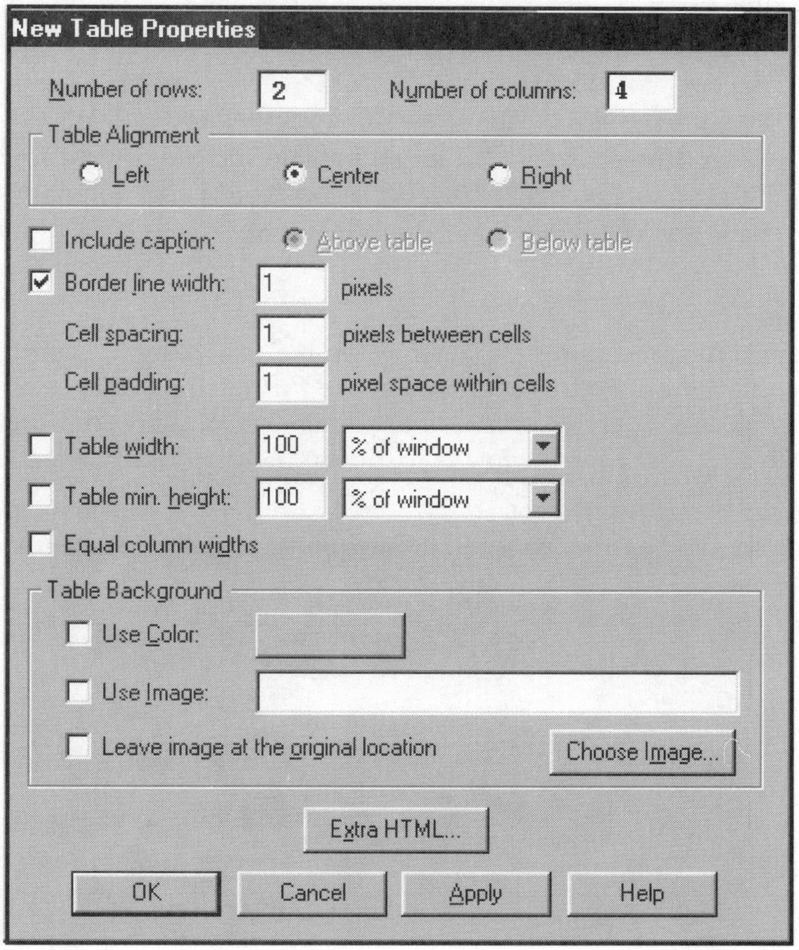

Figure 10-4. New Table Properties

- The **New Table Properties** dialog box (see Figure 10-4) provides the parameters of a new table. The example web page table shows **Number of Rows** 2 and **Number of Columns** 4.
    - **Table Alignment** may be set to Left, Center, or Right. The example shows a table placed at the center of the web page.
    - **Border Line Width** defaults are set at one pixel. Changes to the number of pixels affects the thickness of the borders.
    - **Table Width** allows the table to fill 100 percent of the available web page. However, since the example table is so small, this is not really an issue. Deselect the option to shrink the table to the minimum dimensions necessary to display the text without word wrapping to a second line.
    - **Equal Column Widths** allows the columns to take on an identical width size based on the length of the text.

- **Table Background** provides a color backdrop or an actual image be-hind each cell. Normally, cells should contain the same background as the rest of the web page; however, cell backgrounds may be altered for emphasis and effect.
- **Accept Table Properties**—Click *OK* to accept the table properties. They may be revised, deleted, or new properties added later.
- **Enter Text**—Fill each table cell by entering the desired text. Press the **Tab** key to advance to the next cell or to add additional rows.
- **Save the Web Page** to retain the changes.

Image Hyperlinks

Chapter 6 detailed the procedures for creating text-based and email hyperlinks and should be reviewed before continuing with this chapter. For the Virtual Tour, images oftentimes make the best links to amplified sites. To convert an ordinary image into an active link, insert an appropriate image onto the web page and click the image to indicate a hyperlink.

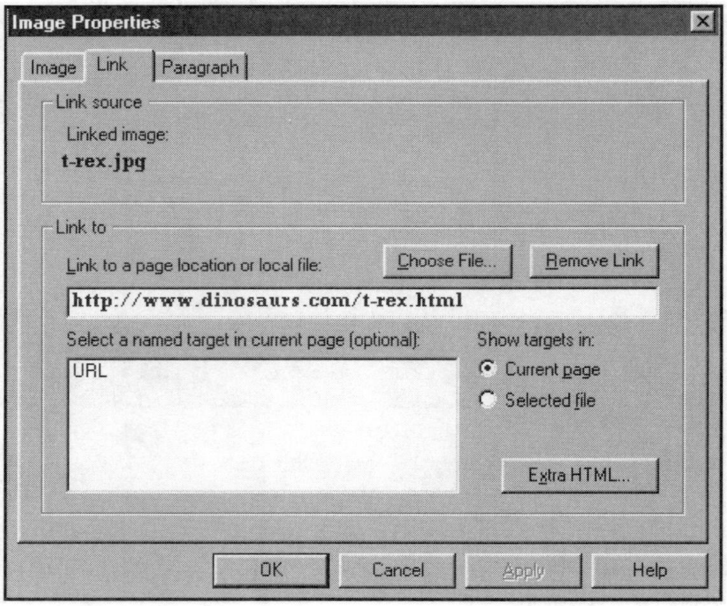

Figure 10-5. Image Properties—Linking to a Page or File

- **Inserting the Link**—Click the *Link icon* from the Tool Bar or the **Insert → Link** pop-down menu. In the Dialog box (see Figure 10-5), locate the window en-titled **Link to a page location or local file**.
  - To *enter an external link*, the URL must begin with the *http://* tag. For example, to send a learner to a site on the Internet the address must include *http://*.
  - To *enter an internal link*, the *http://* prefix is omitted from the URL. An internal link sends the learner to another web page usually created by

the teacher. For an internal link to work correctly, the file name *must* be located in the same physical directory or on the same physical diskette. *If the target html file, along with every image it displays, is not in the same directory, the page will not load properly.*

• **Save the web page** to retain the changes.

Inserting Animated Graphics

Animated graphics are a series of individual images scrolled rapidly by a web browser to give the effect of a moving picture—much like a cartoon. Many Internet sites offer animated images ready for harvesting. Some favorites are included in Table 10-1.

Internet Site Name	URL
Caboodles	**www.caboodles.com/animated**
World of Animation	**members.xoom.com/WoGA/**
Clip Art Collection	**www.clipartconnection.com/**
Clip Art Universe	**nzwwa.com/mirror/clipart/graphics/animated**

Table 10-1. Sites for Harvesting Animated Graphics

In the example web page, the image of the triceratops is an animated graphic. Of course, the animation only works with a web browser. Procedures for inserting animated graphics onto a web page are the same as any other image. First move the cursor to the desired location for the new image.

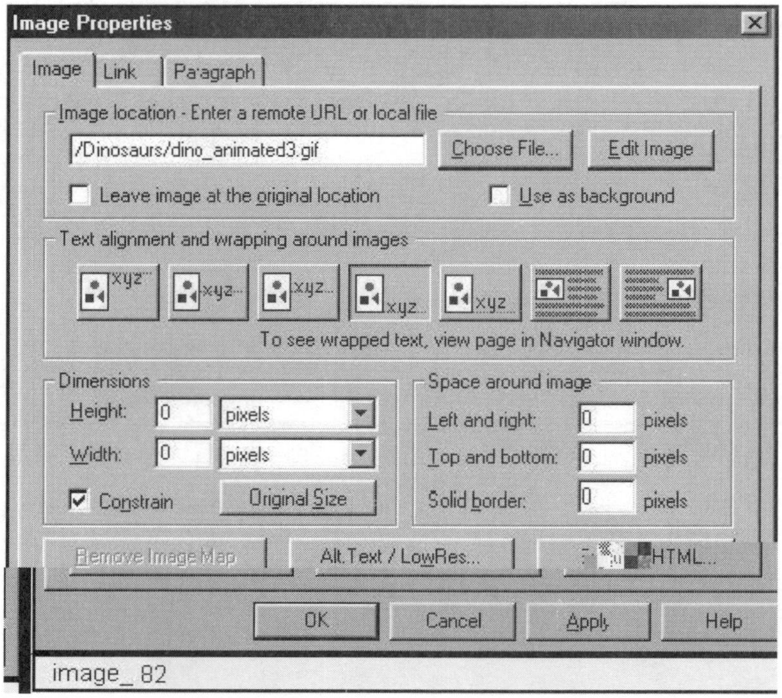

Figure 10-6. Image Properties—Inserting an Animated Graphic

- *Click the Image icon* from the Tool Bar menu or **Insert** → **Image** from the pop-down menu.
- *Click the Choose File* button to open a dialog box (see Figure 10-6) containing the file names of available images. *Click OK* to insert the image.
- *Save the Web Page* to retain the changes.
- *Preview* the animated graphic. *Click the Preview* button to revert to Netscape Navigator and view the animated graphic. (**Note: animated graphics do not work in Netscape Composer. Only previewing with Navigator results in on-screen animation.**)

Creating Targets

A target is an "intra-page" link, navigating the user up and down an exceptionally long web page. Two actions are required to create an active target. First, the target itself must be placed on the web page. Then, a corresponding link to that target must be created.

Figure 10-7. Creating Targets

- **Place the Target**—For the example web page, a target has been placed rather artificially in the middle of the page for demonstration purposes (see Figure 10-7). Position the cursor at the location where the target is to be inserted, usually at the beginning of a line. On the example web page, the cursor is placed immediately before the "B" of the text "Begin Your Virtual Tour Here."

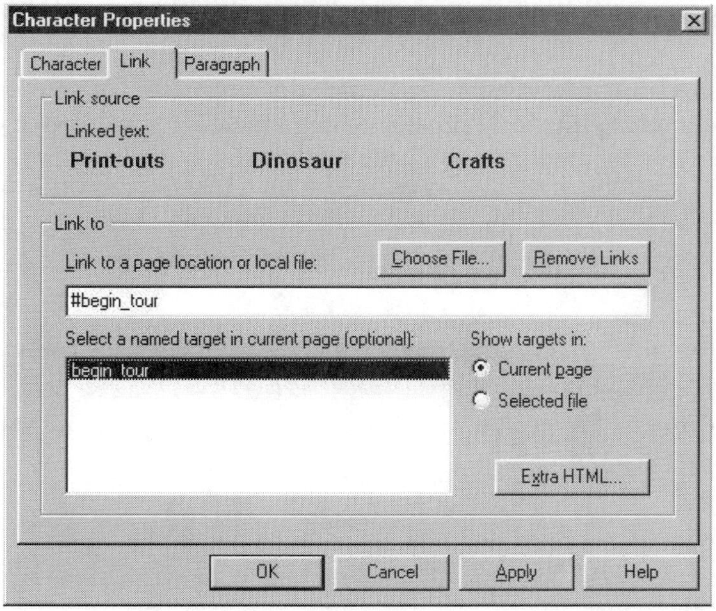

Figure 10-8. Character Properties—Selecting the Target

- *Click the Target icon* or *Insert → Target* from the pop-down menu. *Enter a name for the target* up to 30 characters in the properties window. In the example, the target is called "**begin_tour**" (see Figure 10-8). *Click OK*. Remember, a target icon is visible only in Netscape Composer and disappears when previewing the page in Navigator.

- **Create the Corresponding Link,** either text or image. At the top of the example web page is a line of text that reads "Begin Tour By Clicking Here." After entering the text, click *Insert → Link* and select a named target from the window rather than entering a URL or file name. Click *OK* to insert the link.
- *Save the web page* to retain the changes.
- *Preview* the operation of the target. Keep in mind that targets, like other special features, work only in Netscape Navigator.

Designing web pages, especially for the Virtual Tour, is much easier if you follow some simple advice. When creating a web-based lesson, keep all associated files including the html file and any images in the same physical directory. Internet browsers tend to look for hyperlinks, images, and files on the same media as the originally accessed web page. Any difficulty in locating these files results in incomplete pages, error messages, and missing links. Otherwise, the use of the advanced features described above provides all the necessary elements of a successful Virtual Tour.

Preparing the Virtual Tour Lesson

Objective 10.2: Demonstrate a knowledge of web-base design along with a mastery of advanced web page construction features. Combine these skills with the use of technology resources harvested from the Internet to produce the Virtual Tour lesson.

The Virtual Tour is a humanistic teaching strategy appropriate for elementary school through adult learners who may benefit from a multimedia format. An example of each of the 14 "front doors" is available on the accompanying CDROM. Use **Best Practices #13** to locate the Virtual Tour entitled "Dinosaurs of North America Home Page: The Next Exhibit Front Door."

Best Practices #13

On the CDROM locate the folder entitled Dinosaur_VT. In this folder find the file name dino_01ne.htm containing the Next Exhibit front door.

Click to open the Virtual Tour lesson.

Creating a Virtual Tour Lesson

The Virtual Tour is appropriate for students who learn best when instruction is offered in a student-centered and student-controlled learning environment embracing discovery and cooperative learning techniques. With the advanced features introduced in the previous section, the "Model for Technology-Based Lessons" (see Figure 10-9) continues to offer a step-by-step approach for developing a successful Virtual Tour lesson.

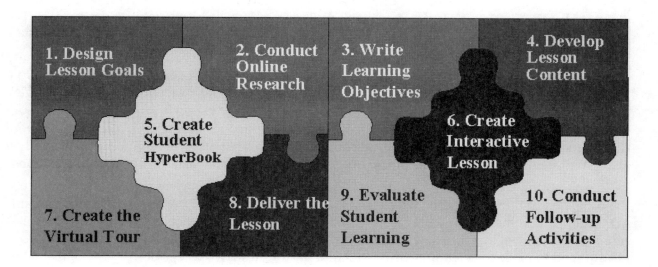

Figure 10-9. The Model for Technology-Based Lessons

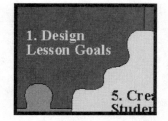

Step 1: Design the Lesson Goals. The initial stage of the development process establishes the appropriate goals for the lesson. While the Virtual Tour makes for the ideal instructional unit because it combines several academic disciplines, this step is also the most time-consuming phase in the preparation of the lesson.

In addition to the academic content offered in the Virtual Tour, two other considerations are paramount to a successful lesson. First, the technical skills of the learner must be considered. Specifically, is the learner able to use browser software to navigate the Internet, bookmark important sites, and harvest images and text? Second, consistent construction of web pages is key to student understanding. In support of these two considerations, the Virtual Tour Front Door includes:

- **Introduction** to the topic written at the student's level. (Note: for early childhood lessons, this may mean pictures rather than words.)
- **Instructions** for completing the Virtual Tour lesson. Students should understand what is required to complete the lesson.
- **Allotted Time**—Lesson goals should clearly state the amount of time available and how much of that time is allotted to the completion of the lesson either in the computer lab or, if available, from home via the Internet.
- **Lesson Goals**—The example Front Doors provided on the CDROM offer the students a range of lesson goals. While not every goal is appropriate for every Front Door, the Virtual Tour affords students opportunities for personal investigation of dinosaurs. Included in this exploration would be selecting your two favorite dinosaurs, distinguishing between the Carnivore and the Omnivore, exploring four major periods of evolution, locating geographic regions, navigating the Internet and locating specific web sites, and downloading and printing images and text.

Step 2: Conduct Online Research. Online research presents a slightly different venue than previous text-based and visual-based materials. The purpose of a Virtual Tour is to address the following questions.

If an existing web site already offers the best selection of images and text to increase student understanding of the lesson goals, why should a new site be created? "Jason's Dinosaur Site" (members.aol.com/Ermine/index.html) and "Zoom Dinosaurs" (www.enchantedlearning.com/subjects/dinosaurs) provide a host of images and textual information about dinosaurs to increase student knowledge of the geographic regions where dinosaurs lived. They also provide numerous images of dinosaurs that students may harvest for their own collections.

If an existing web site already does an outstanding job of explaining the difference between the omnivore and the carnivore, why should a teacher spend time designing repetitious content? "Dinosauria On-line" (www.dinosauria.com/) explains the difference between carnivores and omnivores at a level that fourth graders can readily understand. Students, directed to this site, are encouraged to place the creatures discussed into one of these two categories.

If there is already a web site that provides maps, charts, and statistical tables appropriate for your students, why would teachers ignore this information and spend the time and effort necessary to create new materials? The U.S. Geological Service site (pubs.usgs.gov/gip/dinosaurs/) offers the finest selection of maps depicting famous dinosaur fossil finds throughout the world.

Rather than recreating online materials, the primary goal of the Virtual Tour, then, is to access existing web sites to present lesson content. Students receive a guided tour of the Internet examining sites already found by their teacher. As with the Interactive Lesson and the HyperBook, material on the Internet is so abundant that the challenge to the teacher is limiting the URLs to incorporate into the Virtual Tour.

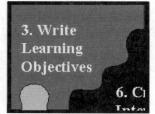

Step 3: Write Learning Objectives. The Virtual Tour places considerable emphasis on the needs of the target learner. Furth (1970) distinguishes between the concrete and abstract learner and brings to light the importance of making instructional material age-appropriate for the learner. For the Virtual Tour, concrete learners (approximately ages 7–11 years) demand tangible experiences with images, sounds, and video clips supported by web-based media. The abstract learner (ages 11 years and older) revels in concepts and ideas and the graphics and hyperlinks which support multisensory exploration.

In this step, specific learning objectives are added to the Virtual Tour after being matched with prior student knowledge and classroom assignments. See Table 10-2 for an example of the "Dinosaur Virtual Tour" and its respective learning objectives.

Lesson Goal: Personal exploration of dinosaurs.	Learning Objective 1: Students will locate, download, and print at least two images of their favorite dinosaurs.
Prior Knowledge: Students will discuss the most familiar dinosaurs depicted in films and television. Students also have map skills from a previous lesson on cartography.	Learning Objective 2: Students will distinguish between the carnivore and omnivore.
	Learning Objective 3: Students will select two dinosaurs from each of the four major periods of evolution.
	Learning Objective 4: Students will locate the geographical regions of the world where Dinosaur fossils have been discovered.
	Assignment 1. Students must select their two favorite dinosaurs. Students must download two images, print them on the black and white laser printer, and color them for classroom display.
	Assignment 2. Students will compile a table of carnivores and omnivores, listing the various animals respectively.
	Assignment 3. Students will distinguish two dinosaurs that represent each period of evolution.
	Assignment 4. Students will plot the regions on a map and reference a table of dinosaurs found in each region.

Table 10-2. Learning Objectives for the "Dinosaur Virtual Tour"

Step 4: Develop Lesson Content. With the lesson goals, online research, and learning objectives firmly in mind, the next step is the advancement of the actual lesson material. The "Dinosaur Virtual Tour" includes content items outlined in Table 10-3.

Learning Objective	Virtual Tour Lesson Content
Learning Objective 1: Students will locate, download, and print at least two images of their favorite dinosaurs.	1. Why are some dinosaurs more popular than others? 2. What characteristics of dinosaurs make them popular? 3. What are some of the most popular dinosaurs?
Learning Objective 2: Students will distinguish between the carnivore and omnivore.	Major characteristics of omnivores • Any animal that eats both animal flesh and vegetable matter. • Omnivores are less specialized in their food gathering habits than carnivores or herbivores. • Many animals that are often considered carnivores are actually omnivorous. • The teeth of omnivorous mammals possess special features resembling the teeth of carnivores.
	Major characteristics of carnivores • General term for any animal that subsists mainly on the flesh of other animals. • The carnivores are at the top of the food chains that make up the food web of the earth's life forms. • They feed on omnivores, or plant-eaters, which in turn feed on the plants at the bottom of the food chains that absorb and store energy directly from the sun. • Carnivores live mainly alone or in small groups and are not preyed upon except by other carnivores.

Learning Objective 3: Students will select two dinosaurs from each of the four major periods of evolution.	• *Triassic Period* 225 Million Years ago
	  • Allosaurus
	  • Plateosaurus
	  • Spinosaurus
	• *Jurassic Period* 215 Million Years ago
	  • Diplodocus
	  • Ceolophysis
	  • Megalosaurus
	• *Cretaceous Period* 140 Million Years ago
	  • Iguanodon
	  • Tyannosaurus
	  • Triceratops
	  • Pteranodon
	  • Stegosaurus
	• *Cenozoic Era* 65 Million Years ago
	  • Crocodile
	  • Birds

Learning Objective 4: Students will locate the geographical regions of the world where dinosaur fossils have been discovered.	Identify the Major Regions of the United States
	• Western North America
	  • Allosaurus
	  • Apatosaurus
	  • Diatryma

cont.

	• Procompsognathus
	• Psittacosaurus
	• Central North America
	• Ankylosaurus
	• Corythosaurus
	• Dimetrodon
	• Pachycephalosaurus
	• Polacanthus
	• Protoceratops
	• Trachodon
	• Northeastern North America
	• Plateosaurus
	• Struthiomimus
	• Tylosaurus
	• Southern North America
	• Iguanodon
	• Sabre Tooth Tiger
	• Yaleasaurus

Table 10-3. Lesson Content for the Dinosaur Lesson

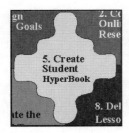

Step 5: Create Student Workbook. Since the HyperBook was completed in chapter 8, it might be a good idea to review its contents at this time. The Virtual Tour uses this text-based tool to provide some of the online exercises required of the students.

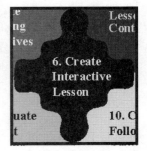

Step 6: Create the Interactive Lesson. The Interactive Lesson was completed in chapter 9. As a reminder, the learning objectives for the Interactive Lesson covered the theories of dinosaur extinction. For this chapter, we move on to the development of the Virtual Tour.

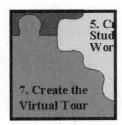

Step 7: Create the Virtual Tour. Selecting a front door commensurate with lesson objectives and individual technical skills is not difficult. With 14 formats available, selection is based first and foremost on an analysis of the lesson goals, followed by the learning styles of the students, and then finally by the technical expertise of the designer.

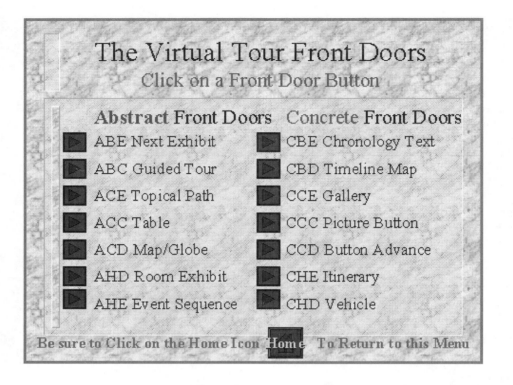

Figure 10-10. Front Doors for the Virtual Tour

There are 14 actual front doors (see Figure 10-10) offering a facade for the Virtual Tour and its amplified sites. Each is tagged with a three-character code to indicate its strength in a particular thinking operation, either Abstract or Concrete (the first character of the code). The second character identifies the most appropriate psychology for learning: Behavioral, Cognitive, or Humanistic. And, since we are dealing with technology, each front door has a third label suggesting Easy, Challenging, or Difficult.

Each Front Door is also assigned a value on a scale from 1 (Very Weak) to 10 (Very Strong), indicating the strengths and weaknesses of this particular format with respect to lesson analysis, design, development, and implementation. The Overall Composite Score provides the reader an indication of the overall vigor of its instructional design. A view of how the "Dinosaurs Virtual Tour" lesson would look using each Front Door precedes each discussion.

1. The Next Exhibit Front Door. One of the most easily mastered formats of the Virtual Tour, the **Next Exhibit** opens with the essential elements of a Virtual Tour: Introduction, Instructions, Time Allotted, Lesson Goals, and, most important, Learning Objectives. Textual material is held to a minimum and images control movement through the lesson. Learners travel sequentially from one exhibit to the next until they reach the final screen.

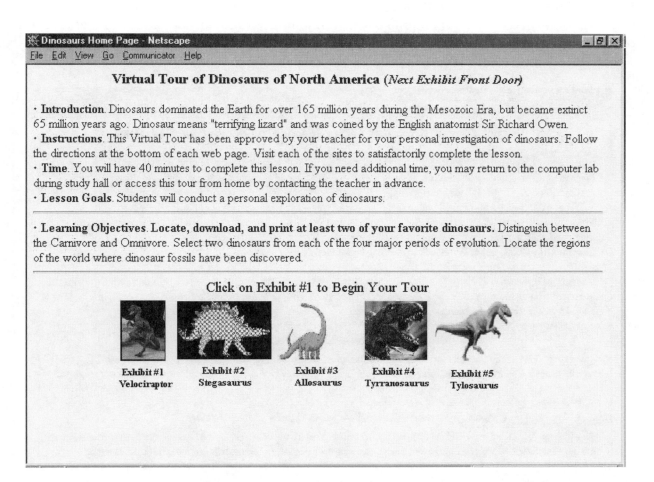

The Evaluation Tag "**ABE**" indicates that the Next Exhibit is most appropriate for teaching (A)bstract content by creating a lasting image in the mind of the learner. It is (B)ehavorial in its focus, presenting information sequentially from first to last. And, the door is technically (E)asy to create. Primarily for the abstract learner, the Next Exhibit is best applied to older students who are able to share their understanding in a classroom discussion format, the primary vehicle for evaluating student understanding using this front door.

Characteristic	Rating	Explanation of Issues with this Front Door Format
Analysis	4	Difficult to address diverse learning styles.
Design	10	Sequencing is paramount, making the design of this front door efficient and fast.
Development	8	Technically easy but requires significant exploration and familiarization with content area.
Implementation	10	Classroom-focused; easily understood by the learner.
Overall Composite Rating	8.0	

2. The Topical Path Front Door. The Topical Path provides learners an opportunity to use their prior knowledge to select amplified sites containing additional instructional material. Text is predominant and images are reserved for subsequent amplified sites.

Dinosaurs Home Page - Netscape

File Edit View Go Communicator Help

Virtual Tour of Dinosaurs of North America (*Topical Path Front Door*)

• **Introduction**. Dinosaurs dominated the Earth for over 165 million years during the Mesozoic Era, but became extinct 65 million years ago. Dinosaur means "terrifying lizard" and was coined by the English anatomist Sir Richard Owen.
• **Instructions**. This Virtual Tour has been approved by your teacher for your personal investigation of dinosaurs. Follow the directions at the bottom of each web page. Visit each of the sites to satisfactorily complete the lesson.
• **Time**. You will have 40 minutes to complete this lesson. If you need additional time, you may return to the computer lab during study hall or access this tour from home by contacting the teacher in advance.
• **Lesson Goals**. Students will conduct a personal exploration of dinosaurs.

• **Learning Objectives**. Locate, download, and print at least two of your favorite dinosaurs. **Distinguish between the Carnivore and Omnivore.** Select two dinosaurs from each of the four major periods of evolution. Locate the regions of the world where dinosaur fossils have been discovered.

Distinguish Between the Carnivore and Omnivore

<u>Carnivores.</u> Jurassic dinosaurs included some of the most powerful of all dinosaurs, massive creatures that towered over their prey. The most famous Jurassic carnosaur is the Tyrannousaurus Rex. They fell into two distinct categories:

- *Predators* attacked other animals and hunted for their food in packs
- *Scavengers* were also meat-eaters and would "clean up" after a predactor's kill

<u>Omnivores.</u> "Plant-eaters" reached as much as 15 tons in weight, these animals would ravage the prehistoric landscape making short work of vegatation and sea plants. As with their predators, omnivores were categorized as either:

- *Land Animals*, eating vegatation found in the primeval forests of the Triassic and Jurassic periods.
- *Water Animals* used the aquatic environment for both food and protection.

The Evaluation Tag "**ACE**" indicates that the Topical Path offers (A)bstract content to the learner using a (C)ognitive approach combining prior student knowledge with amplified sites. The Topical Path is technically (E)asy to design and implement. Target older learners for this front door; it might be too "dry" and too abstract for younger students.

Characteristic	Rating	Explanation
Analysis	6	Addresses diverse learning styles with component topics for consideration by the learner.
Design	10	Follows closely the cognitive teacher's building block lesson plan objectives.
Development	8	Requires significant technology resources to augment existing lesson materials.
Implementation	10	Easy to implement because of its intuitive presentation format.
Overall Composite Rating	8.5	

3. The Event Sequence Front Door. Another approach to the study of dinosaurs is the development of mini-lessons; one for each of the scientific periods of evolution. The Event Sequence focuses on a single unique occurrence in time and place. More often than not, events are historical or geographical in nature, viewed as a sequence of evolving changes or the movement of an object during a designated time period.

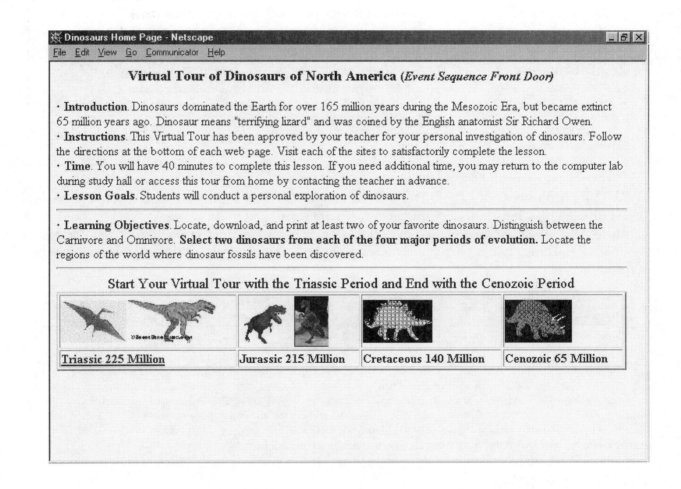

The Evaluation Tag "**AHE**" indicates that the Topical Path blends (A)bstract content with multisensory examples. Use this format to offer the student a more personalized, affective, (H)umanistic view of the subject matter. Text-based links should be the primary construct for the front door of the Event Sequence. Keep the amount of text to a minimum although the insertion of images continues to categorize this front door as one of the (E)asy formats. Remember, this is an abstract thinking tool excellent for introducing the young learner to the world of abstract thinking. The Event Sequence presents age-appropriate content material to all but the youngest student.

Characteristic	Rating	Explanation
Analysis	9	Typically, the subject and lesson topics supply the detailed analysis of content material needed.
Design	8	The designer should augment this front door with considerable supporting instruction.
Development	8	Links are the key. Text-based links are sufficient and highly recommended. Use graphics primarily to elaborate.
Implementation	7	Relatively easy for any concrete learner who might happen onto this site; however, navigation may prove difficult.
Overall Composite Rating	8.0	

4. The Chronology Text Front Door. Chronology Text uses a timeline approach to create text-based links to new information. Time increment are expressed in days, weeks, years, decades, or centuries and links to more detailed material oftentimes created by the teacher. Chronology is an instinctive learning style for a behavioral lesson as it follows the natural time sequence to present information.

Dinosaurs Home Page - Netscape

File Edit View Go Communicator Help

Dinosaurs of North America Home Page (*Chronology Text Front Door*)

• **Introduction.** Dinosaurs dominated the Earth for over 165 million years during the Mesozoic Era, but became extinct 65 million years ago. Dinosaur means "terrifying lizard" and was coined by the English anatomist Sir Richard Owen.
• **Instructions.** This Virtual Tour has been approved by your teacher for your personal investigation of dinosaurs. Follow the directions at the bottom of each web page. Visit each of the sites to satisfactorily complete the lesson.
• **Time.** You will have 40 minutes to complete this lesson. If you need additional time, you may return to the computer lab during study hall or access this tour from home by contacting the teacher in advance.
• **Lesson Goals.** Students will conduct a personal exploration of dinosaurs.

Learning Objectives. Locate, download, and print at least two of your favorite dinosaurs. Distinguish between the Carnivore and Omnivore. **Select two dinosaurs from each of the four major periods of evolution.** Locate the regions of the world where dinosaur fossils have been discovered.

Start Your Virtual Tour with the Triassic Period and End with the Cenozoic Period

Triassic Period 225 Million Years Ago	Jurassic Period 215 Million Years Ago	
Rutiodon	Metriorhynchus	Lesathosaurus
Plateosaurus	Diplodocus	Dimorphodon
	Coelophysis	

Cretaceous Period 140 Million Years Ago		Cenozoic Period 65 Million Years Ago	
Tyrannosaurus	Iguanodon	Crocodile	Stegosaurs
Archaeopteryx	Deinonychus	Ornithomimus	Pterodaktyl
		Birds	

The Evaluation Tag "**CBE**" offers a format to present detailed textual material. Each time increment in the chronology contains a (C)oncrete amount of instruction, (B)ehavioral in its focus, and among the (E)asier formats for the Virtual Tour. Without graphics, the Chronology Text is ill-suited for the pre-school learner. On the other end of the spectrum, however, abstract learners may also find this front door uninteresting. Save it for the middle school years.

Characteristic	Rating	Explanation
Analysis	5	Deciding on an appropriate time increment is key to this front door.
Design	8	With the increment and materials determined, designing the resulting web pages is relatively easy.
Development	10	Very strong. Text links comprise the entire front door.
Implementation	10	The learner needs some prior knowledge to the specific period to explore the linked content.
Overall Composite Rating	8.25	

5. The Gallery Front Door. One of the most popular front doors, the Gallery promotes cognitive learning by organizing a series of images matching the specific learning objectives of a lesson. The Gallery's reliance on graphics promotes concrete learning and fosters the building block approach that cognitive learners relish.

The Evaluation Tag "**CCE**" recognizes the Gallery's reliance on graphics to promote (C)oncrete learning. Each image is a window to additional content material. (C)ognitive learning is fostered by the building block design and closely mirrors how some teachers teach and some students learn. Depending primarily on images linked to textual information, the Gallery front door is relatively (E)asy to design and implement. Appropriate for nearly every age, the Gallery front door provides an intuitive navigational tool for the exploration of lesson objectives via the Internet.

Characteristic	Rating	Explanation
Analysis	8	Designed for literally any age, analysis is the strongest feature of the Gallery front door.
Design	10	The designer should use building blocks to design this front door.
Development	10	Intuitive development of the tour using relatively unsophisticated web-based tools.
Implementation	10	Intuitive for both the teacher and the learner who must use this lesson.
Overall Composite Rating	9.5	

6. The Itinerary Front Door. The Itinerary front door is patterned after a person's (or in this case, a dinosaur's) daily diary, presenting instruction as a series of related activities, appointments, experiences, or personal memories. Most Itinerary front doors simulate the activities of a subject during a "typical" 24-hour period, while others chronicle events over a much longer period of time.

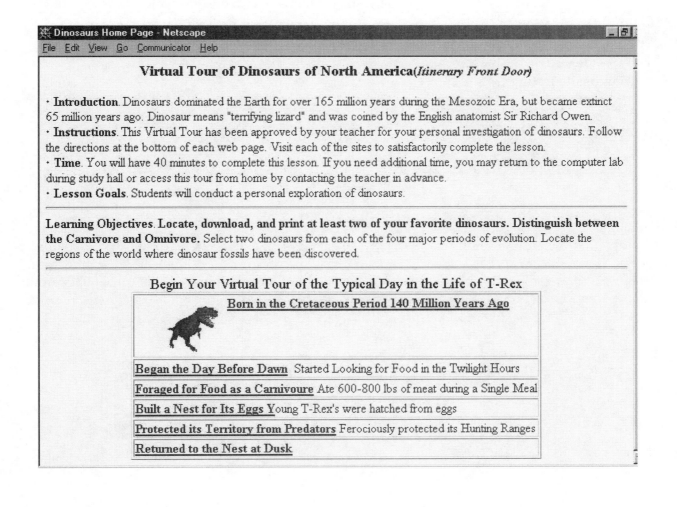

The Evaluation Tag "**CHE**" suggests the Itinerary's format is predominantly text-based with limited use of images. This format is one of the most (C)oncrete front doors with specific information, facts, and events taken from the diary or desktop calendar of an important character in history. (H)umanistic in its focus, the Itinerary encourages affective examination of material—an insider's look at the "rest of the story." Technically (E)asy to create, this front door is also quickly revised or even translated into other languages. The "Dinosaur Virtual Tour" reviews the life of a "typical" dinosaur, motivating the elementary-age student with familiar text and relevant classroom content. For older learners, the diary format appeals to their need for social interaction and interpersonal communication. Intermediate learners tend to view the diary form as boring and irrelevant.

Characteristic	Rating	Explanation
Analysis	10	Format of this front door provides excellent structure for analyzing contents of more complex lessons.
Design	6	Straight forward presentation design; however, selecting the elements which meet learning objectives will be a challenge.
Development	9	Templates provide a strong format for lesson development. In other words, follow the example and substitute your activities to create a new lesson.
Implementation	8	Easy to implement and revise; easy for the learner to understand.
Overall Composite Rating	8.25	

7. The Picture Button Front Door. Appropriate for many age groups, the Picture Button provides a visual menu of sites for exploration. Each site is visited without regard for sequence, allowing the designer to add new features and new sites as they become available.

The Evaluation Tag "**CCC**" recommends that the Picture Button address specific content with a limited number of amplified sites. Primary target is the K–6 (C)oncrete learner. Use of subsequent links fosters the building block design of lesson development and prior student knowledge is employed to construct new learning; both are sure signs of (C)ognitive thinking. This format also integrates a significant amount of images, text, and amplified sites and is therefore categorized as (C)hallenging. Most Picture Button front doors reference a wide variety of external links and require considerable investment of time in content research. A variety of students benefit from the Picture Button format. However, it is particularly appealing to younger learners who readily comprehend what is expected of them when using the buttons to navigate through the material presented.

Characteristic	Rating	Explanation
Analysis	2	An inordinate amount of time must be devoted to analyzing academic content prior to beginning the design phase. To use this front door, considerable planning is required.
Design	2	Teachers will find that the entire tour must be designed before development can begin.
Development	8	Understanding the use of images as links is technically more demanding than some of the other formats.
Implementation	10	Students find this front door easy to understand and use.
Overall Composite Rating	5.5	

8. The Table Front Door. Tables provide a relatively uncomplicated front door for links. The amplified sites are typically text-based with links programmed to change colors after they are visited. Tables foster student understanding of classification, categorization, sorting, and organization.

Dinosaurs Home Page - Netscape

File Edit View Go Communicator Help

Virtual Tour of Dinosaurs of North America (*Table Front Door*)

· **Introduction**. Dinosaurs dominated the Earth for over 165 million years during the Mesozoic Era, but became extinct 65 million years ago. Dinosaur means "terrifying lizard" and was coined by the English anatomist Sir Richard Owen.
· **Instructions**. This Virtual Tour has been approved by your teacher for your personal investigation of dinosaurs. Follow the directions at the bottom of each web page. Visit each of the sites to satisfactorily complete the lesson.
· **Time**. You will have 40 minutes to complete this lesson. If you need additional time, you may return to the computer lab during study hall or access this tour from home by contacting the teacher in advance.
· **Lesson Goals**. Students will conduct a personal exploration of dinosaurs.

· **Learning Objectives**. Locate, download, and print at least two of your favorite dinosaurs. **Distinguish between theCarnivore and Omnivore.** Select two dinosaurs from each of the four major periods of evolution. Locate the regions of the world where dinosaur fossils have been discovered.

What was a Carnivore Like?	What was an Omnivore Like?
Carnivores included some of the most powerful of all dinosaurs, **massive creatures** towering over their prey.	"Plant-eaters" **weighed** as much as 15 tons. The last of the omnivore dinosaurs certainly had **fruit** available to eat.
The most famous Jurassic carnovore is the **Tyrannousaurus Rex**.	Omnivores would ravage the **prehistoric landscape** making short work of vegatation and sea plants.
Some hunted other dinosaurs or **scavenged** dead animals. *Predators* hunted for their food in packs	*Land Animals*, eating vegatation found in the primeval forests of the Triassic and Jurassic periods.
Scavengers were also meat-eaters and would "clean up" after a predactor's kill	*Water Animals* used the aquatic environment for both food and protection.

The Evaluation Tag "**ACC**" indicates how easily the Table front door links diverse aspects of (A)bstract materials leaving the construction of new knowledge in the hands of the learner. The use of multiple Tables is recommended for complex lessons and to organize sites logically for the learner—key characteristics of the (C)ognitive approach. Inserting Tables is (C)hallenging but not much more difficult than inserting links or images. Focus the Table front door on more mature students who learn better with abstract material.

Characteristic	Rating	Explanation
Analysis	8	To establish learning objectives, follow the non-technical classroom presentation or perhaps the delivery layout of textbook-based materials.
Design	7	Once materials are collected, designing this front door requires an "average" amount of effort.
Development	9	Tables present the chief design format making development of the virtual tour relatively simple. Text links add other amplified sites and are easily appended when new material is located. Web browser tools makes the development of tables fairly easy.
Implementation	7	Most students understand Tables. And, using text-based links makes tracking visited sites simple.
Overall Composite Rating	7.75	

9. The Guided Tour Front Door. The Guided Tour presents ideas and concepts in a very logical sequence, constructed much like a tour of the stars' homes in Hollywood. Learning occurs when completed tours trigger student-centered classroom discussions allowing them to share facts, concepts, and ideas in an open forum.

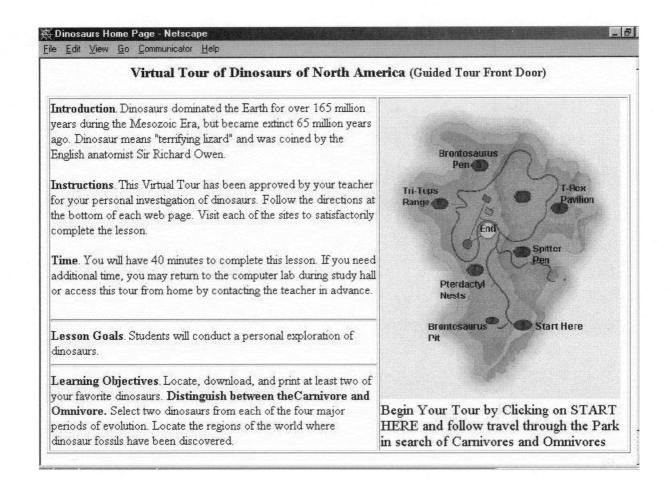

The Evaluation Tag "**ABC**" for the Guided Tour advocates the use of graphic images to teach (A)bstract concepts and ideas with a minimum of textual information. The Guided Tour must be designed with a particular theme in mind. The learner is expected to follow the guide (B)ehaviorally and surface at the end of the lesson with an understanding of the stated learning objectives. Therefore, the learning objectives must be clearly defined and presented prominently somewhere on the front door. Constructing the various pages which link from the Guided Tour is technically (C)hallenging and so is the map that guides student selection. Assessment is particularly critical with this front door; teachers must be alert not to believe learning has occurred when in fact it has not. Guided Tours provide opportunities for students to mature as abstract learners while younger learners benefit from a reliance on the behavioristic sequencing of the instruction.

Characteristic	Rating	Explanation
Analysis	8	Analyzing the contents of the Guided Tour is aided by the needs of the abstract learner for a wide variety of materials.
Design	8	Design follows the logical sequence of any guided tour presentation.
Development	9	Development requires elaborate exploration and harvesting of materials from a variety of diverse sources.
Implementation	10	Easy for the student to master; therefore, one of the most powerful front doors available for the teacher.
Overall Composite Rating	8.75	

10. The Map/Globe Front Door. Well suited to a social studies lesson in geography or history, a Virtual Tour using the Map/Globe literally links students to the world. The designer chooses from many different venues for the amplified sites. Countries, states, and continents are all potential representations of important lesson content. While younger students benefit from a well-prepared lesson using this format, prior knowledge is an important key to successful learning outcomes using this front door.

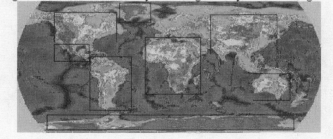

The Evaluation Tag "**ACD**" demonstrates how the Map/Globe front door excels when offering the learner an opportunity to expand personal thinking skills. Link this front door to ideas and concepts for best results and encourage the learner to explore as many aspects of the (C)ognitive content area as time and energy permit. Technical knowledge must be above average since the primary key to exploration involves a technique known as the bitmap image. The map of the world shown in the example Map/Globe front door was created using this technique. Construction of the bitmap image is explained later in this chapter. In addition, an in-depth familiarization with the content area is essential; therefore, the door is tagged with the (D)ifficult label. Older students are better prepared to learn from this front door.

Characteristic	Rating	Explanation
Analysis	2	Considerable effort expended to understand the learner and isolate the lesson objectives.
Design	2	Begins after the teacher first presents the same lesson objectives in a more traditional setting.
Development	4	Best approached by a team of teachers who can share responsibilities for design, development, and implementation.
Implementation	8	Easy for the student; capacity issues (megabytes of storage) for the designer.
Overall Composite Rating	4.0	

11. The Timeline Map Front Door. Most Timeline maps combine a clickable bitmap image with text-based or table-based links to amplified sites. A sophisticated understanding of graphics and web design is required before the Timeline Map may be used effectively. This particular front door presents sequenced instruction designed to focus on drill and practice or tutorial presentation—all content that is behavioral-based.

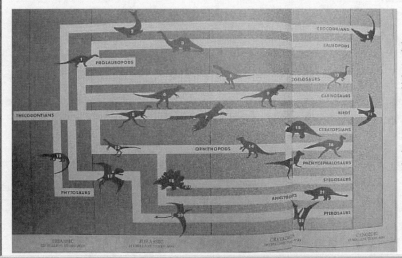

The Timeline Map format is given the Evaluation Tag **"CBD."** Presentation of (C)oncrete instruction requires multi-sensory material as the bitmap image links to a vast array of supplemental material. This front door emphasizes the structured drill and practice approach to learning and is (B)ehavioral in nature. There are tools available for designing the bitmap image. Still, it cannot be recommended for the technical novice. Only those who understand more (D)ifficult aspects of web design should attempt this front door.

Characteristic	Rating	Explanation
Analysis	6	Analysis takes time but is not complex. The Timeline format itself does most of the work.
Design	6	Once materials are collected, designing this front door requires an "average" amount of effort.
Development	2	Weak area. Most of the real learning occurs on the amplified pages which follow.
Implementation	8	Once created, modifications require considerable effort and changes tend to confuse learners.
Overall Composite Rating	5.5	

12. The Button Advance Front Door. Buttons are merely images combined with text to aid the learner with Internet navigation. It takes practice with graphics software to find the right size button and overlay the proper text before inserting the new image directly onto the front door. The Button Advance is an outstanding format for the visually challenged student. Of course, learners must be readers before this front door will work. The designer should vary the imbedded text depending on the reading level of the student; but, buttons tend to bore the more mature learner.

Dinosaurs Home Page - Netscape

File Edit View Go Communicator Help

Virtual Tour of Dinosaurs of North America*(Button Advance Front Door)*

| North |
| Northeast |
| Mid-Atlantic |
| South |
| Mid-West |
| Central West |
| Southwest |
| West |

• **Introduction**. Dinosaurs dominated the Earth for over 165 million years during the Mesozoic Era, but became extinct 65 million years ago. Dinosaur means "terrifying lizard" and was coined by the English anatomist Sir Richard Owen.

• **Instructions**. This Virtual Tour has been approved by your teacher for your personal investigation of dinosaurs. Follow the directions at the bottom of each web page. Visit each of the sites to satisfactorily complete the lesson.

• **Time**. You will have 40 minutes to complete this lesson. If you need additional time, you may return to the computer lab during study hall or access this tour from home by contacting the teacher in advance.

• **Lesson Goals**. Students will conduct a personal exploration of dinosaurs.

Learning Objectives. Locate, download, and print at least two of your favorite dinosaurs. Distinguish between the Carnivore and Omnivore. Select two dinosaurs from each of the four major periods of evolution. **Locate the regions of the world where dinosaur fossils have been discovered.**

Begin Your Virtual Tour by Clicking on any of these regions.

The Evaluation Tag **"CCD"** is specified for the Button Advance format. Click a button, view a site. The designer concentrates on presenting (C)oncrete multi-sensory information with minimal diversion. Increasingly more complex material is offered throughout the lesson—a sure sign of the (C)ognitive approach to learning. Many sites offer pre-designed buttons ready for download. But nearly every lesson demands unique links requiring graphics utility software to create a customized set of buttons. As a result, this front door is labeled as (D)ifficult although most intermediate designers may decide that "challenging" is a better descriptor.

Characteristic	Rating	Explanation
Analysis	4	Analysis requires forethought before design can begin although many integrated thematic units lend themselves nicely to this format.
Design	4	Lesson objectives are the key to a well-structured lesson using the Button Advance front door. And, that stipulation can be either a strength or weakness of this format.
Development	1	Very weak area. Combining standard buttons and creating new ones will tax the designer. A lengthy phase in the development process when time could be better spent in content.
Implementation	4	Challenging to implement, it is highly suggested that a prototype lesson be presented, tested, and evaluated in an actual class setting before making a virtual tour using this front door as part of a permanent lesson.
Overall Composite Rating	3.25	

13. The Room Exhibit Front Door. A bitmap image provides the graphical interface for this front door. Analogous to the rooms of a house or the halls of a museum, the Room Exhibit supports a variety of teaching applications. Each room links the learner to amplified sites that address detailed lesson content.

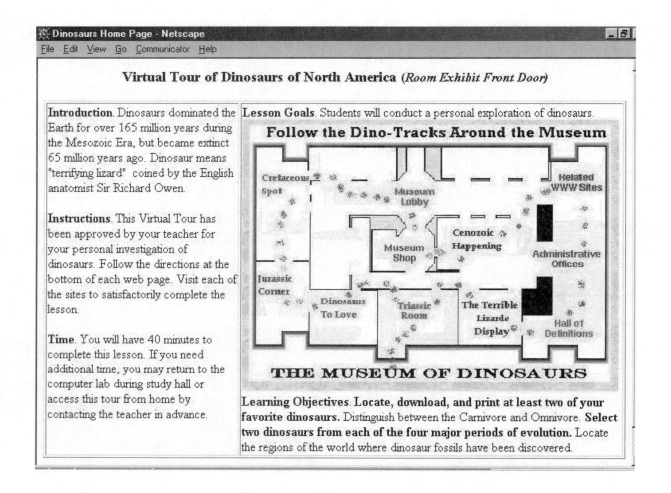

The Room Exhibit front door receives the "**AHD**" Evaluation Tag. As each room is entered, (A)bstract instruction is presented for the learner to connect into a cohesive lesson. Cooperative learning experiences are supported by this (H)umanistic front door and a higher level of technological competence is required. The Room Exhibit is considerably more (D)ifficult to design because of the bitmap image but less difficult for the student because of the inherently obvious use of buttons to navigate the Internet.

Characteristic	Rating	Explanation
Analysis	2	Room exhibit demands considerable analysis to marry this front door with student-appropriate content material.
Design	2	Design requires a detailed consideration of how each piece of the lesson is to produce the desired learning.
Development	1	Development takes considerable time and effort — not to mention technical expertise.
Implementation	9	Once created, the use of this front door is readily understood by the more advanced learner.
Overall Composite Rating	3.5	

14. The Vehicle Front Door. The Vehicle front door is a particularly effective format but difficult (technically) to create and maintain. Imagine a graphic depicting the compartments of a submarine, various systems on-board an airplane, or the newest features of next year's automobiles. Each component of the front door bitmap image is visually separated from the composite graphic and serves to link the learner to amplified sites containing additional instructional content.

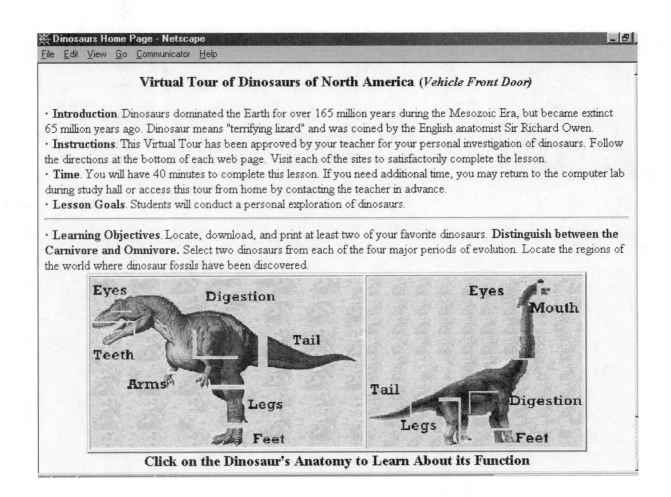

The Evaluation Tag "**CHD**" suggests that the Vehicle front door is best reserved for the (C)oncrete learner. Most effective with younger learners, this front door moves the concrete student towards the realm of abstract thinking. For those already thinking abstractly, this format may be too predictable. One of the few (H)umanistic front doors available, bitmap images require software utilities to digitally isolate a portion of the front door and link these components successfully to subsequent information. This front door is only for the more advanced designer who can handle the technically (D)ifficult format.

Characteristic	Rating	Explanation
Analysis	9	Analysis is simplified by the intuitive nature of the image map.
Design	9	Links to a series of amplified sites, content material is constructed as separate elements. Learners move forward or backward within components.
Development	2	Tricky at best, involving the use of a few technical tricks best left to the more advanced tour guide.
Implementation	9	Once designed and developed, the Vehicle front door is ready to use. Learners take quickly to the format.
Overall Composite Rating	7.25	

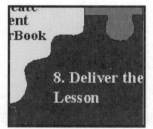

Step 8: Deliver the Lesson. One of the many advantages of the Virtual Tour is the flexibility that web-based lessons offer the classroom teacher. However, as an educator, once the web page is created, the next step is to consider how to make this information available to students. To publish a Virtual Tour (or any web page for that matter), follow these procedures for publishing a web page.

- **Locate All Files In The Same Physical Directory**—To avoid problems associated with directories, all related web files and images should be placed onto a common media, either hard disk or floppy diskettes. Launching a Virtual Tour assumes that all internal links (.htm files) and graphic images (.gif or .jpg files) are located in the same physical directory unless specific paths are designated. Placing all related files into one unique directory is an excellent organizational scheme when uploading an entire web site to a server.

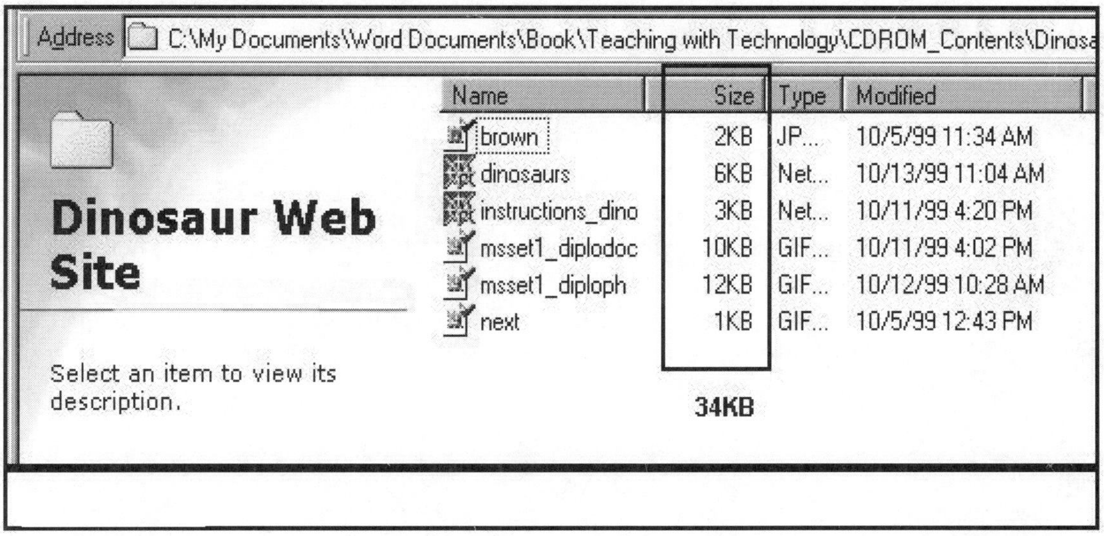

Figure I0-II. Computing the Size of a Web Site

- **Determine Disk Space Required**—To determine the amount of disk space required for a web-based lesson, open the directory that contains the files and simply *add the Size of each file*. Web pages are not particularly large; however, images and animated graphics may require considerable storage. The "Dinosaur Web Site," with its two .htm files and four image files shown in Figure 10-11, takes a mere 34,000 bytes of storage; hardly enough to fill 2.5% of a floppy diskette which would be the recommended storage media for this site.

  - **If the Virtual Tour Requires *less than 1.4 megabytes*,** plan to operate the web site from a 3.5-inch floppy diskette. As the contents of the site approach a megabyte of files and images, consider the next option. If the contents fit onto a single diskette, a floppy is probably the best host. Teachers who produce a diskette for each student or for each work station in a computer lab encourage out-of-class exploration of the subject material from the school library or home. A single floppy also aids in restricting idle exploration and the possibility that younger students might accidentally find inappropriate sites during unsupervised surfing.

  - **If the Virtual Tour Requires *more than 1.4 megabytes*.** If all the files associated with the Virtual Tour do not fit onto a single floppy, consider purchasing a Zip Disk that holds 100-250 megabytes. Larger sites may also be placed directly onto a web server and connected directly to the Internet via a high speed, network link. Internet Service Providers (ISP) are easily located in the yellow pages of a local phone book and offer a variety of services. For comparison purposes, a typical ISP charges $20 a month and offers an array of services including free software updates; toll free, unlimited access; e-mail accounts; personal home pages typically with 5 megabytes of available disk space; 24/7 (24 hours a day, 7 days a week) technical support; and, user-defined URLs for the Virtual Tour.

Each of the issues discussed above contributes to the successful delivery of a Virtual Tour lesson. Some other issues to consider include: scheduled file backups to ensure materials are not lost, student printing needs, periodic maintenance and update of the web site, and continuous improvement of content material based on current research of the latest and best web-based resources.

Step 9: Evaluate Student Learning. Table 10-3 offers a final look at each of the front doors examined in this chapter and offers a few words regarding their strengths and weaknesses in the area of student assessment. The Virtual Tour is the answer to locating, organizing, and incorporating content specific sites into student-centered lessons and, at the same time, evaluating whether learning outcomes were achieved.

Front Door	Rating (1–10)	Comments
1. Next Exhibit	2	Assessment almost non-existent; requires external review via objective tests such as matching, true-false, completion.
2. Topical Path	2	Similar to the Next Exhibit, this front door requires external assessment via class discussion or essay tests.
3. Event Sequence	4	Most effective evaluation for this front door includes authentic assessments such as portfolios and thinking journals.
4. Chronology Text	5	Use a hard-copy, text-based quiz with this front door to assess your student's understanding of the material.
5. Gallery	6	With so many user choices for this format, students are best assessed using typical discovery learning techniques such as group work, reports, and presentations.
6. Itinerary	5	Subjective evaluations are most appropriate here. Assess your student's knowledge with reports.
7. Picture Button	5	Buttons contribute to ready self-evaluation, but it takes some effort to design the assessment.
8. Table	6	Teachers can track student progress by examining visited links. Not a particularly reliable assessment, but significantly more useful than some of the other front doors.
9. Guided Tour	6	Strongest assessment of student learning uses matching objective tests.
10. Map/Globe	10	Essays, objective assessments, and class discussions are best alternatives.
11. Timeline Map	10	Follow-on pages can provide true online assessments.
12. Button Advance	2	Must be supported with outside measurement tools.
13. Room Exhibit	8	Best when using cooperative learning strategies.
14. Vehicle	10	If you can design this front door, creating an assessment to go along with it is easy.

Table 10-3. Evaluating the Front Door Lesson

10. Conduct Follow-up Activities

Step 10: Conduct Follow-up Activities. A total of 14 different front doors are available to present abstract and concrete concepts; behavioral, cognitive, and humanistic content; and, technically challenging or difficult construction. Developing follow-up activities is a matter of creating additional Web pages or identifying great sites already available on the Internet and linking them to the Virtual Tour. Additional examples are provided at the following URLs (see Table 10-4) to increase your understanding of the proposed front doors and to offer some excellent examples of possible follow-up activities.

Front Door	Evaluation Tag	Site Name and URL
1. Next Exhibit	ABE	Chamber of the Holocaust www.mznet.org/chamber/
2. Topical Path	ACE	The Particle Adventure ParticleAdventure.org/spanish/index.html
3. Event Sequence	AHE	Eruption of Mount St. Helens volcano.und.nodak.edu/vwdocs/msh/msh.html
4. Chronology Text	CBE	History of Computing Devices www.llcc.cc.il.us/dbeverid/framtry2.htm
5. Gallery	CCE	National Gallery of Art www.nga.gov/collection/gallery/gg62/gg62-main1.html
6. Itinerary	CHE	Day in the Life of a President www.lbjlib.utexas.edu/ford/library/exhibits /daylife/dailydia.htm
7. Picture Button	CCC	Wonders of the Ancient World ce.eng.usf.edu/pharos/wonders/
8. Table	ACC	Dragonfly Museum tess.uis.edu/www/environmentaled/
9. Guided Tour	ABC	U.S. White House www.whitehouse.gov
10. Map/Globe	ACD	Gordon's Ongoing Journey www.pgordon.com/
11. Timeline Map	CBD	Olympic Games: Victors devlab.dartmouth.edu/olympic/Victors/
12. Button Advance	CCD	Makalu Cyberfest www.mountainzone.com/climbing/makalu/index.html
13. Room Exhibit	AHD	Ancient Olympic Games devlab.dartmouth.edu/olympic
14. Vehicle	CHD	The U-505 Submarine Tour www.msichicago.org/exhibit/U505/U505tour.html

Table 10-4. Example Front Door Sites

Conclusion

Perhaps for the first time since the computer made its debut in the classroom, the teacher is once again in the position to control the technology-based resources used for instruction. Gone are the days when teachers must rely solely on the expertise of computer professionals to create computer-assisted instruction.

Behaviorally, the Virtual Tour is a natural extension of sequential learning with content presented from first to last, simple to complex, general to specific. The cognitive teacher offers content in progressive steps until a schema, or pattern, emerges to aid the learner in the construction of new knowledge. Humanism offers the personalized approach to learning, selecting information determined to be important to the student. The Virtual Tour supports each of these major psychologies perhaps better than any previous teaching strategy ever devised.

With the advent of the World Wide Web, responsibility for creating student-centered, age-appropriate material rests in the hands of the classroom teacher. The design of the Virtual Tour is the newest strategy for linking literally millions of content specific sites that add images, sounds, and video media to an instructional lesson.

Bibliography

Network Wizards. (2000). *Internet Domain Survey*. Capertino, CA: CommerceNet. http://www.commerce.net/research/stats/results.html

Furth, H. (1970). *Piaget for teachers*. Englewood Cliffs, NJ: Prentice-Hall.

Appendix

DINOSAURS OF NORTH AMERICA HOME PAGE

Example Web Page

Begin Tour By Clicking Here

Introduction. Dinosaurs dominated the Earth for over 165 million years during the Mesozoic Era, but mysteriously went extinct 65 million years ago. The term dinosaur (deinos means terrifying; sauros means lizard) was coined by the English anatomist Sir Richard Owen in 1842.

Lesson Objective: Visit each of the Exhibits in this Virtual Tour to **navigate** the Internet. Locate specific Dinosaur Web sites and **download and print** your two favorite dinosaurs.

Begin Your Virtual Tour Here
Click on Any of the Dinosaurs

1 Allosaurus	2 Diplodocus	3 Pterodactyl	4 Stegosaurus
5 Spinosaurus	6 T-Rex	7 Plateosaurus	8 Triceratops

PART 4

ASSESSING INSTRUCTIONAL LESSONS

Chapter 11

EVALUATING
TECHNOLOGY-BASED RESOURCES

Assessment may be defined as "any method used to better understand the current knowledge that a student possesses" (Dietel & Knuth, 1991). Assessment can be as simple as a teacher's subjective judgment of student performance or as complex as a standardized achievement test. The concept of "current knowledge" implies that what a student knows is always changing and therefore teachers are to make assessments about their students' achievements repeatedly throughout the school year.

Instructional technology in general and the elements of technology-based materials and lessons introduced in this book specifically have identical reasons for undergoing the scrutiny of formal evaluation as any other form of valid classroom assessment. The purposes of assessment are many, depending in large measure on the initiators of the evaluation. School administration uses assessment to set standards and policies, direct resources, establish goals, and monitor the quality of education. Parents and students gauge student progress, assess student strengths and weaknesses, measure school accountability, and make informed educational and personal career decisions. And, teachers advocate assessment for individual diagnosis and prescription, curriculum revision and modernization, determination of student mastery, and to establish fairness in grading. In defense of those objectives, chapter 11 completes this examination of technology for teaching and learning by proposing

- **Technology Recap.** Objective 11.1: Review the fundamental contributions of this text to the understanding, selection, preparation, and delivery of technology-based instructional resources.

- **Assessing Technology-Based Resources.** Objective 11.2: Become familiar with the characteristics of good assessment for classroom purposes, important trends in assessing technology-based instruction, and specific assessment activities appropriate for the technology-based classroom teacher.

- **Self-Assessment and the Technology Checklists.** Objective 11.3: Apply the fundamentals of self-assessment checklists for teaching and learning; incorporate specific elements appropriate for the technology-based materials and lessons.

- **Performance-Based Assessment and the Technology Rubric.** Objective 11.4: Apply the fundamentals of performance-based assessment using rubrics for teaching and learning; incorporate specific elements appropriate for the technology-based materials and lessons.

- **Authentic Assessment and the Technology Portfolio.** Objective 11.5: Apply the fundamentals of authentic assessment using portfolios for teaching and learning; incorporate specific elements appropriate for the technology-based materials and lessons.

Technology Recap

Objective 11.1: Review the fundamental contributions of this text to the understanding, selection, preparation, and delivery of technology-based instructional resources.

Technology-based instructional resources have much to offer the educator of the 21st century. For the elementary teacher, handouts and study guides provide an immediate learning tool for students who need the extra help on topics that may be particularly challenging. For the secondary teacher, web-based home pages and classroom presentations excite the high school student with multimedia images, sounds, and video and bring otherwise lackluster content material to life. Distance educators will find the Virtual Tour particularly appropriate for their students who rely on technology as the primary vehicle for their instruction. And, finally, *corporate trainers* will tend toward the HyperBook and Interactive Lesson as they develop instructional resources that can be made available to their organizations to improve their bottom line.

Text-Based Student Materials

Text-based student materials include the classroom handout and the student study guide. Handouts are one-page documents that focus on specific learning objectives and include the instructional steps, content material, procedures for learning, and formative assessment to ensure student learning. Study guides focus on a specific learning style, concentrating on a limited number of learning objectives and matching them to successful teaching strategies.

Visual-Based Presentations

Visual-based presentations offer a multimedia environment for concepts and ideas critical to student understanding. They create powerful slide shows incorporating bulleted lists and numbered text; multimedia clip art, pictures, sounds, and movies; links to teacher-validated web sites and documents; colorful charts and graphs; and a choice of output options tailored to individual learning styles.

Web-Based Home Pages

Web-based home pages host online instruction by presenting actual learning objectives while focusing attention on the most important aspects of the lesson. Perhaps the most exciting aspect of web-based home pages is identifying appropriate web sites for student exploration. Internal as well as external links tie together teacher-made web pages, professional pages found on the Internet, and online handouts and classroom presentations.

The HyperBook Lesson

The HyperBook lesson is a student-centered, teacher-prepared workbook integrating images, real-world exercises, visual charts, graphs, and tables, and real-time links to applicable web sites in a text-based format for learning and assessment. To be successful, the text-based lesson is created using word processing, graphics, and the Internet. However, it may be implemented in a classroom without the aid of a computer or any other form of instructional technology.

The Interactive Lesson

The interactive lesson is a visual-based, classroom-centered teaching strategy appropriate for learners of all ages who find learning easier when confronted with concrete, sequential instruction imbedded with real-time assessment. Lessons are student controlled and offer individualized instruction, remedial or additional practice, or enrichment.

The Virtual Tour Lesson

The virtual tour lesson is a web-based teaching strategy which presents multi-sensory, multimedia instruction appropriate for individual student exploration and group learning experiences. Front doors address particular learning styles, and amplified sites offer the specific content information.

Assessing Technology-Based Resources

Objective 11.2: Become familiar with the fundamentals of good assessment for learning and specific assessment activities appropriate for the technology-based materials and lessons.

Fundamentals of Good Assessment

Traditionally, when questioned about why teachers should learn about assessment, four reasons surface to the front of any discussion. The first most common motive is often to properly diagnose student strengths and weaknesses followed by monitoring student progress, assigning grades, and determining the effectiveness of the instruction. Several additional reasons have emerged with the advent of instructional technology as a teaching strategy. Changing public attitudes about technology is particularly appropriate when the "public" is defined as students and parents, fellow teachers and administrators, and the taxpaying constituency funding the school system. Becoming good stewards of the technology funds entrusted to schools means producing results in the form of higher scores and satisfied customers (i.e., students and their parents). Valid assessment also increases the opportunities to evaluate classroom teaching skills. Teachers who use technology are viewed in a more positive light by the community, especially if that technology has been soundly integrated into the curriculum (Leighton, 1996).

Characteristics of Good Assessment

Good assessment information provides accurate estimates of student performance and enables teachers to make appropriate decisions regarding course content and lesson delivery. Since technology is one of the newest instructional strategies with limited research on which to base design and implementation, assessment indeed takes on special meaning in a text which purports to advocate its use for teaching and learning.

The first important characteristic of good assessment is **validity**; that is, does the assessment tool actually measure what it is intended to measure and does it permit a useful analysis of the student's skills and abilities? A second important characteristic of good assessment is **reliability**. Can assessment results be replicated at some other time, using different measurement tools, when scored by different raters?

Other characteristics of good assessment for classroom purposes include an examination of how well the teacher's educational objectives and instruction match the assessment. A well-designed assessment tool includes criteria that represents the full range of knowledge and skills that are the primary targets of instruction. Expectations for student performance should be clear. Finally, any sound assessment should be free of factors which serve to confuse or cue student responses.

Formats for Effective Assessment of Technology-Based Resources

Experts in the field of technology have selected three common forms of assessment as most appropriate for evaluating technology-based applications: (a) self-assessment, demonstrated by the technology checklist; (b) performance-based assessment, evidenced by the rubric; and (c) authentic assessment, exhibited by the portfolio.

The task is now one of moving from an understanding of how technology-based resources are designed, developed, and delivered to one of assessing how those materials affect student understanding and learning outcomes. The following section of this final chapter offers checklists, rubrics, and portfolios for the instructional materials prepared in part 2 and the instructional lessons presented in part 3.

Self-Assessment and the Technology Checklists

Objective 11.3: Apply the fundamentals of self-assessment checklists for teaching and learning; incorporate specific elements appropriate for the technology-based materials and lessons.

Self-assessment has three integral components: (a) the **criteria** for determining the effectiveness of the materials produced, (b) a valid **methodology** for collecting and analyzing the results of the self-evaluation, and (c) an appropriate **framework** for interpreting the results of the assessment. In support of these components, a series of checklists are proposed for a self-examination of the concepts, skills, and products offered in this text (Leighton, 1996).

First, criteria for assessing technology-based instructional material was provided throughout parts 2 and 3. In each chapter, design guidelines presented the fundamentals integral to the creation of successful materials and effective lessons. In self-assessment, the basic question is, "Does this particular instructional media contain the necessary elements to ensure increased student knowledge and understanding?" The checklists which follow summarize these elements.

Second, while offering a convenient forum for presenting the key elements of a successful lesson, the checklists also provide an excellent tool for tracking whether the materials and lessons contain all the elements necessary to ensure a successful application of technology for teaching and learning. A particular weakness associated with self-assessment is its inherent subjectivity; reviewing one's own efforts is often skewed by familiarity and personal misconceptions. By offering checklists as a methodology for self-assessment, an objective review of technology-based materials and lessons may differ in technical rigor while still providing the learner with the necessary knowledge and understanding of the specific learning objectives established by the teacher.

Third, an analytic approach to assessing student learning should reward important issues. For example, an acknowledgement of the proper uses of classroom handouts, presentations, and web sites is the first step in the successful use of technology. Correct implementation should reap significant points from a valid checklist. Clear and concise directives also contribute to a student-controlled lesson and deserve high marks. The integration of more skills and competencies reflected by a host of technical "bells and whistles" within a visual-based classroom presentation, however, can be highly distracting and actually take away from the student learning opportunity. It should receive a limited number of points on a checklist, perhaps even a negative number.

The true appeal of self-assessment, then, is that it permits an accountability system tailored to the avowed principles of instructional technology. Checklists are aimed specifically at components of student performance deemed crucial by the teacher and the curricular content of the subject matter presented. Review the checklists presented here and consider their use following the development of any technology-based materials resulting from applications presented in this text.

Handouts/Study Guides

SELF-ASSESSMENT LEGEND
Indicate by placing an "X" in the Check Here box if your personal assessment of this item indicates that the Criteria for Self-Assessment is present in the Handout/Study Guide under evaluation.

Check Here	Criteria for Self-Assessment
	1. Did the designer select the correct application of text-based formats (i.e., handouts versus study guides)?
	2. Is the title of the lesson present, and is there a graphic or image appropriate for the content material contained in the resource?
	3. Does the use of a student name identify materials to be used either by the individual student or in learning groups?
	4. Does the use of a lesson date identify multiple sessions over the course of a semester or multiple academic years?
	5. Are page numbers used to avoid student confusion and enhance classroom discussion?
	6. Did the designer use a variety of sensory aids to student learning? Identify the aids included in the Handouts/Study Guides from the following list:
	a. Clip art
	b. Images harvested from the Internet
	c. Text harvested from the Internet
	7. Were the materials spell-checked to avoid unnecessary misspellings?
	8. When printed, did the documents impart a visually appealing presentation?
	9. Were features of appearance (e.g., bold, underline, etc.) used to stress critical items for student understanding?
	10. Were the number of pages used in the Study Guide/Handout appropriate to ensure the lesson objectives were met.

Classroom Presentations

SELF-ASSESSMENT LEGEND
Indicate by placing an "X" in the Check Here box if your personal assessment of this item indicates that the Criteria for Self-Assessment is present in the Classroom Presentation under evaluation.

Check Here	Criteria for Self-Assessment
	1. Do Slides 1 and 2 present the title and topic of the lesson, and is there a graphic or image appropriate for the content material contained in these slides?
	2. Does Slide 3 provide the learning objectives in a way that students (and parents, if appropriate) understand what learning outcomes are expected?
	3. Do Slides 4 through 9 confer the content material of the lesson?
	4. Slides 10 and 11 should summarize new vocabulary words and an opportunity for student assessment. Do they?
	5. The final slides of the presentation should provide pre-selected web sites, additional workbook material, and further research opportunities for students to continue their exploration of the topic. Are these included in the presentation?
	6. Does the designer use a variety of multimedia resources to aid student learning? Identify the aids included in the presentation from the following list:
	a. Clip art
	b. Images harvested from the Internet
	c. Animated images harvested from the Internet
	d. Text harvested from the Internet
	e. Sounds from the gallery or harvested from the Internet
	f. Movies (i.e., video clips) from the gallery or harvested from the Internet
	g. Hyperlinks from the Internet
	7. Were contents of the slides spell-checked to avoid unnecessary misspellings?

cont.

	8. Did the designer select a template different from that supplied by Auto Content Wizard and does the selected template add to the quality of the presentation?
	9. Was the slide presentation offered to students in hard copy format? And, if so, is the printed presentation visually appealing?
	10. Are features of appearance (e.g., bold, underline, etc.) used to stress critical items for student understanding?
	11. Are colors (text, background, hyperlinks, etc.) used effectively and consistently throughout the presentation?
	12. Are the number of slides used in the Presentation appropriate to meet the lesson objectives?

Web Home Pages

SELF-ASSESSMENT LEGEND
Indicate by placing an "X" in the Check Here box if your personal assessment of this item indicates that the Criteria for Self-Assessment is present in the Web Home Pages under evaluation.

Check Here	Criteria for Self-Assessment
	1. Does the web page present the title and topic of the lesson, and is there a graphic or image appropriate for the content material contained on this page?
	2. Are lesson instructions provided so that students (and parents, if appropriate) understand what learning outcomes are expected?
	3. Is the web page appropriate for the specific lesson objectives?
	4. Have all the External web sites been previewed by the teacher prior to the lesson?
	5. Does the web page provide pre-selected web sites, additional workbook material, and further research opportunities for students to continue their exploration of the topic?

cont.

	6. Does the designer use a variety of multimedia resources to aid student learning? Identify the aids included in the web page from the following list:
	
	   a. Clip art
	   b. Images harvested from the Internet
	   c. Animated images harvested from the Internet
	   d. Text harvested from the Internet
	   e. Sounds harvested from the Internet
	   f. Movies (i.e., video clips) harvested from the Internet
	   g. Hyperlinks to External sites on the Internet
	   h. Hyperlinks to Internal sites prepared by the teacher

	7. Were contents of the web page spell-checked to avoid unnecessary misspellings?
	8. Did the designer select a background color or image that adds to the quality of the web page?
	9. When printed, is the web page visually appealing?
	10. Are features of appearance (e.g., bold, underline, etc.) used to stress critical items for student understanding?
	11. Are bullets effectively used as an organizational scheme?
	12. Are colors (text, background, hyperlinks, etc.) used effectively and consistently throughout the presentation?
	13. Is the length of the web page appropriate to ensure lesson objectives are met?

HyperBook Lessons

> ### SELF-ASSESSMENT LEGEND
> Indicate by placing an "X" in the Check Here box if your personal assessment of this item indicates that the Criteria for Self-Assessment is present in the HyperBook Lesson under evaluation.

Check Here	Criteria for Self-Assessment
	1. Does the lesson overview contain indicative information, introduction to the topic, student instructions, time allotted, and lesson goals?
	2. Do initiating, developing, and concluding activities match specific learning objectives, student assignments, and student evaluation and feedback?
	3. Are additional resources such as videotapes, audiocassettes, and publications cited and recommended?
	4. Are any of the following aids included in the HyperBook ? a. Clip art b. Images harvested from the Internet c. Text harvested from the Internet d. Hyperlinks to External sites on the Internet (optional) e. Hyperlinks to Internal sites prepared by the teacher (optional)
	5. Are the materials spell-checked to avoid unnecessary misspellings?
	6. When printed, does the HyperBook impart a visually appealing presentation?
	7. Are features of appearance (e.g., bold, underline, etc.) used to stress critical items for student understanding?
	8. Are the number of pages used in the HyperBook appropriate to meet the lesson objectives?
	9. Do the instructional goals of the lesson tie new learning opportunities to prior student knowledge?
	10. Are instructional objectives developed at increasingly advanced levels of higher order thinking, including knowledge, comprehension, application, analysis, synthesis, and evaluation?
	11. Is the HyperBook provided in both hard copy and personal (i.e., diskette) formats?

cont.

	12. Are both formative and summative assessments evidenced in the HyperBook lesson, as well as traditional and authentic assessment styles?
	13. Does the designer integrate additional technical and non-technical activity resources into the lesson?
	14. Are follow-on activities provided to supply additional information for remedial students and enrichment activities for faster students?

Interactive Lessons

> **SELF-ASSESSMENT LEGEND**
> Indicate by placing an "X" in the Check Here box if your personal assessment of this item indicates that the Criteria for Self-Assessment is present in the Interactive Lesson under evaluation.

Check Here	Criteria for Self-Assessment
	1. Does the lesson overview contain indicative information, introduction to the topic, student instructions, time allotted, and lesson goals?
	2. Does the lesson review prior student knowledge and provide feedback before further student exploration?
	3. Are transition slides used to move the learner through the lesson?
	4. Is each learning objective used in the Interactive Lesson composed of a title slide, content slide(s), and a formative assessment slide(s)?
	5. Is the summative assessment slide readily identifiable and does it measure student learning outcomes over the entire lesson?
	6. Identify the multimedia resources included in the Interactive Lesson:
	a. Clip art
	b. Images harvested from the Internet
	c. Animated images harvested from the Internet
	d. Text harvested from the Internet
	e. Sounds from the gallery or harvested from the Internet
	f. Movies (i.e., video clips) from the gallery or harvested from the Internet
	g. Hyperlinks from the Internet

cont.

	7. Do the final slides of the lesson provide pre-selected web sites, additional workbook material, and further research opportunities for students to continue their exploration of the topic?
	8. Is the Interactive Lesson delivered using the kiosk mode?
	9. Is the lesson designed to integrate formative assessments using action buttons, hidden slides, and positive and negative reinforcement slides?
	10. Is the lesson designed to integrate summative assessment either online or with other resources such as the HyperBook or the Virtual Tour?
	11. Are contents of the slides spell-checked to avoid unnecessary misspellings?
	12. Does the designer personalize a template different from that supplied by Auto Content Wizard and does the template add to the quality of the presentation?
	13. Is the Interactive Lesson visually appealing?
	14. Are features of appearance (e.g., bold, underline, etc.) used to stress critical items for student understanding?
	15. Are colors (text, background, hyperlinks, etc.) used effectively and consistently throughout the lesson?
	16. Are the number of slides used in the lesson appropriate to meet the learning objectives?
	17. Do the instructional goals of the lesson tie new learning opportunities to prior student knowledge?
	18. Are instructional objectives developed at increasingly advanced levels of higher order thinking, including knowledge, comprehension, application, analysis, synthesis, and evaluation?

Virtual Tour Lessons

> **SELF-ASSESSMENT LEGEND**
> Indicate by placing an "X" in the Check Here box if your personal
> assessment of this item indicates that the Criteria for Self-Assessment
> is present in the Virtual Tour under evaluation.

Check Here	Criteria for Self-Assessment
	1. Does the Virtual Tour present the title and topic of the lesson, and is there a graphic or image appropriate for the content material contained on this page?
	2. Are lesson instructions provided so that students (and parents, if appropriate) understand what learning outcomes are expected?
	3. Is the Virtual Tour appropriate for the specific lesson objectives?
	4. Have all the external web sites been previewed by the teacher prior to the tour?
	5. Does the Virtual Tour provide pre-selected web sites, additional workbook material, and further research opportunities for students to continue their exploration of the topic?
	6. Does the designer use a variety of multimedia resources to aid student learning? Identify the aids included in the web page from the following list:
	a. Clip art
	b. Images harvested from the Internet
	c. Animated images harvested from the Internet
	d. Text harvested from the Internet
	e. Sounds harvested from the Internet
	f. Movies (i.e., video clips) harvested from the Internet
	g. Hyperlinks to External sites on the Internet
	h. Hyperlinks to Internal sites prepared by the teacher
	7. Were contents of the Virtual Tour spell-checked to avoid unnecessary misspellings?
	8. Did the designer select a background color or image that adds to the quality of the tour?

cont.

	9. When printed, is the Virtual Tour visually appealing?
	10. Are features of appearance (e.g., bold, underline, etc.) used to stress critical items for student understanding?
	11. Are bullets effectively used as an organizational scheme?
	12. Are colors (text, background, hyperlinks, etc.) used effectively and consistently throughout the presentation?
	13. Is the length of the Virtual Tour appropriate to meet the lesson objectives? And are the objectives reflective of increasingly advanced levels of higher order thinking?
	14. Does the designer apply a Front Door appropriate for the thinking operation, psychology for learning, and technical difficulty?
	15. Are exploration pages within the Virtual Tour matched with specific learning objectives?
	16. Does the designer make good use of internal links to expand the content material presented to the student?
	17. Is the Virtual Tour provided to the student in both an online (i.e., web server) and personal (i.e., diskette) format?

Performance-Based Assessment and the Technology Rubric

Objective 11.4: Apply the fundamentals of performance-based assessment using rubrics for teaching and learning; incorporate specific elements appropriate for the technology-based materials and lessons.

NA	1	2	3	4	5	6	7	8	9	10	Score: _____

RUBRIC LEGEND

Not Applicable Weak ————————————— Strong   Recap Score Here

A rubric differs from the checklist in that it helps to accommodate both collaboration and authenticity with respect to the instructional materials produced. Rubrics address three areas of assessment concern that attempt to answer the question, "Does this particular instructional media pose the necessary questions, required research, and personal collaboration to increase student knowledge and understanding?"

First, they promote performance and understanding by demonstrating why the content material is important to the student. Some of the criteria for evaluating instructional resources using a rubric include a focus on

- Relevant and meaningful problems
- Specific research ideas and problem-solving skills
- Data from a variety of sources, first-hand and other
- Efforts to accommodate individual learning styles
- Follow-on activities for remedial and enrichment instruction
- Communication skills, personal and interpersonal
- Practical applications of abstract concepts
- Application of knowledge to new situations

Second, rubrics require more clarity regarding the criteria evidencing student understanding. Checklists often relegate the list of possible responses to "yes" and "no" alternatives. Rubrics, on the other hand, offer a much broader range of alternatives along a continuum. For example, on a scale from 1 to 10,

10 =   Outstanding problem or question raised by the materials or lesson
          Accurate material gleaned from course content and online research
          Clear, concise organization of the web site or classroom presentation
          Outstanding use of multimedia materials
          Outstanding use of student-controlled and student-centered format

8 =   Significant strengths in above areas
          Very good application of course content and online research
          Well designed web site or classroom presentation

Excellent use of multimedia materials
Primary use of student-controlled and student-centered format

6 = Many strengths listed above
Good application of course content and online research
Web site design or classroom application clear
Good contributions from multimedia materials
Evidence of student control of lesson content

4 = Adequate use of course content material and online research
Consistent use of multimedia materials
Student control of lesson content weak

2 = Not adequate in the above categories

Third, rubrics bring the student into the evaluation process by sharing the criteria upon which the assignment is to be graded. When communicated to the student, rubrics bring an end to the frustrating experience of submitting an assignment without knowing how it will be evaluated or whether it will measure up to the standards that remain known only to the instructor.

Rubrics are presented here for each of the technology-based resources included in this text. Select the format of the resource and locate the applicable rubric for assessing the quality of the material and its potential for increasing student understanding and knowledge.

Handouts/Study Guides

RUBRIC LEGEND											
NA	1	2	3	4	5	6	7	8	9	10	Score: _____

Not Applicable Weak ——————————— Strong   Recap Score Here

1. **Satisfaction of Lesson Goals.** Rate the effectiveness of the text-based materials to meet the established purpose of the lesson:

a. Rate how well the materials are linked to specific learning objective(s).

NA	1	2	3	4	5	6	7	8	9	10	Score: _____

b. Guage whether the number of pages used in the Study Guide/Handout was appropriate to meet the lesson objectives.

NA	1	2	3	4	5	6	7	8	9	10	Score: _____

2. **Construct of the Instruction**. Rate the occurrence and comprehensiveness of each of the following key elements:

    a. Title of the Lesson.

NA	1	2	3	4	5	6	7	8	9	10	Score: _____

    b. Demographic Information (e.g., Student Name, Date, Teacher's Name, etc.).

NA	1	2	3	4	5	6	7	8	9	10	Score: _____

    c. Quantity/Quality of the Textual Content for the Lesson.

NA	1	2	3	4	5	6	7	8	9	10	Score: _____

    d. Richness of Activities and Exercises for Student Assessment.

NA	1	2	3	4	5	6	7	8	9	10	Score: _____

3. **Structure of the Text-Based Materials**. Rate how well the designer integrated word processing aids to student learning:

    a. Page numbers, if appropriate.

NA	1	2	3	4	5	6	7	8	9	10	Score: _____

    b. Bullets, numbering, and indents.

NA	1	2	3	4	5	6	7	8	9	10	Score: _____

    c. Grammar and spell-checker.

NA	1	2	3	4	5	6	7	8	9	10	Score: _____

    d. Appropriate Multimedia for Lesson Content (e.g., clip art, images, and text).

NA	1	2	3	4	5	6	7	8	9	10	Score: _____

    e. Use of Textual Content Harvested from the Internet.

NA	1	2	3	4	5	6	7	8	9	10	Score: _____

Classroom Presentations

RUBRIC LEGEND												
NA	1	2	3	4	5	6	7	8	9	10	Score: _____

Not Applicable Weak ——————————— Strong   Recap Score Here

1. **Satisfaction of Lesson Goals.** Rate the effectiveness of the visual-based presentation to meet the established purpose of the lesson:

    a. Rate how well the visual-based materials are linked to specific learning objective(s).

NA	1	2	3	4	5	6	7	8	9	10	Score: _____

    b. Gauge whether number of slides used for the presentation was appropriate to meet the lesson objectives.

NA	1	2	3	4	5	6	7	8	9	10	Score: _____

    c. Assess whether the slides were well designed and age-appropriate for the target student population.

NA	1	2	3	4	5	6	7	8	9	10	Score: _____

2. **Construct of the Instruction**. Rate the occurrence and comprehensiveness of each of the following key elements:

    a. Lesson introduction: Slides 1 and 2.

NA	1	2	3	4	5	6	7	8	9	10	Score: _____

    b. Delivery of learning objectives: Slide 3.

NA	1	2	3	4	5	6	7	8	9	10	Score: _____

    c. Lesson content: Slides 4 through 9.

NA	1	2	3	4	5	6	7	8	9	10	Score: _____

d. Student Assessment: Slides 10 and 11.

NA	1	2	3	4	5	6	7	8	9	10	Score: _____

e. Richness of Activities and Exercises for Student Assessment.

NA	1	2	3	4	5	6	7	8	9	10	Score: _____

3. **Structure of the Visual-Based Materials**. Rate how well the designer integrated graphics design aids to student learning.

a. Sound design concepts for preparing visual materials (e.g., use of colors, backgrounds, images, etc.).

NA	1	2	3	4	5	6	7	8	9	10	Score: _____

b. Appropriate Multimedia for Lesson Content (e.g., clip art, images, and text).

NA	1	2	3	4	5	6	7	8	9	10	Score: _____

c. Use of Multimedia Content Harvested from the Internet.

NA	1	2	3	4	5	6	7	8	9	10	Score: _____

d. Use of Hyperlink Content Harvested from the Internet.

NA	1	2	3	4	5	6	7	8	9	10	Score: _____

e. Application of New Design Template/Backgrounds.

NA	1	2	3	4	5	6	7	8	9	10	Score: _____

Web Home Pages

RUBRIC LEGEND

NA	1	2	3	4	5	6	7	8	9	10	Score: _____

Not Applicable Weak ————————————— Strong   Recap Score Here

1. **Satisfaction of Lesson Goals.** Rate the effectiveness of the web home pages to meet the established purpose of the lesson:

   a. Rate how well the web-based materials are linked to specific learning objective(s).

NA	1	2	3	4	5	6	7	8	9	10	Score: _____

   b. Gauge whether length of the web page was appropriate to meet the lesson objectives.

NA	1	2	3	4	5	6	7	8	9	10	Score: _____

   c. Assess whether the web page was well designed and age-appropriate for the target student population.

NA	1	2	3	4	5	6	7	8	9	10	Score: _____

2. **Construct of the Instruction.** Rate the occurrence and comprehensiveness of each of the following key elements:

   a. Introduction and Student Instructions.

NA	1	2	3	4	5	6	7	8	9	10	Score: _____

   b. Statement of Learning Objectives.

NA	1	2	3	4	5	6	7	8	9	10	Score: _____

   c. Web sites for Student Exploration.

NA	1	2	3	4	5	6	7	8	9	10	Score: _____

d. Student Assessment .

NA	1	2	3	4	5	6	7	8	9	10	Score: _____

3. **Structure of the Web-Based Materials**. Rate how well the designer integrated web-based elements in support of student learning:

a. Banner Title and Opening Image.

NA	1	2	3	4	5	6	7	8	9	10	Score: _____

b. Appropriate Use of Multimedia Content (e.g., clip art, images, and text).

NA	1	2	3	4	5	6	7	8	9	10	Score: _____

c. Use of Internal (i.e., Teacher-made) Hyperlinks.

NA	1	2	3	4	5	6	7	8	9	10	Score: _____

d. Use of External (i.e., Internet-ready) Hyperlinks.

NA	1	2	3	4	5	6	7	8	9	10	Score: _____

e. Use of E-Mail Hyperlink for Student Inquiries and Access to the Teacher.

NA	1	2	3	4	5	6	7	8	9	10	Score: _____

f. Use of the Address Block with Author's Name and Contact Information, Fair Use Statement, and a Created and Revised Date Stamp.

NA	1	2	3	4	5	6	7	8	9	10	Score: _____

HyperBook Lessons

RUBRIC LEGEND

| NA | 1 | 2 | 3 | 4 | 5 | 6 | 7 | 8 | 9 | 10 | Score: _____ |

Not Applicable Weak ————————————— Strong   Recap Score Here

1. **Design the Lesson**. Rate how well the designer specified the overall instructional goals of the lesson and attempted to tie new learning opportunities to prior student knowledge.

| NA | 1 | 2 | 3 | 4 | 5 | 6 | 7 | 8 | 9 | 10 | Score: _____ |

2. **Conduct Online Research**. Rate how well the designer emphasized technology when introducing content into the lesson and whether the teacher recognized the value of more traditional (i.e., non-technical) sources of instructional materials.

| NA | 1 | 2 | 3 | 4 | 5 | 6 | 7 | 8 | 9 | 10 | Score: _____ |

3. **Writing Learning Objectives**. Rate how well the designer developed instructional objectives at increasingly advanced levels of higher order thinking, including knowledge, comprehension, application, analysis, synthesis, and evaluation.

| NA | 1 | 2 | 3 | 4 | 5 | 6 | 7 | 8 | 9 | 10 | Score: _____ |

4. **Developing Lesson Content**. Rate whether the designer offers appropriate initiating, developing, and concluding activities based on student needs, interests, and lesson objectives within the lesson. Also, rate how well the designer connected learning objectives from the previous step with content material in this step.

| NA | 1 | 2 | 3 | 4 | 5 | 6 | 7 | 8 | 9 | 10 | Score: _____ |

5. **Create the HyperBook**. Rate how well the designer constructed the HyperBook lesson. As a minimum, consider the following factors:

    a.   Lesson overview containing indicative information, introduction to the topic, student instructions, time allotted, and lesson goals.

| NA | 1 | 2 | 3 | 4 | 5 | 6 | 7 | 8 | 9 | 10 | Score: _____ |

b. Exercise Pages. Initiating, developing, and concluding activities should correlate with specific learning objectives, student assignments, and any student evaluation and feedback.

NA	1	2	3	4	5	6	7	8	9	10	Score: _____

c. Follow-on Activities with additional information for remedial students and enrichment activities.

NA	1	2	3	4	5	6	7	8	9	10	Score: _____

d. Additional Resources such as videotapes, audiocassettes, and publications.

NA	1	2	3	4	5	6	7	8	9	10	Score: _____

e. Use of External Student Materials.

NA	1	2	3	4	5	6	7	8	9	10	Score: _____

6. **Create the Interactive Lesson**. Do not rate the Interactive Lesson using this rubric. Rather, circle "NA" for Step 6 and rate the Interactive Lesson in the subsequent rubric.

(NA)	1	2	3	4	5	6	7	8	9	10	Score: _____

7. **Create the Virtual Tour Lesson**. Do not rate the Virtual Tour lesson using this rubric. Rather, circle "NA" for Step 7 and rate the Virtual Tour in the subsequent rubric.

(NA)	1	2	3	4	5	6	7	8	9	10	Score: _____

8. **Deliver the Lesson**. Rate the presentation of the instruction, the technology incorporated into the lesson, nature of the content material, learning styles implemented, and the technical competency of the designer. Award additional points for HyperBooks which are provided in both hard copy and personal (i.e., diskette) formats.

NA	1	2	3	4	5	6	7	8	9	10	Score: _____

9. **Evaluate Student Learning**. Rate how well the designer integrated an effective process of student evaluation based on this lesson format. Both formative and summative assessments should be evidenced along with a variety of traditional and authentic assessment styles.

NA	1	2	3	4	5	6	7	8	9	10	Score: _____

10. **Conduct Follow-up Activities**. Rate how well the designer integrated additional resources into the lesson, award additional points for using both technical and non-technical activities.

NA	1	2	3	4	5	6	7	8	9	10	Score: _____

Interactive Lessons

RUBRIC LEGEND											
NA	1	2	3	4	5	6	7	8	9	10	Score: _____

Not Applicable Weak ———————————— Strong   Recap Score Here

1. **Design the Lesson**. Rate how well the designer specified the overall instructional goals of the lesson and attempted to tie new learning opportunities to prior student knowledge.

NA	1	2	3	4	5	6	7	8	9	10	Score: _____

2. **Conduct Online Research**. Rate how well the designer emphasized technology when introducing content into the lesson and whether the teacher recognized the value of more traditional (i.e., non-technical) sources of instructional materials.

NA	1	2	3	4	5	6	7	8	9	10	Score: _____

3. **Writing Learning Objectives**. Rate how well the designer developed instructional objectives at increasingly advanced levels of higher order thinking, including knowledge, comprehension, application, analysis, synthesis, and evaluation.

NA	1	2	3	4	5	6	7	8	9	10	Score: _____

4. **Developing Lesson Content**. Rate whether the designer offers appropriate initiating, developing, and concluding activities based on student needs, interests, and lesson objectives within the lesson. Also, rate how well the designer connected learning objectives from the previous step with content material in this step.

NA	1	2	3	4	5	6	7	8	9	10	Score: _____

5. **Create the HyperBook**. Do not rate the HyperBook lesson using this rubric. Rather, circle "NA" for Step 5 and rate the HyperBook Lesson using the previous rubric.

NA	1	2	3	4	5	6	7	8	9	10	Score: _____

6. **Create the Interactive Lesson**. Rate how well the designer constructed the Interactive Lesson. As a minimum, consider the following factors:

   a. Lesson overview containing indicative information, introduction to the topic, student instructions, time allotted, and lesson goals.

NA	1	2	3	4	5	6	7	8	9	10	Score: _____

   b. Review of prior student knowledge including selected questions to arrive at the level of student understanding of the topic, a positive feedback slide to reinforce the correct response, and a negative feedback slide to provide the correct response and encourage further student exploration.

NA	1	2	3	4	5	6	7	8	9	10	Score: _____

   c. Transition slide to move the learner from the pre-lesson to the body of new material.

NA	1	2	3	4	5	6	7	8	9	10	Score: _____

   d. Learning objectives composed of a title slide, content slide(s), and formative assessment slide(s).

NA	1	2	3	4	5	6	7	8	9	10	Score: _____

   e. Summative assessment slide(s) to recap lesson goals and measure student learning outcomes over the entire lesson.

NA	1	2	3	4	5	6	7	8	9	10	Score: _____

   f. Follow-on Activities with additional information (e.g., web sites) for student enrichment activities.

NA	1	2	3	4	5	6	7	8	9	10	Score: _____

   g. Use of additional resources such as videotapes, audiocassettes, and publications.

NA	1	2	3	4	5	6	7	8	9	10	Score: _____

7. **Create the Virtual Tour Lesson**. Do not rate the Virtual Tour lesson using this rubric. Rather, circle "NA" for Step 7 and rate the Virtual Tour in the subsequent rubric.

| (NA) | 1 | 2 | 3 | 4 | 5 | 6 | 7 | 8 | 9 | 10 | Score: _____ |

8. **Deliver the Lesson**. Rate the presentation of the instruction, the technology incorporated into the lesson, nature of the content material, learning styles implemented, and the technical competency of the designer. Award additional points for Interactive Lessons which are delivered in a kiosk mode and offered in both a computer lab setting and for home/personal exploration.

| NA | 1 | 2 | 3 | 4 | 5 | 6 | 7 | 8 | 9 | 10 | Score: _____ |

9. **Evaluate Student Learning**. Rate how well the designer integrated formative assessments into the lesson using action buttons, hidden slides, and positive and negative reinforcement slides. Award additional points for effective summative assessment whether online or with other resources (handouts or the HyperBook, for example).

| NA | 1 | 2 | 3 | 4 | 5 | 6 | 7 | 8 | 9 | 10 | Score: _____ |

10. **Conduct Follow-up Activities**. Rate how well the designer integrated additional resources into the lesson, award additional points for using both technical and non-technical activities.

| NA | 1 | 2 | 3 | 4 | 5 | 6 | 7 | 8 | 9 | 10 | Score: _____ |

Virtual Tour Lessons

RUBRIC LEGEND

| NA | 1 | 2 | 3 | 4 | 5 | 6 | 7 | 8 | 9 | 10 | Score: _____ |

Not Applicable Weak ——————————— Strong   Recap Score Here

1. **Design the Lesson**. Rate how well the designer specified the overall instructional goals of the lesson and attempted to tie new learning opportunities to prior student knowledge.

| NA | 1 | 2 | 3 | 4 | 5 | 6 | 7 | 8 | 9 | 10 | Score: _____ |

2. **Conduct Online Research**. Rate how well the designer emphasized technology when introducing content into the lesson and whether the teacher recognized the value of more traditional (i.e., non-technical) sources of instructional materials.

| NA | 1 | 2 | 3 | 4 | 5 | 6 | 7 | 8 | 9 | 10 | Score: _____ |

3. **Writing Learning Objectives**. Rate how well the designer developed instructional objectives at increasingly advanced levels of higher-order thinking, including knowledge, comprehension, application, analysis, synthesis, and evaluation.

NA	1	2	3	4	5	6	7	8	9	10	Score: _____

4. **Developing Lesson Content**. Rate whether the designer offers appropriate initiating, developing, and concluding activities based on student needs, interests, and lesson objectives within the lesson. Also, rate how well the designer connected learning objectives from the previous step with content material in this step.

NA	1	2	3	4	5	6	7	8	9	10	Score: _____

5. **Create the HyperBook**. Do not rate the HyperBook lesson using this rubric. Rather, circle "NA" for Step 5 and rate the HyperBook Lesson using the previous rubric.

(NA)	1	2	3	4	5	6	7	8	9	10	Score: _____

6. **Create the Interactive Lesson**. Do not rate the Interactive Lesson using this rubric. Rather, circle "NA" for Step 6 and rate the Interactive Lesson in the subsequent rubric.

(NA)	1	2	3	4	5	6	7	8	9	10	Score: _____

7. **Create the Virtual Tour Lesson**. Rate how well the designer constructed the Interactive Lesson. As a minimum, consider the following factors:

    a. Selection of a suitable Front Door based on an appropriate thinking operation, psychology for learning, and technical difficulty.

NA	1	2	3	4	5	6	7	8	9	10	Score: _____

    b. Lesson overview containing indicative information, introduction to the topic, student instructions, time allotted, and lesson goals.

NA	1	2	3	4	5	6	7	8	9	10	Score: _____

    c. Exploration pages which match with specific learning objectives.

NA	1	2	3	4	5	6	7	8	9	10	Score: _____

    d. Appropriate Use of Multimedia Content (e.g., clip art, images, and text).

NA	1	2	3	4	5	6	7	8	9	10	Score: _____

e. Use of Internal (i.e., Teacher-made) Hyperlinks.

NA	1	2	3	4	5	6	7	8	9	10	Score: _____

f. Use of External (i.e., Internet-ready) Hyperlinks.

NA	1	2	3	4	5	6	7	8	9	10	Score: _____

g. Follow-on Activities with additional information for student enrichment.

NA	1	2	3	4	5	6	7	8	9	10	Score: _____

h. Use of additional resources such as videotapes, audiocassettes, and publications.

NA	1	2	3	4	5	6	7	8	9	10	Score: _____

8. **Deliver the Lesson**. Rate the presentation of the instruction, the technology incorporated into the lesson, nature of the content material, learning styles implemented, and the technical competency of the designer. Award additional points for Virtual Tours which are provided online and in personal (i.e., diskette) formats.

NA	1	2	3	4	5	6	7	8	9	10	Score: _____

9. **Evaluate Student Learning**. Rate how well the designer integrated an effective process for student evaluation based on this lesson format. Both formative and summative assessments should be evidenced along with a variety of traditional and authentic assessment styles. Give additional points for selecting a Front Door with a particularly high level of effective student assessment (see Table 10-3).

NA	1	2	3	4	5	6	7	8	9	10	Score: _____

10. **Conduct Follow-up Activities**. Rate how well the designer integrated additional resources into the lesson, award additional points for using both technical and non-technical activities.

NA	1	2	3	4	5	6	7	8	9	10	Score: _____

Authentic Assessment and the Technology Portfolio

Objective 11.5: Apply the fundamentals of authentic assessment using portfolios for teaching and learning; incorporate specific elements appropriate for the technology-based materials and lessons.

At the top of the assessment ladder is the use of portfolios to evaluate student learning outcomes. Effective portfolio assessment centers around the identification of five essential ingredients of learning: reading, writing, thinking, interacting, and demonstrating. Together, these elements represent the foundations of teaching and learning (Wilcox & Tomei, 1999).

Reading

Reading is primary; the first of the foundations. It is concerned with gathering new knowledge and developing new perspectives on prior knowledge, both critical to the successful implementation of technology-based resources. Whether the information is presented to the student using text books, journals, teacher-prepared handouts, or online avenues, reading provides the underpinning for a successful technology-based program. Technology encourages virtual journeys to the largest accumulation of knowledge since the encyclopedia: the Internet. Online searches, electronic journals, and digital libraries contribute to support of the reading foundation. Electronic mail, list servers, and online subscriptions increase the domain of readily available reading resources. Reading remains the most encompassing foundation for technology-based instructional resources and must be evident during examination of a portfolio for assessment.

Writing

New thinking is presented, defended, and extended via writing. Especially with regards to technology, writing is often overlooked in favor of demonstrating, yet writing remains the primary evidence that prior knowledge has been accumulated, integrated, and transferred to practical classroom applications. Writing is worthy of inclusion in any well designed instructional technology-based lesson. Formal papers, publication submissions, and classroom materials require the most commonly used personal computer application: word processing. A writing exercise should include a submission free of misspelled words with proper grammar and appropriate reading levels. Mastery of the spell checker, thesaurus, reading level gauge, and grammar checker should become necessary skills for students using instructional technology.

Thinking

Student understanding becomes visible in thinking-centered elements of an instructional program. Teachers must provide for this foundation when integrating technology into instructional resources. Exercises which require personal reflection and journal writing confirm student thinking and are authentic indicators of student learning. Certain technology tools are available to assist the thinking student and should be evidenced in any well designed technology-based lesson. Database software manages the drudgery of tracking phone numbers, personal and professional contacts, bibliographic citations, and web site addresses, leaving time to think about the contents, implications, and applications of the information collected. Spreadsheets manipulate numeric information and present "what if" scenarios for deeper student exploration. Project management software aids in scheduling and time management and oftentimes becomes a classroom management tool for teachers and a valuable technology skill for students. Finally, most multimedia computers come with a host of utility programs which further encourage investigation of downloaded images, sounds, and video clips that are augmenting the multimedia resources of appropriate classroom materials.

Interacting

Artifacts from this foundation include discovery learning exercises and underline the importance of group inquiry and problem solving. Interacting discusses and defends, constructs and criticizes, and the most apparent examples of successfully integrated technology rest with this foundation. Appropriate communication tools include electronic mail with mentors and peers which allow students to share their learning and brainstorm new ideas. Newsgroups and chat rooms offer more online interaction with a broader scope of teachers, students, and content experts. Lastly, distance learning is opening new venues for video-supported interaction in the medium of the virtual classroom. A well designed lesson includes ample opportunity for technology-based interaction.

Demonstrating

Demonstrating exposes the student to the specific learning objectives of the target lesson. Practical applications of content material offer students a variety of learning styles from which to choose. Chapters 5 and 9 have amply demonstrated the potential of a graphics design and delivery package (i.e., Power Point) to combine materials containing images, sounds, text, and video into a multimedia and multi-sensory presentation. In addition, Netscape Composer offers the web design features necessary to create Internet-based course materials.

Handouts/Study Guides

AUTHENTIC ASSESSMENT LEGEND
Circle the Letter Grade (A, B, or C) in the Portfolio Folder
assessing the strength of the foundation item
present in the Handout/Study Guide under evaluation.

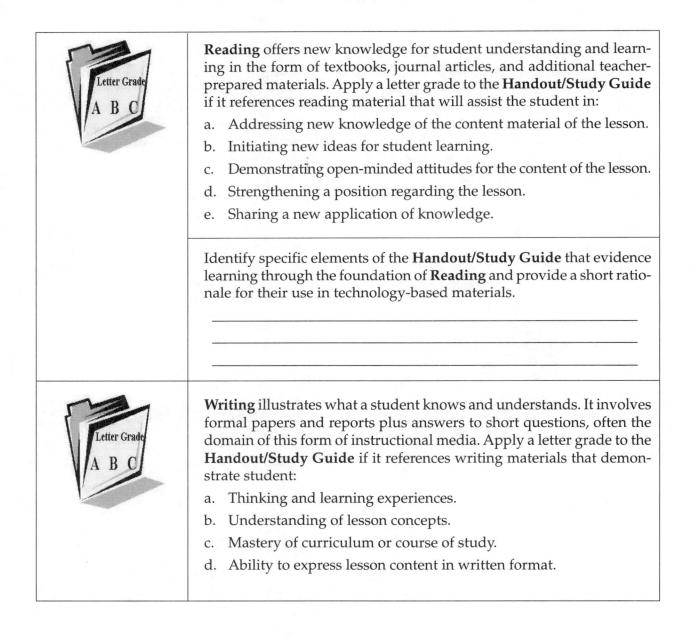

Letter Grade A B C	**Reading** offers new knowledge for student understanding and learning in the form of textbooks, journal articles, and additional teacher-prepared materials. Apply a letter grade to the **Handout/Study Guide** if it references reading material that will assist the student in: a. Addressing new knowledge of the content material of the lesson. b. Initiating new ideas for student learning. c. Demonstrating open-minded attitudes for the content of the lesson. d. Strengthening a position regarding the lesson. e. Sharing a new application of knowledge.
	Identify specific elements of the **Handout/Study Guide** that evidence learning through the foundation of **Reading** and provide a short rationale for their use in technology-based materials. _____ _____ _____
Letter Grade A B C	**Writing** illustrates what a student knows and understands. It involves formal papers and reports plus answers to short questions, often the domain of this form of instructional media. Apply a letter grade to the **Handout/Study Guide** if it references writing materials that demonstrate student: a. Thinking and learning experiences. b. Understanding of lesson concepts. c. Mastery of curriculum or course of study. d. Ability to express lesson content in written format.

Identify specific elements of the **Handout/Study Guide** that evidence learning through the foundation of **Writing** and provide a short rationale for their use in technology-based materials.

_____

_____

_____

Thinking occupies the heart of the portfolio and stirs student thoughts and ideas while providing a place to discuss lesson concepts, consider alternative viewpoints, and self-assess understanding and learning. Apply a letter grade to the **Handout/Study Guide** if they reference thinking material that evidences student:

a. Comprehension of lesson content.

b. Advancement in patterns of thinking.

c. Integration of thinking into personal learning strategies.

d. Problem-solving skills.

e. New concepts that contribute to the knowledge base of the lesson.

Identify specific elements of the **Handout/Study Guide** that evidence learning through the foundation of **Thinking** and provide a short rationale for their use in technology-based materials.

_____

_____

_____

Interacting addresses the responsibility of students to argue, defend, and share their ideas. Of course, this responsibility depends to a great degree on the age, experience, and inclination of the individual. Still, group learning is too important to ignore this important aspect of personal growth. Apply a letter grade to the **Handout/Study Guide** if they reference reading material that indicates students' ability to:

a. Consider the ideas of others.

b. Articulate and defend ideas in classroom discussions.

c. Share ideas and concepts via classroom participation.

d. Flourish in both formal and informal classroom environments.

Identify specific elements of the **Handout/Study Guide** that evidence learning through the foundation of **Interacting** and provide a short rationale for their use in technology-based materials.

_____

_____

_____

Demonstrating completes the portfolio with evidence of application and transfer of knowledge. If the student truly understands the lesson content and has mastered its learning objectives, the artifacts contained in this portion of the portfolio should exhibit a growing expertise in both knowledge and skills. Apply a letter grade to the **Handout/Study Guide** if they reference interacting by way of:

a. Formal papers, presentations, and exhibition of personal knowledge.

b. Traditional evaluations of lesson content mastery.

c. Authentic assessments of student performance.

Identify specific elements of the **Handout/Study Guide** that evidence learning through the foundation of **Demonstrating** and provide a short rationale for its use in technology-based materials.

_____

_____

_____

Classroom Presentations

AUTHENTIC ASSESSMENT LEGEND
Circle the Letter Grade (A, B, or C) in the Portfolio Folder
assessing the strength of the foundation item
present in the Classroom Presentations under evaluation.

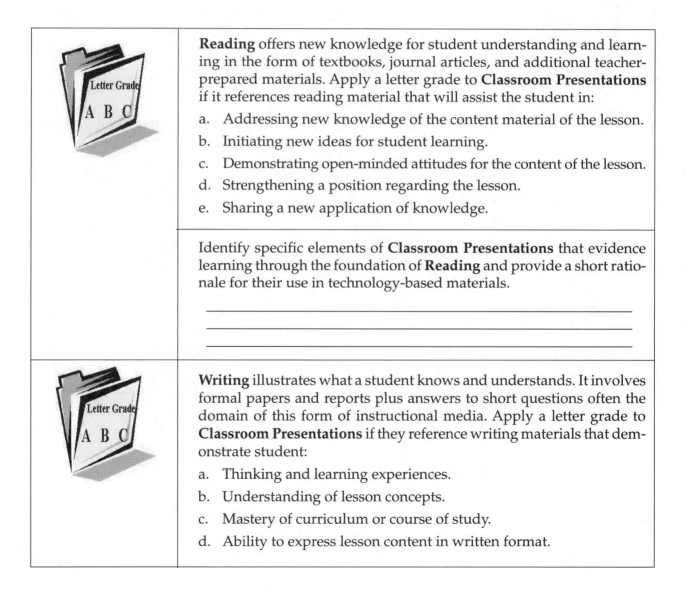

Reading offers new knowledge for student understanding and learning in the form of textbooks, journal articles, and additional teacher-prepared materials. Apply a letter grade to **Classroom Presentations** if it references reading material that will assist the student in:

a. Addressing new knowledge of the content material of the lesson.

b. Initiating new ideas for student learning.

c. Demonstrating open-minded attitudes for the content of the lesson.

d. Strengthening a position regarding the lesson.

e. Sharing a new application of knowledge.

Identify specific elements of **Classroom Presentations** that evidence learning through the foundation of **Reading** and provide a short rationale for their use in technology-based materials.

_____

_____

_____

Writing illustrates what a student knows and understands. It involves formal papers and reports plus answers to short questions often the domain of this form of instructional media. Apply a letter grade to **Classroom Presentations** if they reference writing materials that demonstrate student:

a. Thinking and learning experiences.

b. Understanding of lesson concepts.

c. Mastery of curriculum or course of study.

d. Ability to express lesson content in written format.

Identify specific elements of **Classroom Presentations** that evidence learning through the foundation of **Writing** and provide a short rationale for their use in technology-based materials.

_____

_____

_____

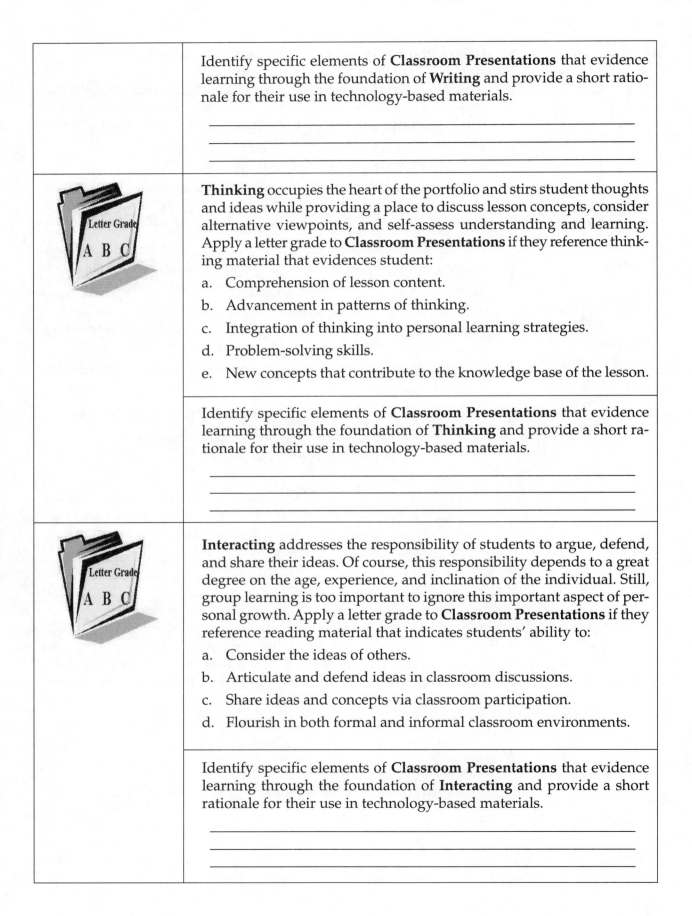

Thinking occupies the heart of the portfolio and stirs student thoughts and ideas while providing a place to discuss lesson concepts, consider alternative viewpoints, and self-assess understanding and learning. Apply a letter grade to **Classroom Presentations** if they reference thinking material that evidences student:

a. Comprehension of lesson content.

b. Advancement in patterns of thinking.

c. Integration of thinking into personal learning strategies.

d. Problem-solving skills.

e. New concepts that contribute to the knowledge base of the lesson.

Identify specific elements of **Classroom Presentations** that evidence learning through the foundation of **Thinking** and provide a short rationale for their use in technology-based materials.

_____

_____

_____

Interacting addresses the responsibility of students to argue, defend, and share their ideas. Of course, this responsibility depends to a great degree on the age, experience, and inclination of the individual. Still, group learning is too important to ignore this important aspect of personal growth. Apply a letter grade to **Classroom Presentations** if they reference reading material that indicates students' ability to:

a. Consider the ideas of others.

b. Articulate and defend ideas in classroom discussions.

c. Share ideas and concepts via classroom participation.

d. Flourish in both formal and informal classroom environments.

Identify specific elements of **Classroom Presentations** that evidence learning through the foundation of **Interacting** and provide a short rationale for their use in technology-based materials.

_____

_____

_____

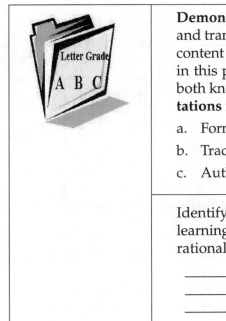

Demonstrating completes the portfolio with evidence of application and transfer of knowledge. If the student truly understands the lesson content and has mastered its learning objectives, the artifacts contained in this portion of the portfolio should exhibit a growing expertise in both knowledge and skills. Apply a letter grade to **Classroom Presentations** if they reference interacting by way of:

a.   Formal papers, presentations, and exhibition of personal knowledge.

b.   Traditional evaluations of lesson content mastery.

c.   Authentic assessments of student performance.

Identify specific elements of **Classroom Presentations** that evidence learning through the foundation of **Demonstrating** and provide a short rationale for its use in technology-based materials.

_____

_____

_____

Web Home Pages

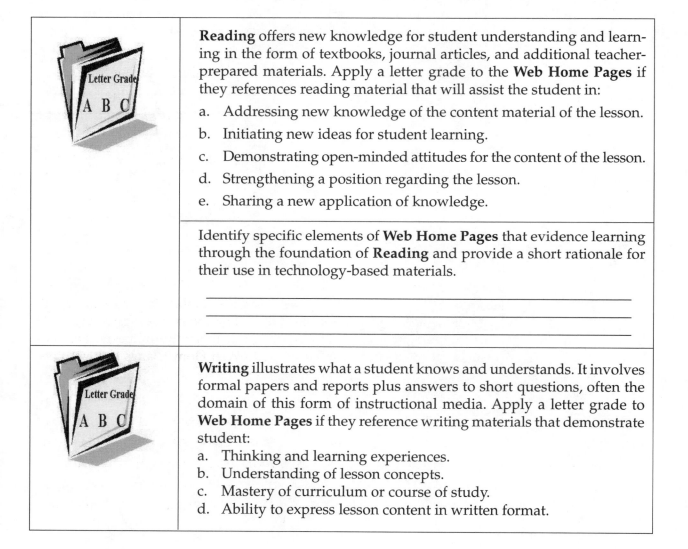

Reading offers new knowledge for student understanding and learning in the form of textbooks, journal articles, and additional teacher-prepared materials. Apply a letter grade to the **Web Home Pages** if they references reading material that will assist the student in:

a. Addressing new knowledge of the content material of the lesson.

b. Initiating new ideas for student learning.

c. Demonstrating open-minded attitudes for the content of the lesson.

d. Strengthening a position regarding the lesson.

e. Sharing a new application of knowledge.

Identify specific elements of **Web Home Pages** that evidence learning through the foundation of **Reading** and provide a short rationale for their use in technology-based materials.

_____

_____

_____

Writing illustrates what a student knows and understands. It involves formal papers and reports plus answers to short questions, often the domain of this form of instructional media. Apply a letter grade to **Web Home Pages** if they reference writing materials that demonstrate student:

a. Thinking and learning experiences.

b. Understanding of lesson concepts.

c. Mastery of curriculum or course of study.

d. Ability to express lesson content in written format.

Identify specific elements of **Web Home Pages** that evidence learning through the foundation of **Writing** and provide a short rationale for their use in technology-based materials.

_____

_____

_____

Thinking occupies the heart of the portfolio and stirs student thoughts and ideas while providing a place to discuss lesson concepts, consider alternative viewpoints, and self-assess understanding and learning. Apply a letter grade to **Web Home Pages** if they reference thinking material that evidences student:

a. Comprehension of lesson content.

b. Advancement in patterns of thinking.

c. Integration of thinking into personal learning strategies.

d. Problem-solving skills.

e. New concepts that contribute to the knowledge base of the lesson.

Identify specific elements of **Web Home Pages** that evidence learning through the foundation of **Thinking** and provide a short rationale for their use in technology-based materials.

_____

_____

_____

Interacting addresses the responsibility of students to argue, defend, and share their ideas. Of course, this responsibility depends to a great degree on the age, experience, and inclination of the individual. Still, group learning is too important to ignore this important aspect of personal growth. Apply a letter grade to **Web Home Pages** if they reference reading material that indicates students' ability to:

a. Consider the ideas of others.

b. Articulate and defend ideas in classroom discussions.

c. Share ideas and concepts via classroom participation.

d. Flourish in both formal and informal classroom environments.

Identify specific elements of **Web Home Pages** that evidence learning through the foundation of **Interacting** and provide a short rationale for their use in technology-based materials.

_____

_____

_____

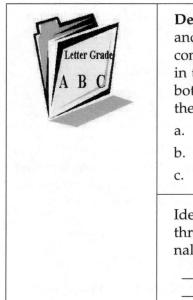

Demonstrating completes the portfolio with evidence of application and transfer of knowledge. If the student truly understands the lesson content and has mastered its learning objectives, the artifacts contained in this portion of the portfolio should exhibit a growing expertise in both knowledge and skills. Apply a letter grade to **Web Home Pages** if they reference interacting by way of:

a. Formal papers, presentations, and exhibition of personal knowledge.

b. Traditional evaluations of lesson content mastery.

c. Authentic assessments of student performance.

Identify specific elements of **Web Home Pages** that evidence learning through the foundation of **Demonstrating** and provide a short rationale for its use in technology-based materials.

_____

_____

_____

HyperBook Lessons

AUTHENTIC ASSESSMENT LEGEND
Circle the Letter Grade (A, B, or C) in the Portfolio Folder
assessing the strength of the foundation item
present in the HyperBook Lesson under evaluation.

Reading offers new knowledge for student understanding and learning in the form of textbooks, journal articles, and additional teacher-prepared materials. Apply a letter grade to **HyperBook Lessons** if they reference reading material that will assist the student in:

a. Addressing new knowledge of the content material of the lesson.

b. Initiating new ideas for student learning.

c. Demonstrating open-minded attitudes for the content of the lesson.

d. Strengthening a position regarding the lesson.

e. Sharing a new application of knowledge.

Identify specific elements of **HyperBook Lessons** that evidence learning through the foundation of **Reading** and provide a short rationale for their use in technology-based materials.

_____

_____

_____

Writing illustrates what a student knows and understands. It involves formal papers and reports plus answers to short questions often the domain of this form of instructional media. Apply a letter grade to **HyperBook Lessons** if they reference writing materials that demonstrate student:

a. Thinking and learning experiences.

b. Understanding of lesson concepts.

c. Mastery of curriculum or course of study.

d. Ability to express lesson content in written format.

Identify specific elements of **HyperBook Lessons** that evidence learning through the foundation of **Writing** and provide a short rationale for their use in technology-based materials.

_____

_____

_____

Thinking occupies the heart of the portfolio and stirs student thoughts and ideas while providing a place to discuss lesson concepts, consider alternative viewpoints, and self-assess understanding and learning. Apply a letter grade to **HyperBook Lessons** if they reference thinking material that evidences student:

a. Comprehension of lesson content.

b. Advancement in patterns of thinking.

c. Integration of thinking into personal learning strategies.

d. Problem-solving skills.

e. New concepts that contribute to the knowledge base of the lesson.

Identify specific elements of **HyperBook Lessons** that evidence learning through the foundation of **Thinking** and provide a short rationale for their use in technology-based materials.

_____

_____

_____

Interacting addresses the responsibility of students to argue, defend, and share their ideas. Of course, this responsibility depends to a great degree on the age, experience, and inclination of the individual. Still, group learning is too important to ignore this important aspect of personal growth. Apply a letter grade to **HyperBook Lessons** if they reference reading material that indicates students' ability to:

a. Consider the ideas of others.

b. Articulate and defend ideas in classroom discussions.

c. Share ideas and concepts via classroom participation.

d. Flourish in both formal and informal classroom environments.

Identify specific elements of **HyperBook Lessons** that evidence learning through the foundation of **Interacting** and provide a short rationale for their use in technology-based materials.

_____

_____

_____

Demonstrating completes the portfolio with evidence of application and transfer of knowledge. If the student truly understands the lesson content and has mastered its learning objectives, the artifacts contained in this portion of the portfolio should exhibit a growing expertise in both knowledge and skills. Apply a letter grade to **HyperBook Lessons** if they reference interacting by way of:

a. Formal papers, presentations, and exhibition of personal knowledge.

b. Traditional evaluations of lesson content mastery.

c. Authentic assessments of student performance.

Identify specific elements of **HyperBook Lessons** that evidence learning through the foundation of **Demonstrating** and provide a short rationale for its use in technology-based materials.

_____

_____

_____

Interactive Lessons

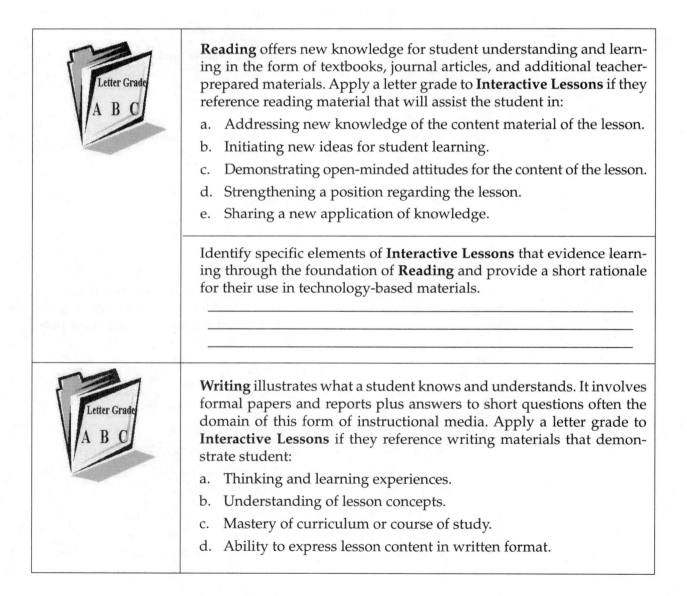

AUTHENTIC ASSESSMENT LEGEND
Circle the Letter Grade (A, B, or C) in the Portfolio Folder
assessing the strength of the foundation item
present in the Interactive Lesson under evaluation.

Reading offers new knowledge for student understanding and learning in the form of textbooks, journal articles, and additional teacher-prepared materials. Apply a letter grade to **Interactive Lessons** if they reference reading material that will assist the student in:

a. Addressing new knowledge of the content material of the lesson.

b. Initiating new ideas for student learning.

c. Demonstrating open-minded attitudes for the content of the lesson.

d. Strengthening a position regarding the lesson.

e. Sharing a new application of knowledge.

Identify specific elements of **Interactive Lessons** that evidence learning through the foundation of **Reading** and provide a short rationale for their use in technology-based materials.

_____

_____

_____

Writing illustrates what a student knows and understands. It involves formal papers and reports plus answers to short questions often the domain of this form of instructional media. Apply a letter grade to **Interactive Lessons** if they reference writing materials that demonstrate student:

a. Thinking and learning experiences.

b. Understanding of lesson concepts.

c. Mastery of curriculum or course of study.

d. Ability to express lesson content in written format.

Identify specific elements of **Interactive Lessons** that evidence learning through the foundation of **Writing** and provide a short rationale for their use in technology-based materials.

_____

_____

_____

Thinking occupies the heart of the portfolio and stirs student thoughts and ideas while providing a place to discuss lesson concepts, consider alternative viewpoints, and self-assess understanding and learning. Apply a letter grade to **Interactive Lessons** if they reference thinking material that evidences student:

a. Comprehension of lesson content.

b. Advancement in patterns of thinking.

c. Integration of thinking into personal learning strategies.

d. Problem-solving skills.

e. New concepts that contribute to the knowledge base of the lesson.

Identify specific elements of **Interactive Lessons** that evidence learning through the foundation of **Thinking** and provide a short rationale for their use in technology-based materials.

_____

_____

_____

Interacting addresses the responsibility of students to argue, defend, and share their ideas. Of course, this responsibility depends to a great degree on the age, experience, and inclination of the individual. Still, group learning is too important to ignore this important aspect of personal growth. Apply a letter grade to **Interactive Lessons** if they reference reading material that indicates students' ability to:

a. Consider the ideas of others.

b. Articulate and defend ideas in classroom discussions.

c. Share ideas and concepts via classroom participation.

d. Flourish in both formal and informal classroom environments.

Identify specific elements of **Interactive Lessons** that evidence learning through the foundation of **Interacting** and provide a short rationale for their use in technology-based materials.

_____

_____

_____

Demonstrating completes the portfolio with evidence of application and transfer of knowledge. If the student truly understands the lesson content and has mastered its learning objectives, the artifacts contained in this portion of the portfolio should exhibit a growing expertise in both knowledge and skills. Apply a letter grade to **Interactive Lessons** if they reference interacting by way of:

a. Formal papers, presentations, and exhibition of personal knowledge.

b. Traditional evaluations of lesson content mastery.

c. Authentic assessments of student performance.

Identify specific elements of **Interactive Lessons** that evidence learning through the foundation of **Demonstrating** and provide a short rationale for its use in technology-based materials.

_____

_____

_____

Virtual Tour Lessons

AUTHENTIC ASSESSMENT LEGEND
Circle the Letter Grade (A, B, or C) in the Portfolio Folder
assessing the strength of the foundation item
present in the Virtual Tour under evaluation.

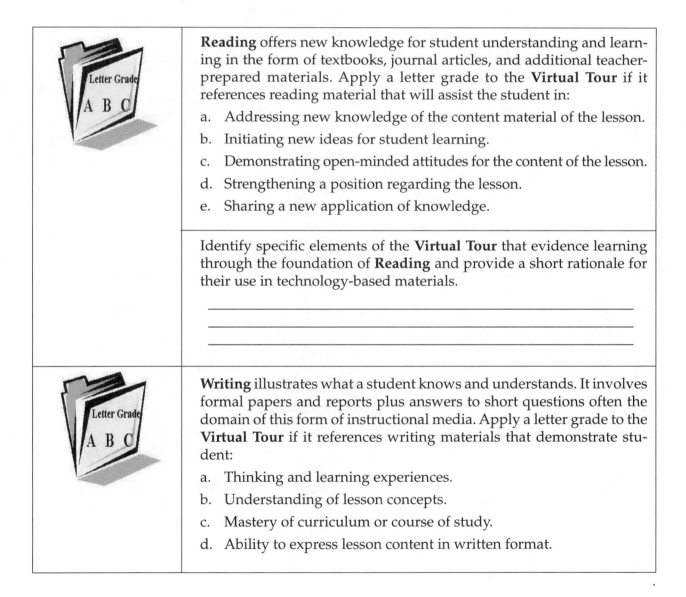

Reading offers new knowledge for student understanding and learning in the form of textbooks, journal articles, and additional teacher-prepared materials. Apply a letter grade to the **Virtual Tour** if it references reading material that will assist the student in:

a. Addressing new knowledge of the content material of the lesson.

b. Initiating new ideas for student learning.

c. Demonstrating open-minded attitudes for the content of the lesson.

d. Strengthening a position regarding the lesson.

e. Sharing a new application of knowledge.

Identify specific elements of the **Virtual Tour** that evidence learning through the foundation of **Reading** and provide a short rationale for their use in technology-based materials.

_____

_____

_____

Writing illustrates what a student knows and understands. It involves formal papers and reports plus answers to short questions often the domain of this form of instructional media. Apply a letter grade to the **Virtual Tour** if it references writing materials that demonstrate student:

a. Thinking and learning experiences.

b. Understanding of lesson concepts.

c. Mastery of curriculum or course of study.

d. Ability to express lesson content in written format.

Identify specific elements of the **Virtual Tour** that evidence learning through the foundation of **Writing** and provide a short rationale for their use in technology-based materials.

_____

_____

_____

Thinking occupies the heart of the portfolio and stirs student thoughts and ideas while providing a place to discuss lesson concepts, consider alternative viewpoints, and self-assess understanding and learning. Apply a letter grade to the **Virtual Tour** if it references thinking material that evidences student:

a. Comprehension of lesson content.

b. Advancement in patterns of thinking.

c. Integration of thinking into personal learning strategies.

d. Problem-solving skills.

e. New concepts that contribute to the knowledge base of the lesson.

Identify specific elements of the **Virtual Tour** that evidence learning through the foundation of **Thinking** and provide a short rationale for their use in technology-based materials.

_____

_____

_____

Interacting addresses the responsibility of students to argue, defend, and share their ideas. Of course, this responsibility depends to a great degree on the age, experience, and inclination of the individual. Still, group learning is too important to ignore this important aspect of personal growth. Apply a letter grade to the **Virtual Tour** if it references reading material that indicates students' ability to:

a. Consider the ideas of others.

b. Articulate and defend ideas in classroom discussions.

c. Share ideas and concepts via classroom participation.

d. Flourish in both formal and informal classroom environments.

Identify specific elements of the **Virtual Tour** that evidence learning through the foundation of **Interacting** and provide a short rationale for their use in technology-based materials.

_____

_____

_____

Demonstrating completes the portfolio with evidence of application and transfer of knowledge. If the student truly understands the lesson content and has mastered its learning objectives, the artifacts contained in this portion of the portfolio should exhibit a growing expertise in both knowledge and skills. Apply a letter grade to the **Virtual Tour** if it references interacting by way of:

a. Formal papers, presentations, and exhibition of personal knowledge.

b. Traditional evaluations of lesson content mastery.

c. Authentic assessments of student performance.

Identify specific elements of the **Virtual Tour** that evidence learning through the foundation of **Demonstrating** and provide a short rationale for its use in technology-based materials.

_____

_____

_____

Bibliography

Dietel, R. J., Herman, J. L., & Knuth, R. A. (1991). *What does research say about assessment?* Oak Brook, IL: NCREL.

Leighton, M. S. (July 1996). *Developing a self-assessment system. The role of leadership in sustaining school reform: Voices from the field.* Washington, DC: U.S. Department of Education: www.ed.gov/pubs/Leadership

Wilcox, B., & Tomei, L. A. (1999). *Professional portfolios for teachers.* Norwood, MA: Christopher-Gordon.

GLOSSARY OF TERMS

Definition (Chapter)

Abstract Learning (7) Less structured environment with more student control and personal exploration. Technology offers effective formats for this type of learning.

Action Button (9) A Power Point feature that integrates hyperlink connections to other slides within the presentation, to other presentations, to the World Wide Web, or to inserted sound and video files.

Address Block (6) In web page design, the address block provides the policies regarding use of web-based materials including author citation (with name, affiliation, and email address), copyright and Fair Use statement, and a created and revised on date.

Alias (2) A Macintosh-specific term for a special file that points to another file or device. You can place shortcuts on the desktop to conveniently access files that may be stored deep in the directory structure. Clicking the shortcut icon is the same as double clicking the actual file.

Amplified Sites (10) From the Virtual Tour format, to draw additional, up-to-date, appropriate subject matter area content from sites throughout the Internet. Using the portion of a web site that addresses the particular lesson objective in the precise format best suited to your students.

Authentic Assessment (11) Incorporates the essential ingredients of learning: reading, writing, thinking, interacting, and demonstrating. Common forum is the portfolio.

AutoContent Wizard (5) A utility within Power Point that walks the user through the steps of producing different types of presentations.

Behaviorism (1) A school of psychology that views the environment as key to learning. Environment factors are seen in terms of stimuli and its resultant behavior or response. Reward or reinforcement links the stimuli and response. The behavior of students is a response to their past and present environment and all behavior is learned.

Best Practices (Foreword) Suggest how technologies are implemented in an actual classroom environment; increase understanding of technology applications; and, encourage professional development in technology. Identified by their green borders.

Bookmark (3) To track a document or a specific place in a document for later retrieval. Nearly all Web browsers support a bookmarking feature that lets you save the address (URL) of a Web page so that you can easily re-visit the page at a later time.

CDROM (2) Abbreviation for compact disk; a computer storage media containing a large amount of data, including text and images, that can be viewed using a computer but cannot be altered or erased.

Clip Art (4) Electronic illustrations (i.e., cartoons) that can be inserted into a document.

Clipboard (6) A special file or memory area (buffer) where data is stored temporarily before being copied to another location. Many word processors, for example, use a clipboard for cutting and pasting. When a block of text is cut or copied, the word processor copies the block to the clipboard. When the block is pasted, the word processor copies it from the clipboard to its final destination.

Cognitivism (1) A school of educational psychology that focuses on the learner as an active participant in the teaching-learning process. Proponents believe that teachers can be more effective if they know what prior knowledge the student already possesses and how information is processed and structured in an individual's memory.

Concluding Activities (7) Offer closure by allowing students an opportunity to apply what they have learned. Not all concluding activities must include technology.

Concrete Instruction (7) Sequential, highly teacher-controlled learning, containing as many hands-on exercises as technically possible. Technology offers effective formats for this type of learning.

Copyrightable Resources (3) Any of the following items can receive the protection of U.S. copyright laws as currently enforced: literary works, musical works, dramatic works, pictorial, graphic and sculptural works, motion pictures, sound recordings, and other intellectual works.

Demonstrating (11) Assessment foundation; exposes the student to the specific learning objectives of the target lesson. Practical applications of content material offers students a variety of learning styles.

Design Template (5) A Power Point feature designed to give your slide presentations a consistent appearance. There are four ways that Power Point helps you control the look of your slides—with design templates, masters, color schemes, and slide layouts.

Developing Activities (7) Provide the majority of projects in the lesson and present new material for student understanding and learning. Selection of appropriate activities is based on student needs, interests, and lesson objectives. Not all developing activities must include technology.

Domain (3) Group of computers and devices on a network, administered as a unit with common rules and procedures. Common domains for the Internet include .com, .edu, .gov, .org., and .net.

Educational Technology (1) The combination of instructional, developmental, managerial, and other technologies as generally applied to the solution of educational problems.

Email (2) Electronic mail; email consists of messages, often just text, sent from one user to another via a network. Email can also be sent automatically to a number of addresses.

Evaluation Tag (10) From the Virtual Tour, a rubric for assessing the most appropriate application of a front door to an actual learning situation. The first character of the Tag indicates (A)bstract or (C)oncrete learning styles. The second character indicates (B)ehavioral, (C)ognitive, or (H)umanistic psychology of learning. The third character suggests whether the front door format is technically (E)asy, (C)hallenging, or (D)ifficult to design.

Fair Use Laws (3) Allow for educational application of a reasonable quantity of resources without the need for obtaining permission from the copyright holder.

Front Door (10) From the Virtual Tour format, one of 14 teacher-developed formats that matches an instructor's preferred teaching strategy to a student's ideal learning style.

Groupware (2) Software for people working together on a project; makes it possible for several people to work on the same file at once, via a network. It also helps with scheduling meetings and other kinds of group planning.

Handouts (4) Text-based technology resource. Concise, one or two-page documents that focus on a specific learning objective providing specific instructional steps, student materials, procedures for learning, and a short assessment. Typically completed within a single learning class period.

Harvesting the Internet (3) The ability to capture (i.e., cut, copy, and paste) and download (i.e., file save) images, charts, graphics, and text from any web page to a personal computer.

Home Page (6) The main page of a Web site. Typically, the home page serves as an index or table of contents to other documents stored at the site. The first page viewed upon entering a web site.

Humanism (1) A school of psychology that believes that how a person feels about learning is as important as how the person thinks or even behaves. Behavior is viewed from the vantage point of the student who is performing the activity. The humanist creates an educational environment that fosters self-development, cooperation, positive communications, and personalization of information.

HyperBook (7) A text-based instructional resource combining word processing skills with practical exercises and activities to guide the student through a *cognitive* learning experience. A workbook-centered teaching strategy integrating images, real-world exercises, visual aids, and real-time links appropriate for learning and assessment.

Hyperlink (5) An element in an electronic document that links to another place in the same document or to an entirely different document. An essential ingredient of the World Wide Web.

Initiating Activities (7) Prepare students to learn by creating interest in the subject matter. Not all initiating activities must include technology.

Instructional Information (3) Online information prepared by the academic community for students, fellow educators, or research. Often take the form of online journals, magazines, and periodicals.

Instructional Technology (1) The application of technology to the solution of explicit instructional problems. Instructional technology deals with the practice of using technology to teach.

Interacting (11) Assessment foundation; discusses, defends, constructs, and criticizes; includes communication with mentors and peers to share the learning experience and brainstorm new ideas. Most common technical form of interacting is electronic mail.

Interactive Lesson (7) A behavioral learning experience using the strengths of visual-based classroom presentations with the teacher controlling the sequence of the instruction while the student controls the pace. A visual-based, classroom-centered teaching strategy appropriate for learners of all ages who benefit from concrete, sequential instruction imbedded with real-time assessment necessary to assure student learning.

Internet (2) A global network that connects more than tens of thousands of networks, millions of large multiuser computers, and tens of millions of users in more than 100 countries.

Internet Browsers (2) Programs that let you navigate to and view the various Internet resources.

Internet-Ready Computer System (3) A multimedia-equipped personal computer with enhanced, state-of-the-art capabilities with respect to processor speed, memory, hard disk, sound system, video display, high speed connectivity, and Internet browser software.

ISTE (1) The International Society for Technology in Education. A nonprofit professional organization with a worldwide membership of leaders and potential leaders in educational technology. Promotes the appropriate uses of information technology to support and improve learning, teaching, and administration in K–12 education and teacher education.

Kiosk (9) A Power Point feature that provides a simple user interface that can be used as an unattended presentation option for long periods of time. Also, the primary media format for Interactive Lessons.

Link (5) An element in an electronic document that links to another place in the same document or to an entirely different document. An essential ingredient of the World Wide Web.

Master Slides (9) Allows the designer to customize a presentation. Includes titles, main text, and any background items. A change to the Master Slide affects all slides in the presentation.

Megabyte (2) Also "mb"; 1,048,576, or about one million, bytes.

Megahertz (2) Also mhz; one million hertz (cycles per second); measure of computer processor speed.

Metasearch Engines (7) The metasearch engine relies on other Internet search engines to do the work. Each metasearch examines multiple databases before retrieving any results saving time by investigating a variety of search engines without connecting separately to each one.

Model for Technology-Based Lessons (7) A rubric especially for teachers interested in preparing their own instructional lessons. A step-by-step rubric for designing, developing, implementing, delivering, and evaluating full-blown technology-based curriculum.

Modem (2) Acronym for MOdulator-DEModulator device used to convert computer-compatible signals to signals that can be transmitted over the telephone lines, then back again to computer signals at the other end of the line.

Multimedia Application (2) Computer applications that involve the integration of text, sound, graphics, motion video, and animation.

NCATE (1) The National Council for Accreditation of Teacher Education promotes high quality teacher preparation through the process of professional accreditation of schools, colleges, and departments of education.

Non-Copyrightable Resources (3) Includes the following: ideas or concepts; lists showing no originality, including alphabetically sorted lists; factual information; public records, court transcripts, and statistics; and titles or short phrases.

Notorious Information (3) Online information intended to create disbelief or induce a reaction. Chief cause of schools and districts installing Internet filtering software to ward off student access to such material.

Office Productivity Software (4) An integrated applications package typically offering tools such as: word processing, spreadsheet, database, desktop publishing, and graphics design and presentation.

On-Demand Search Engines (7) Search engines that continuously update their databases by locating documents and capturing selected text from home pages, then adding links to the text to summarize the contents of the page.

Pedagogy (1) The science or profession of teaching. Specifically, the teaching of children.

Performance-Based Assessment (11) Employs relevant and meaningful problems to evaluate student learning outcomes. Possible venues include: specific research ideas and problem-solving; follow-on activities for remedial and enrichment instruction; communication skills, personal and interpersonal; practical applications of abstract concepts; and application of knowledge to new situations.

Perfunctory Information (3) Online information containing illustrations written at a level that the casual reader understands. Primary purpose is to entertain, sell products, or advocate a particular viewpoint.

Pre-Selected Search Engines (7) Human-generated databases; a machine-generated search engine might initially explore the web pages, but humans choose what will and will not be included in the final results.

Reading (11) Assessment foundation; the primary foundation concerned with gathering new knowledge and developing new perspectives on prior knowledge; presented using text books, journals, teacher-prepared handouts, or online avenues; provides the underpinning for a successful technology-based program.

Rubric (11) In assessment terms, a model that allows more objective and consistent assessment; clearly shows the student how their work will be evaluated and what is expected; promotes student awareness of the criteria to be used in assessment; and, demands teacher focus to clarify outcome in specific terms.

Scholarly Information (3) Online information generally covering news and other similar events often reported in a way that is easily understood by the larger audience of educated people. Often contains illustrations for the layperson.

Search Engine (7) A program that searches documents for specified keywords and returns a list of the documents where the keywords are found. Often used to specifically describe systems that enable users to search for documents on the World Wide Web.

Self-Assessment (11) Requires criteria for determining the effectiveness of the materials produced, a valid methodology for collecting and analyzing the results of the self-evaluation, and an appropriate framework for interpreting results.

Shortcut (2) A Windows term; a special file that points to another file or device. You can place short-cuts on the desktop to conveniently access files that may be stored deep in the directory structure. Double-clicking the shortcut icon is the same as double-clicking the actual file.

Study Guides (4) Text-based technology resource focusing on one or more lesson objectives. Often addresses several objectives, but limited to a single instructional strategy appropriate for a majority of classroom students.

Taxonomy for Instructional Technology (7) A corresponding level of progressive technical complexity from literacy to communications, decision-making, instruction, integration, and acculturation.

Taxonomy of Educational Objectives (7) A Krathwohl and Bloom (1984) model; theory of six progressively complex steps for developing instructional objectives at increasingly advanced levels of higher order thinking: knowledge, comprehension, application, analysis, synthesis, and evaluation.

Teacher Educator Portfolio (1) A collection of artifacts specific to the three phases of teacher development: teacher as learner, teacher as expert, and teacher as scholar. A collection of reading, writing, thinking, interacting, and demonstrating artifacts for use in the classroom.

Technology Bursts (Foreword) Introduce skills and competencies, provide detailed instruction and examples, and aid in developing instructional materials. Identified by their blue borders.

Technology for Acculturation (7) A level of the Taxonomy for Instructional Technology; concerns itself with the ability to judge the value of technology.

Technology for Communication (7) A level of the Taxonomy for Instructional Technology; the ability to use technology to interact, including written and verbal communication, the professional exchange of information, and interpersonal collaboration.

Technology for Decision-Making (7) A level of the Taxonomy for Instructional Technology; the ability to use technology in new and concrete problem-solving situations. Includes such important tools as spreadsheets, brainstorming software, statistical analysis packages, and gradebook programs.

Technology for Instruction (7) A level of the Taxonomy for Instructional Technology; learning outcomes center around identifying instructional materials, analyzing their component parts, integrating these components, and understanding the organizational principles involved in their application.

Technology for Integration (7) A level of the Taxonomy for Instructional Technology; use of technology to act upon the component parts of content material and re-assembles them for better learner understanding.

Technology for Literacy (7) A level of the Taxonomy for Instructional Technology; the minimum level of competency expected of teachers and students with respect to computers, educational programs, office productivity software, and the Internet.

Technology (1) The systemic and systematic application of behavior and physical sciences concepts and other knowledge to the solution of problems.

Thinking (11) Assessment foundation; personal reflection which confirms student understanding; authentic indicators of student learning.

URL (3) Acronym for Uniform Resource Locator; the global address of documents and other resources on the World Wide Web. The first part of the address indicates what protocol to use, and the second part specifies the IP address or the domain name where the resource is located.

Virtual Tour (7) Concentrates on the strengths of the humanistic approach to learning by integrating Internet sites specifically selected to focus attention on content important to the learner.

Watermark (9) Allows the designer to import a scanned picture, set the background to transparent, crop the picture, add special effects, and adjust its brightness, contrast, and color.

Windows (2) A section of a display screen that is dedicated to a specific document, activity, or application; simultaneous display of subareas of a particular window; a software product by Microsoft Corporation that provides a graphical user interface and multi-tasking.

Wizard (5) A utility within an application that helps the user perform a particular task. For example, Power Point's AutoContent Wizard walks the user through the steps of producing different types of presentations.

World Wide Web (2) An Internet server that offers multimedia and hypertext links.

Writing (11) Assessment foundation; the primary evidence that prior knowledge has been accumulated, integrated, and transferred to student classroom applications. Writing activities are worthy of inclusion in any well designed instructional, technology-based lesson, as are formal papers, publication submissions, and classroom materials.

Index

CD DIRECTORY

Teaching Digitally comes with a CDROM of directories, folders, and files that enhance the practical understanding of how technology can be used effectively in the classroom. Each chapter references examples found on the CDROM corresponding to student-appropriate handouts, study guides, and workbooks; classroom presentations and interactive lessons; and, course web pages and virtual tours. Exact instructions are found in the various Technology Bursts and Best Practice icons and lead you directly to these files.

Readers may also examine these files at any time by inserting the CDROM into a multimedia-capable computer using either the Macintosh or Windows operating systems A short synopsis of the most important elements captured on the CDROM follows.

CDROM Name	Type	Description	Instructions
Dinosaur_Handout	Folder	Contains the file dinohandout.doc which demonstrates the use of word processing to create a text-based student handout.	Click on Dinosaur_Handout, then click on dinohandout.doc
Dinosaur_Hyperbook	Folder	Contains the file hyperdino.doc which demonstrates the advanced use of word processing to create a text-based student workbook	Click on Dinosaur_Hyperbook, then click on hyperdino.doc
Dinosaur_Interactive	Folder	Contains the file ildino.ppt which demonstrates the advanced use of graphics presentation to create a a visual-based student lesson	Click on Dinosaur_Interactive, then click on ildino.ppt
Dinosaur_Page	Folder	Contains the file dinosaur.htm which demonstrates the use of web page design to create a web-based course page	Click on Dinosaur_Page, then click on dinosaur.htm
Dinosaur_Presentation	Folder	Contains the file dinosofna.ppt which demonstrates the use of graphics presentation to create a visual-based classroom presentation	Click on Dinosaur_Presentation, then click on dinossofna.ppt
Dinosaur_VT	Folder	Contains the file index.htm which provides a table of contents for the advanced use of web page design to create a web-based virtual tour	Click on Dinosaur_VT, then click on index.htm
Example	Folder	Contains the file page.htm which provides an example for practicing web page design	Click on Example, then click on page.htm

Example_Text	Folder	Contains the file text.htm which provides a table of contents for 17 examples of text-based student handouts, study guides, and workbooks created by classroom teachers	Click on Example_Text, then click on text.htm
Example_Visual	Folder	Contains the file visual.htm which provides a table of contents for 20 examples of visual-based classroom presentations and interactive lessons created by classroom teachers	Click on Example_Visual, then click on visual.htm
Example_Web	Folder	Contains the file web.htm which provides a table of contents for 18 examples of web-based course home pages and virtual tours created by classroom teachers	Click on Example_Web, then click on web.htm
IT_Reports	Folder	Contains the file reports.htm which provides a table of contents for 23 reports covering various topics of instructional technology	Click on IT_Reports, then click on reports.htm
Learning_Theories	Folder	Contains the file theories.htm which provides a comprehensive discussion of educational learning theories appropriate for designers of instructional technology lessons	Click on Learning_Theories, then click on theories.htm
Pedagogy	Folder	Contains the file pedagogy.htm which provides a concurrent discussion of instructional technology as a pedagogy for the future	Click on Pedagogy, then click on pedagogy.htm
Portfolios	Folder	Contains the file portfolio.htm which provides an online examination of professional portfolios for the teacher as learner, expert, and scholar	Click on Portfolios, then click on portfolio.htm
copy4a.ppt	File	Features of copyright protection and the issues of Fair Use are discussed in this Power Point presentation that can be shown at in-service assemblies for faculty	Click on copy4a.ppt
www-sites.htm	File	Excellent web page depicting a few of the best World Wide Web Sites for Educators; an excellent starting point for teachers wishing to locate the best content material on the Internet	Click on www-sites.htm